SYRIA ————————

SECOND EDITION

T0056393

Hot Spots in Global Politics

SYRIA ——————————

SECOND EDITION

Samer N. Abboud

Polity

First published in 2015 by Polity Press

This second edition published in 2018 by Polity Press

Polity Press
65 Bridge Street
Cambridge CB2 1UR, UK

Polity Press
101 Station Landing
Suite 300
Medford, MA 02155, USA

ISBN-13: 978-1-5095-2240-8
ISBN-13: 978-1-5095-2241-5(pb)

A catalogue record for this book is available from the British Library.

Library of Congress Cataloging-in-Publication Data
Names: Abboud, Samer Nassif, author.
Title: Syria / Samer N. Abboud.
Description: Second edition. | Cambridge, UK ; Medford, MA : Polity Press, 2018. | Series: Hot spots in global politics series
Identifiers: LCCN 2017058009 (print) | LCCN 2018004384 (ebook) | ISBN 9781509522446 (Epub) | ISBN 9781509522408 | ISBN 9781509522408q(hardback) | ISBN 9781509522415q(pbk.)
Subjects: LCSH: Syria--History--Civil War, 2011- | Syria--History--Civil War, 2011---Participation, Russian. | Syria--Politics and government--2000-
Classification: LCC DS98.6 (ebook) | LCC DS98.6 .A233 2018 (print) | DDC 956.9104/23--dc23
LC record available at https://lccn.loc.gov/2017058009

Typeset in 10.5 on 12 pt Sabon
by Fakenham Prepress Solutions, Fakenham, Norfolk NR21 8NL
Printed and bound in Great Britain by Clays Ltd, Elcograf S.p.A

For further information on Polity, visit our website:
politybooks.com

To the memory of Obaida al-Habbal, and all of Syria's Martyrs

Contents

Acknowledgments

There is no easy way to tell the story of the Syrian crisis. There is no linear story to be captured or a singular experience that all Syrians can relate to. For Syrians, the experiences of the last six years have been multiple and unique and betray the simple ways in which we regularly choose to speak of what has happened since 2011 when we focus on things like regime and rebel territorial gains, or the question of what went wrong with the revolution. In the course of my research in and on Syria since the early 2000s, I was fortunate to have met and befriended so many people, all of whom I regularly and often think of even if we are not always in touch. I retain the most wonderful memories of my time in Syria and my friendships, especially with Obaida al-Habbal, to whom this book was dedicated, and Zaher al-Sagheer, who is as good a friend as anyone can ask for.

It is these friendships and others that I often think about when my thoughts turn to Syria's slow descent into this catastrophe. I am neither an impartial nor a dispassionate observer of the conflict but I am also quite removed from the day-to-day experiences and hardships of Syrians. I have spoken at length with others who write and research about Syria; we speak of how the feelings of being both detached and attached often compound the sadness and helplessness one feels in telling stories about the conflict. Without the support of so many, I would not have had the personal or intellectual strength to tell the story that you will read in the coming pages.

My utmost gratitude is reserved for Louise Knight and Nekane Tanaka Galdos at Polity for their patience and commitment to this project and for providing me the opportunity to tell this story. Ann Klefstad was as patient and precise a copy editor as I could have asked for, and her regular words of encouragement as I stumbled to the finish line were always received warmly. My former research assistant, Josephine Lippincott, contributed significant time to the first edition of the book and her imprint is also felt on the second. Since the publication of the first edition, I have been invited to many campuses, radio shows, and classrooms to talk about Syria. These were all wonderful opportunities to meet with people, especially young people, who were interested in deepening their understanding of the conflict. These engagements were also spaces for me to think through some of the ideas that appear in the second edition. I am grateful to all of those who thought I had something to say about Syria and who were willing to listen.

As I completed this edition of the book, I also embarked on a professional transition and a new position at Villanova University's Global Interdisciplinary Studies program. During the completion of this book, I was fortunate enough to have spent time as a Visiting Scholar at Villanova's Center for Arab and Islamic Studies. When I initially approached Dr. Hibba Abugideiri and Dr. Catherine Warrick about affiliation with the Center, all I hoped for was a broom closet and a Wi-Fi password. They have given me so much more and have provided a welcoming space for me to read, write, and think as I completed the book. Many others at Villanova, including Dr. Fr. Kail Ellis, Nadia Barsoum, and Jerusha Conner, have made me feel very much at home and a member of their community and have helped ease my transition and make it very exciting for me. My colleagues at Arcadia University where I taught for many years, Kira Baker-Doyle, Kerr Messner, Gregg Moore, Warren Haffar, Jennifer Riggan, and Peter Siskind, are some of the most wonderful people I have ever been around and I am very appreciative for the many ways in which they show care for me, make me laugh, and are always willing to listen to my ideas and occasional complaints.

I am also deeply grateful and indebted to my colleagues in the Beirut Security Studies Collective: Omar Dahi, Nicole Sunday Grove, Waleed Hazbun, Sami Hermez, Coralie Hindawi, Jamil Mouawad, and Seteney Shami, who are some of the most brilliant and interesting people I have had the pleasure of working with. Although we spend more time talking about when to launch our website than we do talking about Syria, the comradery and intellectual engagement that our work together provides energizes and motivates me. For this, I am forever indebted to the Arab Council for the Social Sciences (ACSS) for providing the support and vision for the Collective and for making our exciting work possible.

I am very fortunate to have friends like Miguel de Larrinaga, Marc Doucet, Benjamin J. Muller, Can Mutlu, and Mark Salter, who sustain me in numerous ways. My admiration for them as scholars and fathers is beyond words. I count myself as very lucky to have friendships that can vacillate between discussions of hockey, academic debates, our family lives, and the latest giggles from the far corners of the Internet. While we are very rarely in the same place, I am grateful for when we are together and the multiple electronic exchanges that fill in the times between. Bob Vitalis never ceases to make me laugh with his jokes or amaze me with his brilliance and insight. As long as we are not stuck in a car together, I always look forward to our conversations. Bassam Haddad, whose sharpness is only matched by his tenacity, has been a constant source of professional support for which I am deeply grateful. Finally, I would be remiss if I ignored Michael Collins, Jim (Doc) Davis, and the many others from hockey whose friendships outside the dressing room are so meaningful and important to me.

My final thanks are reserved for my family. Fred and Rabia Rosen are very supportive in-laws and while I know they are never bothered to be with their grandchildren, it means a great deal that they are always ready to help when needed. My parents, Rabab and Nassif, have always provided me with unconditional love and support in all of my endeavors, and for this I am eternally grateful. The respect and admiration that I have for them is immense and it is on the back of their love and hard work that I am able to live the life that I live. I blame them for my interest in politics and in Syria in particular, as we never went a day in our house—and we still do not—without talking about either. My children, Kalila, Nadim, and Maysa, have brought me immeasurable joy and given so much meaning to my life. Our morning cuddle routines, walks in the woods with our sling-shots, regular games of Subway Surfer, and general silliness make the day-to-day so pleasurable. Watching them engage in various activities, develop friendships, and learn how to be themselves in this world is one of the greatest joys of my life. And I am eternally grateful that I get to share all of this with my spouse, Sonia Rosen. From the moment we met, Sonia changed my sense of possibility in this world. I am reminded of this each and every day when I reflect on the wonderful life that we share together and the love that envelops our home.

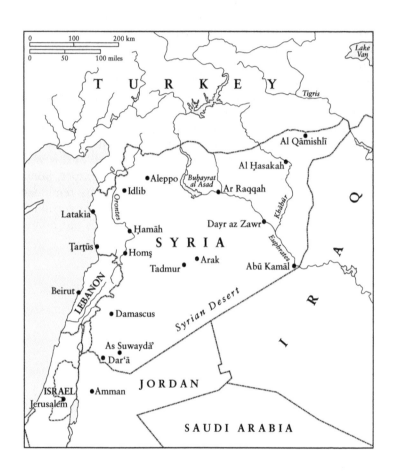

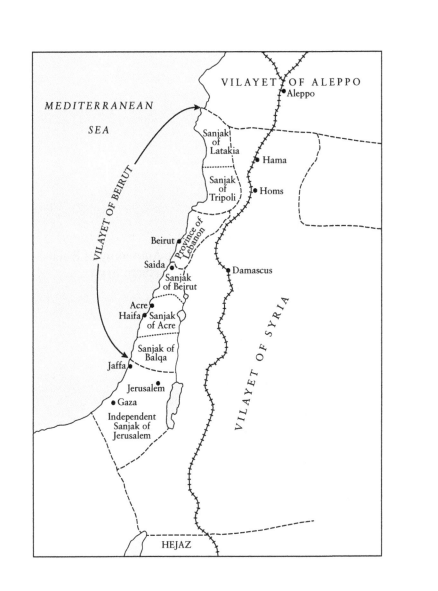

VILAYET OF ALEPPO

MEDITERRANEAN

SEA

Aleppo

Sanjak
of
Latakia

Hama

Sanjak
of
Tripoli

Homs

VILAYET OF BEIRUT

Beirut

Province of Lebanon

Saida

Damascus

Sanjak
of Beirut

Acre
Haifa
Sanjak
of Acre

VILAYET OF SYRIA

Sanjak of
Balqa

Jaffa

Jerusalem

Gaza

Independent
Sanjak of
Jerusalem

HEJAZ

Abbreviations

AQI—al-Qaeda in Iraq
CPA—Coalition Provisional Authority
CBDAR—Canton Based Democratic Autonomy of Rojava
DFNS—Democratic Federation of Northern Syria
FRB—Free Raqqa Brigade
FSA—Free Syrian Army
GCC—Gulf Cooperation Council
HNC—Higher Negotiations Committee
HTS—Hayat Tahrir al-Sham
IF—Islamic Front
ILF—Islamic Liberation Front
ISIS—Islamic State of Iraq and as-Sham
JAN—Jabhat an-Nusra
KDP—Kurdish Democratic Party
KNC—Kurdish National Council
KRG—Kurdish Regional Government
LAS—League of Arab States
LC—Local Councils
LCC—Local Coordination Committees
MB—Muslim Brotherhood
MSM—Majlis Shura al-Mujahideen
NATO—North Atlantic Treaty Organization
NCB—National Coordination Body for Democratic Change
NDF—National Defence Force
NRC—Norwegian Refugee Council

NSF—National Salvation Front
PKK—Kurdistan Workers Party
PPC—People's Protection Committees
PYD—Kurdish Democratic Union Party
SAA—Syrian Arab Army
SAMS—Syrian American Medical Society
SDF—Syrian Defense Forces
SIG—Syrian Interim Government
SHRC—Syrian Human Rights Committee
SIF—Syrian Islamic Front
SILF—Syrian Islamic Liberation Front
SKC—Supreme Kurdish Council
SNC—Syrian National Council
UAR—United Arab Republic
UNHCR—United Nations High Commission on Refugees
UNSC—United Nations Security Council
UNSCR—United Nations Security Council Resolution
UOSSM—Union of Syrian Medical Relief Organizations
YPG—People's Defense Corps
YPJ—Kurdish Women's Protection Units

Introduction

When negotiations between the Syrian regime and some opposition groups began in Geneva in 2016, Mohammed Alloush, a commander of the armed Islamist group Jaysh al-Islam, was designated as lead negotiator for the opposition. Many Syrians and observers of the conflict, especially those who were captivated by the possibilities that the uprising created, would have been excused if they had to rub their eyes to make sure that they were witnessing reality. Alloush, who was told by regime negotiators that they would not talk to him "until he shaved his beard" (Wintour, 2016), was perhaps not the expected, let alone ideal, choice of Syrians who took to the streets en masse in 2011 demanding political change. That a leader of an Islamist armed group would have been the lead negotiator for the Syrian opposition is not an accident, of course; it is the outcome of years of struggle, betrayal, intervention, and profound violence, which shaped the trajectory of the Syrian conflict and its main protagonists. How did the Syrian revolution evolve this way? Why was Alloush chosen to lead peace negotiations? What happened to the revolution? What explains regime survival? The book that follows tries to capture this story and answer these questions about one of the most brutal conflicts in recent memory.

The daily lives of Syrians have changed dramatically since March 2011 when protests against the fifty-year rule of the Ba'ath Party began in the southern city of Dar'a. What began as a movement of sustained protest demanding regime change and political reforms has morphed into one of the most brutal and horrific conflicts in the post–World War II era. The conflict had evolved toward a political and military stalemate as all major domestic and regional subjugating actors aimed toward a decisive military solution—until a decisive military solution arrived in the form of Russian intervention that has moved the conflict from stalemate to what I call later in the book an "authoritarian peace." In the context of this trajectory, the humanitarian crisis wrought by the conflict is worsening: more than half of the total population killed, maimed, or displaced within only six years. The human tragedy of the Syrian conflict has no current end in sight despite proclamations from regime loyalists and oppositionists that the conflict is nearing its military end. The damage has been wrought, and as we know from most conflicts what appears to be the end may simply be the beginning of something else equally catastrophic and violent. From the Syrian regime itself, which bears ultimate culpability and responsibility for the descent into maddening violence; to the various rebel groups; to Saudi Arabia, Qatar, Turkey, and Iran, the inability to end the conflict has ushered in decades of future struggle for Syrians.

Telling the story of the Syrian conflict is a complicated endeavor, especially in a context in which popular understandings of Syria reduce the conflict to simple binaries (Sunni/Shi'a or regime/rebel) that misrepresent both the complexity of Syrian society and the conflict itself. In the pages that follow I attempt to confront these simplistic dichotomies and to introduce instead a broader picture of the Syrian conflict, one that moves back and forth between the meta-issues (such as regional rivalries, international involvement, and ideological and sectarian calculations) and the micro-issues (such as intra-rebel cooperation and conflict, the humanitarian crisis, and the administrative fragmentation of the country) that are shaping and driving the military and political dynamics of the conflict. A major theme throughout the book is how a military and political stalemate emerged and how the Russian intervention broke this, and what it may mean for the future of Syria. This is not to suggest in any way that the post-Russian intervention period is bringing the conflict to an end. I suggest instead that this is the latest stage in an evolving conflict that has many dynamics and subjugating actors. In introducing the dynamics driving the conflict I also answer questions about who the main actors are, including the Islamic State of Iraq and as-Sham (ISIS), whose rise and fall reflects broader trends in the complicated dynamics of the conflict, as well as the impossibilities of reaching a solution in the short term. One of my central goals is not only to trace the rise of groups like ISIS but to give insight into the constantly shifting nature of alliances among rebel groups, the issues driving the political elements of the conflict, and the main actors (both local and international) who are playing key roles in the conflict. The goals for this book are to help the reader understand the broader dynamics driving the conflict, why it has persisted, who the main actors are, and why it has evolved in the way that it has.

In the popular understanding of the Syrian conflict, it has morphed from a revolution into a civil war (see Hughes, 2014), but the conflict is not as linear as this suggests. There remains an active, robust, and committed movement of Syrians trying to rebuild their country, and to lead it free of the regime and the armed groups that now control it. They have become peripheral and rendered invisible by the profound violence inflicted on civilians and by the presence of so many armed groups, but they exist. Thus the Syrian conflict is more than an uprising that morphed into a civil war; it is a conflict with multiple dimensions that include, among other things, a revolutionary project to restructure society; an international effort to destroy Syria; war profiteers and criminals who fuel conflict; and regime loyalists, from within and outside Syria, intent on countering what they perceive as a conspiracy to overthrow the Assad regime.

Thus the Syrian conflict does not have a definitive beginning or a linear trajectory. What is at stake, analytically speaking, is the understanding of the parallel processes of revolution

and civil war, as well as the antecedent processes of intervention and criminality, and their short- and long-term
effects on Syrian state and society. This requires attentiveness
to the nuances and complexities of the Syrian conflict
that most popular understandings lack (Rawan and Imran,
2013). From my perspective, such attentiveness requires
an examination of the interplay of many factors: historical
analysis, political economy, the role of international actors,
the structure of networks of violence, and so on. With
this in mind, the story I tell in the pages below begins
in the Ottoman era with the formation of a landed elite
that controlled the political and economic levers of society
right through to the Mandate period. In the post-Mandate
period of independence, mobilization of the socially disaffected classes overthrew the pre-existing order. Out of the
remnants emerged the Ba'ath Party, which has ruled Syria
since 1963. The subsequent decades witnessed the consolidation of Ba'athist control of Syria and state institutions
and the emergence of an authoritarian regime that ruled
Syria through a combination of repression and clientelism.
The lack of any sort of political freedoms, and the massive
socioeconomic changes wrought in the 2000s by a shift away
from socialist-era policies toward market-driven ones, fueled
societal grievances that eventually propelled the protests that
began in March 2011. The Syrian state and society have
undergone three seismic shifts in the last century: the collapse
of the Ottoman Empire, the Mandate period, and the era of
Ba'athist authoritarianism.

Intersecting with this historical evolution are the social
realities consequent on changes in the nature and structure
of the Syrian state. The expansion of the state under the
Mandate authorities fundamentally changed the relationship
between state and citizen and brought the political authorities into the everyday lives of Syrians. Under the Ba'ath, the
state was reoriented toward the dual goals of regime preservation and social mobilization through state institutions that
would link different segments of Syrian society, especially
those on the peripheries of Mandate politics, to the state and
regime. The incorporation of new social actors transformed

the material and political basis of Syria's social stratification and brought to political power a regime that was dominated by leaders from Syria's minority communities and rural areas. Ba'athist rule involved the distribution of social welfare in exchange for political quietism in Syria's incorporated social forces. By the 1990s this model had exhausted itself, and the regime slowly turned toward the market. By the time the uprising began in 2011, Syria had undergone a decade of dramatic economic transformation that had ruptured the economic links between state and society established from the 1960s to the 1990s.

Syria played a major regional role during this period as well, having fought two wars with Israel (in 1967 and 1973) and then intervening in Lebanon's civil war later in the 1970s. The Syrian presence in Lebanon lasted until 2005, when a series of protests led to the withdrawal of the Syrian troops and security personnel who had exercised control over the Lebanese political system after the end of the country's civil war in 1991. The Middle East Peace Process in the early 1990s never realized a return of the occupied Golan Heights from Israel and a cold peace prevailed between the two countries up until today. Syria's regional alliances shifted considerably in the decades prior to the uprising, with the regime supporting various Palestinian factions against one another, Kurdish separatist groups in Turkey, and the Islamic Republic of Iran in its eight-year war with neighboring Iraq.

The legacies of Syria's historical evolution as a state, the transformation of its social stratification and political economy, and the changing geopolitical situation in the Middle East have all contributed to shaping the conflict today. The conflict itself has injected its own complexities into the Syrian arena with the arrival of armed groups such as ISIS and the emergence of Syrian Kurdish parties as major actors in the war. The role of regional actors in fomenting violence and supporting regime and rebel forces has internationalized the conflict in ways that de-center local actors from decision-making and power on the ground. Violence, fragmentation, and displacement are radically reshaping Syrian society.

Who are the Syrians?

Syria is an extremely heterogeneous society, with Sunnis, Alawi, Ismailis, Druze, Shi'a, as well as Greek Orthodox, Maronite, and other Christian sects. Population breakdowns by religion are not entirely accurate, but close to 10 percent of the population was Christian and the remaining 90 percent Muslim, the majority of which are Sunni Muslims. In addition to religion or sect, class, ethnicity, and geography are also determinants of Syrian political and social identity. Syria is dominated by Arabs with a sizable Kurdish minority, which is no more than 8 percent of the total population. Prior to the uprising, Syria's population was around 22 million, with more than half of the population formerly concentrated in urban centers.

Syria shares borders with Iraq, Palestine/Israel, Lebanon, Jordan, and Turkey. The Golan Heights has been occupied by Israel since the 1967 war but is still home to many Syrian Druze who live under Israeli occupation. In the post-Mandate period, Syria's economy has been dependent on agriculture and oil production. Agricultural production was central to the nation's social stratification in the Ba'ath period and oil revenues provided the regime with substantial rents to establish a strong central state and public sector. During the 1990s, there was a slow shift away from dependence on oil revenues and an attempt to diversify the economy. These reforms were accelerated in the 2000s when Syrian planners enacted policies to shift economic activity toward services. The shift in economic policy away from agriculture paralleled severe environmental degradation in the agricultural regions, including drought, which decreased agriculture's productivity and led to the transformation of the social basis around which agricultural activity occurred.

The social shifts produced during this period have been violently disrupted by the conflict, which has produced a humanitarian crisis that will forever shape Syrian society, and has problematized the question "who are the Syrians?" Today, Syrians and their families have been split, torn apart by war, violence, insecurity, and displacement, in many cases spread around the region and the world, distanced from loved ones and any sense of stability and hope. It is these changes in the individual, familial, and communal life of Syrians that will continue to shape the question of who the Syrians are in the decades to come.

A war of narratives

As war raged on the Syrian battlefield, another war, one of narratives, raged on the Internet and in print. While virtually inconsequential to alleviating the trauma of conflict on Syrians, these narrative wars became very ugly and unproductive, with vitriol tossed back and forth across political lines. These lines, for anyone who followed the narrative wars, were quite clearly demarcated: they separated those who were perceived to be either regime or opposition loyalists. The space for critical thinking, for the grey zone so to speak, shrank, and analysts of Syria were forced into these camps, in which friends and adversaries treated their politics and their assumptions alike as knowable. A common retort about Syrian analysts was whether they were pro-regime, pro-armed groups, pro-intervention, pro-barrel bombs, and, in the worst-case scenarios, pro-ISIS, with the assumption being that analysts wished the horrors brought by ISIS on the Syrian population.

An excellent example of the nastiness of these narrative wars was the reaction to Bassam Haddad's widely circulated article in *The Nation*, "The Debate Over Syria Has Reached a Dead End" (Haddad, 2016). The main claim in the article was that pro-regime and pro-opposition supporters had reached maximalist positions in their politics, positions in which any space for compromise and understanding was virtually nil. What amounted to a call for productive dialogue was largely, and wrongly, treated as a blueprint for regime apologists. Pro-opposition supporters decried the perception of a "two sides" argument as tantamount to collaboration with a brutal Assad regime. In many ways the debate over

Haddad's article proved the point of his argument: debate, discussion, and compromise were no longer possible in a context of maximalist political positions.

Unfortunately, the kind of unproductive debates Haddad referred to in his article remain prominent in debates about Syria, even as former supporters of the opposition turn their sights to what horrors and possibilities the reconstruction period may bring, and regime loyalists celebrate the coming of "peace," no matter how authoritarian and violent it will be. It would thus be misleading and unproductive to begin a book about Syria without acknowledging the dynamics of the narrative wars, no matter how inconsequential I believe them to be to the average Syrian's life. With that said, I do not intend to stake out some sort of analytical high ground or, even worse, to defend some sort of objectivity toward the conflict. Instead, I want to stress the compatibility of an analysis about Syria that recognizes the horrors of the regime and its allies, as well as of the armed groups that have infiltrated the country. This is no plea for moral equivalency: the regime and its allies bear sole responsibility for the Syrian catastrophe. Rather, this is to say that over the course of the conflict, supporters of the uprising have often tied their politics and the political possibilities of the uprising to unsavory and destructive actors, including reactionary, exclusionary Islamists who served to undermine the revolution and its possibilities as much as anything else that happened after March 2011.

I also hope that such positions will not be misread as optimism for the return of the Syrian revolution or the revival of revolutionary actors as the vanguards of a progressive Syria. I do not believe that the possibilities for a progressive Syria, a progressive postconflict Syria that was envisioned by activists in the early stages of the uprising, is possible today under the current circumstances. Nor do I believe that a progressive politics can emerge out of the coming authoritarian peace. None of these positions are incompatible to me: one can simultaneously oppose the regime and the armed groups its brutality spawned while mourning the vision for Syria that emerged after 2011. The analysis that follows is driven by these commitments.

Unraveling the conflict

The complexity and fluidity of the Syrian conflict does not lend itself to any quick-fix theoretical models. Larger questions about why it has evolved in this particular way, why a stalemate took root, and how the Russian intervention in 2015 decisively shifted the conflict away from stalemate, are not easily answered. Much of the academic literature on wars and conflicts focuses on variables and measurements that do not remotely fit the realities of Syria's conflict. More nuanced studies have drawn on different approaches to the study of the Syrian conflict (el-Hokayem, 2013; Lesch, 2013a, b; Sahner, 2014). The background of the protests and the early mobilization period encouraged many to draw on Social Movement Theory (SMT) (Durac, 2015) to help understand the organization and strategies of the early protest movement that morphed into the Local Coordination Committees (LCC). This research, which I will deal with substantially below, has been important in helping us understand the main players fueling the protests, what their socioeconomic backgrounds were, how they organized and mobilized protesters, and what their key roles were in the early stages of the uprising.

Other studies of the conflict attempted to explain the causes and background of the uprising by focusing on the long trajectory and exhaustion of Ba'athist politics in Syria (Wieland, 2012). Further research has been conducted into the causes of the uprising, with some arguing that environmental factors such as climate change and drought were major drivers of the protests, or that the mismanagement of resources led to political unrest (De Châtel, 2014). Others point to Syria's socioeconomic situation on the eve of the uprising, especially the effects of unemployment and declining standards of living, as causes of the protests (Dahi and Munif, 2012) while others argue that the contagion effect of initially successful Arab uprisings in such places as Tunisia and Egypt inspired Syrians to protest (Kahf, 2014; Lynch et al., 2013).

While the study of the causes of the uprising is important, the uprising cannot be reduced to one or two variables. Instead, it is the outcome of the interplay of all of these factors. Some research has focused on explaining the trajectory of the uprising through changes in the regime's behavior and its subsequent mutations during the conflict (Heydemann, 2013a, b; Seeberg, 2014). The regional geopolitical situation can explain some dynamics of the Syrian conflict, and further studies have focused on the interplay between domestic and regional politics by privileging the penetrative role of regional actors in Syria (Salloukh, 2013; el-Hokayem, 2013). Finally, others, such as Khashanah (2014), have argued that the confluence of ideological and geopolitical interests of outside entities induced the Syrian crisis in an attempt to realign the country's foreign relations. More explanations for the conflict, especially from Arabic sources, are taken up in the second chapter of the book.

All of these explanations have been substantial and useful interventions into the study of the Syrian conflict and all serve to inform much of the analysis that follows below. The multilayered complexity of the conflict necessarily produces intellectual and analytical blind spots and an exhaustive study of this complexity would be impossible given the rapidly changing dynamics of the conflict. In order to address these larger questions about the Syrian crisis, I have drawn on some of the dominant approaches to the study of the conflict but sought to look beyond them. Rather than focusing exclusively or predominantly on the trans-formations of the regime or on international roles in the conflict, I have drawn significantly on the idea of wartime political orders to explain the key patterns of the conflict, including cooperation and conflict between different actors, governance, politics, military activity, regional intervention, war economies (Staniland, 2012), and so on. In drawing on this notion of a wartime order, I am trying to explicate some of the more nuanced questions that help parse the conflict: Why do rebels sometimes cooperate and sometimes engage in conflict? What do the political and administrative structures of non-regime areas look like? Who is exercising violence and to what end? How did the Russian intervention break the stalemate?

The study of wartime political orders typically relies on analysis of two variables: territorial control and regime–rebel relations (Staniland, 2012). Most literature on wars tends to ignore how the diverse and contradictory interactions between regimes and rebels serve to construct political authority and control. Regime and rebel actors are not locked in a zero-sum game to control the monopoly of violence; rather, they engage in both cooperative and conflict relationships that shape patterns of violence against civilians, governance, war economies, and, in important ways, postconflict politics. In this study of the Syrian conflict I highlight the diversity of interactions between regime and rebel groups, and also among rebel groups themselves. I look at how these groups control territory, administer that territory, and exercise political power and authority therein. I locate in these dynamics both the causes of a stalemate and the reasons behind the successful Russian intervention to break that stalemate.

From the outset, then, it is important to clarify the meaning of "regime," "rebel," and "opposition," which are often conflated. In the pages that follow, the homogeneity of these categories will be broken down in favor of more pluralistic and heterogeneous explanations of what we call "the regime," "rebels," or "the opposition." In Syria today, there are multiple actors who constitute the parts of what we mean when we refer to these categories. The analysis below highlights the fragmentation of these categories and what that fragmentation means for the conflict.

The Syrian conflict is not simply about military wins and losses or the contraction of regime territorial control. The conflict has produced a political order structured by relations among the different groups that produces patterns of violence, and governance that produced a stalemate. The relations produced by the conflict are themselves shaped by a number of factors, including the role of outside actors, sectarianism, territorial fragmentation, and the humanitarian crisis. In the pages that follow the story of the Syrian conflict is told through these lenses.

Structure of the book

Chapter One begins with a historical overview of Syria's post-Mandate state up until the period of the Ba'athist coup in 1963. The chapter looks at the rise and consolidation of Ba'athist power from 1963 until the outbreak of the uprising in March 2011. In this period, the social and material basis of Ba'athist power shifted dramatically, especially in the period of Bashar al-Assad's rule (from 2000 onwards), during which the regime engaged in marketization, which accelerated the Ba'athist shift away from its traditional social support base. The role of the regime's pillars of power—the Ba'ath Party, the security apparatus, and the state—are discussed throughout. Specific attention is paid to the wide range of social forces in Syria—the peasants, urban bourgeois, workers, and so on—and their differential positioning vis-à-vis the longtime Ba'athist regime. This will provide a substantive background on which to understand the context of the uprising and the social forces driving the movement to topple the regime.

Chapter Two covers the first months of the uprising until the period in which militarization began to take root and an armed opposition emerged. Here we examine the background of the protesters and of the uprising and answer questions about how the protesters organized and mobilized in the context of sustained regime repression. The central role of the Local Coordination Committees (LCCs) is highlighted, as is how the conflict gave rise to civil activity and organization more generally. The regime's response to the protests was to engage in a dual policy of repression and reform. This reform included substantial constitutional changes but had no immediate effect on the ground.

Continued repression forced the uprising to emerge as a nonhierarchical, decentralized movement loosely linking activists together throughout the country. In addition to the LCCs, a political opposition made up mostly of Syrian exiles formed outside of the country and attempted to generate international support for the overthrow of the regime. As armed groups emerged inside the country within the first year, the movement against the regime suffered from "multiple leaderships" and the lack of a centralized structure that could serve as a serious and legitimate alternative to the regime. The failure of the protests of the first months of the uprising to initiate regime change would propel the conflict toward increasing militarization.

The main violent actors are introduced in Chapter Three. In Syria, violence is highly fragmented and decentralized, and there are two different armed actors: fighting units and brigades. The former are usually small armed groups with limited mobility who usually operate in smaller areas of towns or cities, while brigades have hundreds of members and are active across Syrian governorates. These units and brigades are connected to larger networks of violence that are determined by the interplay of many factors: resource access, control of checkpoints and supply routes, ideology, and so on. These networks of violence are very fluid and there remains mistrust between many of the armed factions. Chapter Three explores the networked structure of violence and how this manifests within the Jabhat an-Nusra, ISIS, the Kurdish Democratic Union Party (PYD), and regime networks.

How these networks of violence produced both territorial fragmentation and a military and political stalemate is taken up in Chapter Four. Here, I explore two parallel and reinforcing developments: first, the increased intervention of regional states into the conflict, and, second, the territorial fragmentation of the country and the emergence of alternative and competing models of governance that accelerated Syria's political and social fragmentation. Thus, the chapter aims to bring together analysis of the domestic and regional levels of the Syrian conflict to answer the question of how a stalemate emerged.

The subsequent chapter (Chapter Five) answers how the Russian intervention broke the stalemate and how the intervention made a political process toward peace possible in Syria. The chapter thus reviews the attempts to produce a peace agreement in Syria, why they failed in the context of a military stalemate, and how the Russian intervention produced the momentum toward the design of an "authoritarian peace." In outlining the failures of previous peace plans and the ways in which the Russian intervention broke the stalemate, the chapter identifies and discusses three major long-term consequences of the Russian intervention: the rise of the PYD and Syrian Kurdish politics as major players in Syria; the rise of Hizbollah; and the regime survival. The final chapter, Chapter Six, is concerned with the humanitarian crisis, specifically the displacement of millions of Syrians and the effect this is having on the health care and education access of Syrians. This discussion opens issues and challenges associated with refugee protection in neighboring countries. Chapter Six concludes with a discussion of the failings of the international community to adequately address the Syrian humanitarian crisis. The book concludes with some reflections on the coming authoritarian peace.

What's new in this edition

The first edition of this book was primarily concerned with the question of how a military and political stalemate emerged in the Syrian conflict. The second edition remains concerned with this but also with the question of how the stalemate was broken by the Russian intervention and what its consequences may be as an "authoritarian peace" emerges in Syria. The second edition of the book may thus read as a more periodized discussion of Syria, as divided between before and after periods of the intervention. This is intentional insofar as it allows me to identify and answer key questions about the conflict and to identify key moments that shifted the conflict toward its current state. The issues of regime–rebel relations, for example, are significantly different before and after the intervention. Similarly, the possibilities of revolutionary upheaval and overthrow of the regime were much stronger in 2011 than they were in 2017. All this is to say that the second edition attempts to capture the many changes that have happened in Syria since 2011 by structuring them around the question of how a stalemate emerged and was broken. Importantly, armed groups have evolved considerably throughout the conflict. Jabhat an-Nusra, for example, has now morphed into Hayat Tahrir al-Sham (HTS) and ISIS has virtually disappeared from the battlefield. I refer to the groups by their contemporaneous titles and try to identify their antecedents when possible.

Other changes have been made throughout the book that will be of benefit to the second-time reader. In addition to a total restructuring of the later chapters around the before and after of the stalemate, the book provides more analysis of the evolution of Syrian Kurdish politics during the conflict, especially as it relates to the Democratic Federation of Northern Syria (DFNS), or Rojava, and the prominence of the Kurdish-led Syrian Democratic Forces (SDF) in a post-intervention Syria. More Arabic sources have been included, especially in Chapters Two and Three, which incorporate material on the early stages of the conflict and different perspectives on social forces in the early stages of the uprising. The changing dynamics of regional intervention and involvement, especially shifting positions from states such as Turkey, are taken into account throughout. The final chapter contains updated material about the humanitarian crisis.

1 | The Rise and Fall of the Ba'ath Party

The Ba'ath Party has dominated Syrian politics since a bloodless coup brought military officers loyal to the party to power in 1963. The assumption of Ba'athist power in the 1960s initiated a period of relative political calm in Syria after decades of instability that had followed independence from France in 1946. The social and economic transformations in Syria that made possible the rise of the Ba'ath Party are rooted in the contradictions and consequences of the country's transitions from Ottoman governance to the French Mandate and then through the independence period. These three seismic political shifts have had profound impacts on the shaping of Syrian politics, society, economy, and the state. It is within the context of these major changes in political power and foreign suzerainty in Syria that the ideological and political conditions in which the Ba'ath Party came to power should be understood.

The shaping of contemporary Syria began in the later Ottoman period, when a series of reforms created and empowered a landlord-merchant class that formed the political elite of Syrian society at the turn of the century. The period of the French Mandate was one of relative continuity in the social composition of Syria's political elite, as the Mandate powers proved unwilling and unable to initiate major transformations in Syria's distribution of political power. It is not surprising, then, that after the collapse of the French Mandate, these same landlord-merchant classes continued to rule Syria and dominate political and parliamentary life. Syria's other major social forces, however, increasingly challenged rule by the nobility. Workers, peasants, and other social groupings that were effectively outside of politics and decision-making began to represent a threat to the nobility order. Such tensions between the ruling classes and the social forces that were on the periphery of political life generated tremendous instability in the decades following independence. Indeed, the instability of the independence period that preceded the seizure of power by the Ba'ath was mostly the result of three parallel processes in Syria that would have substantial effects on society: first, rapid social transformation wrought by integration into the global capitalist system; second, the expansion of state capacity and penetration of the state into society; and, finally, widespread social discontent and, eventually, mobilization, which would challenge and ultimately destroy the existing political structure. Out of the aftermath of the post-independence instability arose the Ba'ath Party. From 1963 until 1970 the party pursued a radical political agenda that reflected its leadership's commitment to comprehensive social transformation. In 1970, a "corrective revolution" led by Hafiz al-Assad would moderate some of the party's positions and initiate a process of consolidated state-building.

Having assumed power in 1963, the Ba'ath Party consolidated its rule over Syria and was effective at suppressing and containing any major political challenges by domestic actors (such as the Muslim Brotherhood) and external conflicts, such as the Iraqi and Lebanese wars. One of the key features of Syrian political life since Ottoman times is the differential incorporation of Syria's social forces into political power and the often destabilizing and revolutionary implications of political peripheralization. The Ba'ath Party was largely successful in initiating major social transformation in Syria and uprooting the nobility-based order. This transformation was grounded in an attempt to overthrow the vestiges of nobility rule and to incorporate the disaffected classes, such as peasants, minorities, rural communities, and the petit bourgeoisie, into a new political order. The costs of such transformation, however, were high, and came at the expense of political democratization. During the period of Hafiz al-Assad's rule, a patrimonial state emerged whose stability revolved around key pillars of authoritarian control: mainly the security apparatus, army, the Ba'ath Party, corporatized actors, and the public sector.

The pillars of authoritarian rule in Syria provided the institutions through which political mobilization of the disaffected classes and loyalty to the party could occur. By the 1980s, however, Ba'athist authoritarianism had shown signs of exhaustion. Conflict between the party and the Muslim Brotherhood in the late 1970s and early 1980s represented a major threat to Ba'athist rule, and the financial crisis of the mid-1980s exposed the weak fiscal and institutional grounding of the Syrian development model. Thereafter, gradual liberalization occurred and became a vehicle for the slow reintegration of commercial and bourgeois interests into the ruling coalition as a way to spur development. By 2000, Hafiz al-Assad had died and bequeathed power to his son, Bashar al-Assad. Initially considered to be a reformer capable of steering Syria toward a more democratic system, Bashar al-Assad in the 2000s instituted further political contraction and a crackdown coterminous with economic liberalization. The decade preceding the uprising was one of intense and substantive economic change in Syria, in which the pressures of demographic growth, statist retreat, economic stagnation, and a shift toward marketization generated socioeconomic discontent with the regime that had no legitimate outlet. By the 2000s, the space for incorporation of social forces into the political system had shrunk and the social base that the regime had been based on from the 1970s had shrunk. Workers, peasants, rural communities, small business owners, and the increasingly shrinking middle class no longer had an outlet from which to derive material benefits from the state. Once again, in Syria, the peripheralization of social forces would have dramatic political consequences.

From Ottoman to Mandate politics

The Ottoman Empire underwent substantial change in the 1800s. The period of reforms, known as the Tanzimat (1839–1876), attempted to wholly reorganize the state and the relationship between the Sultan and his subjects. A series of military defeats and nationalist movements that set European provinces on the path toward independence led to the territorial contraction of the Empire. In response, the state initiated the Tanzimat reforms to stave off internal collapse and to confront external pressures associated with European encroachment and the Empire's increasing integration into the global capitalist economy. These reforms were wide ranging and had profound effects on social and political identities in the Empire, principally by reorienting the relationship between state and sultan and introducing new modes of citizenship as well as a series of reforms that accelerated capitalist relations throughout the Empire. The attempt to eliminate distinctions between Muslims and non-Muslims and to transform Ottoman subjects into citizens who would have a stake in the defense and continuity of the Empire would radically alter relations among political leaders and lay people within the Empire. There would be, however, two main outcomes of the reform that would shape political life in Syria for years to come. The first was the centralization of power in the expanding Ottoman state and the stronger, penetrative role for the state in the affairs of the provinces. Such centralizing measures proved to be both a threat and an opportunity to local provincial leaders who had grown accustomed to relative autonomy and distance, both politically and geographically, from the central Ottoman state. The second was the introduction of private property and landownership. The introduction of private landownership would ultimately form the economic basis of a new class that would assume greater political power in the final decades of the Empire and which had positioned itself for a role after its collapse.

By the mid-1800s, the Syrian provinces of the Ottoman Empire were being integrated into the global capitalist system.

Such integration meant increasing European penetration of the provinces and economic pressure against traditional industries. Such pressures stimulated the growth of agriculture, particularly for export to European markets. The importance of agriculture for the finances of the Empire was evident in the passing of the Land Code of 1858, a policy meant to encourage peasants to register state-owned land so that intermediaries could not concentrate control over the productivity of land (Khoury, 1983, p. 27). In fact, the opposite happened. Peasants so feared the encroachment of the state that they resorted to registering lands in the names of urban patrons or rural notables, thus having precisely the opposite effect of the Land Code. Even those peasants who attempted to register their land found the costs prohibitive, and their lands reverted to auction, where rural notables could easily acquire them. Because the peasants were unable to bear the costs associated with registration or agricultural production, they were transformed into sharecroppers and laborers on land that they had recently controlled. The effect of the Land Code, then, was the gradual concentration of land in the ownership of urban families who had more secure property rights and who could officially engage in commerce and trade.

As peasant proprietorship declined, land concentrations increased, and, after a series of political reforms, so did the political power of the landowning classes. In subsequent decades, class conflict became more apparent in the provinces, especially in agriculturally rich areas of Syria such as the Hawran, where conflict between peasants and landowners increased. In 1864, the Empire passed the Law of the Provinces, which established new administrative councils that would incorporate notables into the political system. P. S. Khoury (1983) held that the introduction of private property, the expanding Ottoman state, and new administrative councils provided the basis for the creation of a new kind of political leadership in Syria tethered to landownership. These leaders would be drawn from two sectors: first, the landowning scholars, religious families who controlled key religious posts in Syria; second, the landowning bureaucrats, who controlled the key political and administrative posts in the expanding Ottoman bureaucracy. The emergence of landowning classes would consolidate class structure in the Syrian provinces and more clearly demarcate divisions and conflict between landowners and peasants.

The Tanzimat reforms ultimately could not stave off Ottoman collapse and by the end of WWI, the victorious European powers were granted Mandates by the League of Nations to control former Ottoman lands and to midwife the new states into self-government. A unique form of suzerainty created by the League of Nations, the Mandates led to the creation of the modern states of Lebanon, Syria, Jordan, Iraq, and Palestine. Having assumed the Mandate for Syria and Lebanon (the British had a Mandate for the remaining countries), the French reinforced, rather than undermined, the landed elite. In particular, the French authorities accelerated the private ownership of land through distributing formerly collectively held lands to the landed elite and tribal leaders in exchange for political subservience and commitment to the French project. In addition to increasing land holdings and wealth of the existing elite, they expanded the institutions of political representation to include a parliament, which, for the duration of the Mandate period, was dominated by landed interests. As the main site of political deliberation and decision-making, Parliament became a site of inter-elite negotiation where landed interests were nearly exclusively represented. Thus, the political and economic control of the landed elite was never seriously threatened during the Mandate period. It was not until the post-independence period that a political coalition would emerge that would challenge the authority of the landed elite.

French rule and independence

By the time the French had assumed the Mandate over post-Ottoman Syria in 1922–1923 after the deposition of the Syrian King Faisal in 1920, the country's social structure had begun to crystallize. The period preceding the deposition of King Faisal was one of mass politics and popular mobilization (Gelvin, 1999) in which new ideas about politics and nationhood permeated Syria's social and political landscape. During the immediate period of Ottoman collapse, popular committees emerged that reflected Syria's plural social mosaic and which began to articulate ideals of national community, a concept that was largely foreign until the late Ottoman period (Gelvin, 1999). As ideas of nationalism spread throughout (mainly urban) Syria, social stratification took shape around agricultural production and exchange, which dominated the country's economic activity. Owing to the active discouragement of industrialization by the French authorities, the class structure of Syrian society at the time revolved around landownership and the marketing and exchange of agriculture (Hinnebusch, 1990, pp. 39–40). At the top were the large landowners, numbering around 3,000 notable families who represented less than one percent of the total population but owned more than half of all private land in the country (Hinnebusch, 1990: 39). The landed families also dominated all major political, professional, and bureau-cratic positions. Immediately below the landowners were the merchants who controlled trade. Agricultural exchange provided the basis for the emergence of a new commercial class who facilitated Syria's entry into global capitalism. Merchants who were further removed from landowners and agricultural production and who were concentrated in and around urban areas made up the middle strata of society. These merchants held some land and positions within various professions and the bureaucracy, mirroring those of the landowners and commercial merchants. As such, they did not develop social interests that could challenge the landed nobility–based order. The lower strata of urban Syrian society were made up of the petit bourgeoisie, artisans, and laborers who were at the extreme economic peripheries of the benefits of agricultural production. Finally, Syria's rural areas consisted of a very small group of rural notables who had either acquired some wealth from commercial activities or the zu'ama (political leaders). By far the overwhelming majority of rural Syrians, however, were either sharecroppers (around 30 percent of the total population) or landless peasants (around 60 percent) (Hinnebusch, 1990, p. 40) who earned wages cultivating land owned by the landed notables.

Syria's social stratification and the elite politics it underpinned would remain economically and politically dependent on agricultural production and the elite's control of land. The relative continuity of the composition of the elite from the Ottoman through the Mandate period could not, however, remain stable amidst more substantive political and economic changes introduced by the Mandate authorities. The growth of the state bureaucracy had created an entirely new class of middle-class professionals, mostly Western educated and urban. The increasing penetration of the state into all facets of Syrian life and, more specifically, the increasing control of rural affairs by the urban political center, would further divide rural and urban Syria and breed hostility and resentment from rural communities against increasing state encroachment. Perhaps the most important change under the French authorities was the introduction of formal institutions of political deliberation that would provide the framework for the exercise of a new kind of class cohesion among the landed notables. Unsurprisingly, the concentration of economic power in the landowning and commercial classes was mirrored in the new Syrian Parliament. While political parties did emerge, they entirely reflected landed interests and did not seriously incorporate peasant or rural interests into the political system.

Beginning immediately after the Mandate authorities took power in the mid-1920s, there was signs of resistance to French rule from both the urban elite and the rural peasants. On the one hand, the elite found that French interests were increasingly inimical to their nationalism and that the French authorities had little interest in fulfilling the Mandate of midwifing Syrian self-government. Although the elite had benefitted tremendously from the French reluctance to upset the social structure and balance that had developed under the Ottomans, there was a contentious division between the French authorities and the elite that they ruled Syria through. Such tensions would ultimately culminate in the establishment of various institutions of political representation that offered the elite some degree of autonomy from their French overlords. On the other hand, peasants in the rural areas had become increasingly discontent with their socio-economic plight, as well as with French intervention into Syrian affairs. Such grievances were both complementary and contradictory, and, as such, did not provide the basis for cross-class mobilization against the French. Nor did they provide the basis for horizontal linkages among the lower classes and the development of a class consciousness that could mobilize peasants. Syria's many layered identities—clan, sect, geography—prevented such a development. Clientelism and the dependence of many peasants on the landed elite for social and political gains further ensured that such mobilization could not occur and that peasants would remain subordinate to the elite-dominated system.

By 1925, barely a few years after the Mandate took effect, there was a Great Revolt that lasted until 1927. This cross-sectarian, cross-class revolt occurred throughout Syria and Lebanon and was largely uncoordinated and decentralized but had the common aim of overthrowing French rule. Peasants, tribespeople, rural notables, nationalists, and the elite had all developed grievances against the French after the deposition of King Faisal in 1920. By 1925, a call to arms by a Syrian Druze leader named Sultan al-Atrash led to battles against French forces. In the first weeks of the revolt the Syrian forces were successful and al-Atrash and the nationalists had formed an alliance that led to a National Provisional Government. However, reinforcements from France eventually pushed the Syrian forces into retreat and by 1927 the rebellion had been crushed and along with it the experiment in transitional government. The rebellion had changed French attitudes toward Syria and had encouraged authorities to reform the political system and to begin responding to nationalist demands.

A series of policies followed that were meant to do precisely this, but they had not satisfied nationalist interests. In early 1936, National Bloc leaders had begun to publicly denounce the French authorities, which prompted the closing of the Bloc's offices and the arrest of two of its prominent leaders.

The Bloc responded by calling for a national strike that began on 20 January and led to work stoppages and student protests in all the major cities and towns throughout the country. The strikes paralyzed the country. Initially, French authorities responded with violence against the protesters, which left many dead and forced the Bloc's leaders into exile. By March 1936, the French authorities began negotiations with the National Bloc that led to the signing of the Franco-Syrian Treaty of Independence.

Ideologically speaking, the Syrian elite had begun gravitating toward Arab nationalism. In the 1920s in the aftermath of the collapse of the Ottoman Empire, the elite had not yet distinguished between Arab (transnational) and Syrian (territorial) nationalism nor advocated for either, as their main political interests lay in keeping their position as intermediary between the French authorities and Syrian society (Mufti, 1996, p. 45). The Nationalist Bloc, a proto-party representing nationalist interests, had actively rejected Arab unionist plans, first by renouncing claims to Lebanon in 1936, and second by rejecting unionist overtures from Hashemite Iraq and Transjordan (Mufti, 1996). The elite that controlled politics were thus navigating the space between French suzerainty and Syrian society, the latter of which was increasingly being influenced by nationalism and the possibilities of mass politics.

By 1946, the French occupation of Syria had ended and the National Bloc elites had assumed control. The Bloc, however, immediately disintegrated into different factions—the National Party (Damascus-based), the Republic Party (Damascus-based), and the People's Party (Aleppo-based)—that represented the various interests of the elite. In addition to the remnants of the National Bloc, the Communist Party, the Muslim Brotherhood, and the Youth Party all were in play, all of which had ideological orientations inimical to Arab nationalism. Finally, the Syrian Socialist Nationalist Party (SSNP) and the Ba'ath Party represented transnational ideological interests, with the SSNP advocating for the integration of Syria into a greater Syrian political entity inclusive of Iraq, Lebanon, Palestine, and Jordan, and the Ba'ath Party advocating for Arab nationalism.

From independence to the United Arab Republic

The post-independence period was one of tremendous political instability. Divisions between the political elite and agitation from the political parties opposed to elite rule made governance of the new state and the expansion of its political institutions difficult. The loss of Palestine in 1948 to Zionist forces had profound impacts on the radicalization of Syrian politics, especially for the nationalists. Meanwhile, the old elite had fragmented and was in political decline, while the new parties had begun to enjoy the support of large segments of the population. They could not, however, affect the distribution of power in society. They had not developed the distributive and patronage networks of the elite, which allowed them to maintain support in both rural and urban areas. There was an emergent tension, then, between the elites governing the state and the political interests, demands, and ideological orientation of much of society. Such tensions led to different forms of political protest, and, with remarkable frequency, coup attempts.

The 1950s was a period of intense political debate within Syria, mobilization of different societal interests, and the radicalization of Syrian politics. The elite political coalition that had sustained Syria from Ottoman times through the French Mandate had begun to collapse, and was being replaced with wider political coalitions that were inclusive of Syria's diverse political interests: rural peasants, the middle class, pan-Arab nationalists, and so on. The growth of state institutions created different centers of power beyond the elite-controlled institutions, and the army and bureaucracy emerged as two important sites of political control outside of elite capture. The army in particular, after a series of officer purges by loyalists of Adib Shishakli (President of Syria between 1953–1954), was dominated by Ba'athist officers.

Ba'athist influence was not confined to the army but had stretched to government, Parliament, and many individual Syrians, making the party a formidable force in Syria's emergent political landscape. The rise of Arab nationalism among Syrians had similarly benefitted the Ba'ath Party. The rise of mass politics and Arab nationalism in the 1950s was also shaped by the advancement of economic interests outside of those of the traditional elite. Increasing, the Ba'ath Party and others had adopted progressive social and economic policies that reflected the base of their support. This was especially the case in their advocacy of comprehensive agrarian reform and other policies that sought to break the economic stranglehold of the elites.

At the forefront of the rise of peasant politics in this period was Akram al-Hawrani, who first became engaged in politics in the 1930s. Al-Hawrani came from Hama, an area in which feudal practices persisted and the landed elite remained strong. As al-Hawrani became a prominent figure in Syrian politics in the 1940s and then 1950s, he was a staunch advocate of agrarian reform aimed at breaking the strength of the landed elite. His calls for reform made him an extremely popular figure among Syria's peasantry. By 1950, al-Hawrani had established the Arab Socialist Party (ASP) and was credited with providing the space for the mobilization of Syria's peasantry against the old order (Batatu, 1999, p. 370). His influence on the Ba'ath Party was not only through his advocacy of peasant politics. In the aftermath of his exile in the early 1950s after the banning of the ASP, al-Hawrani agreed to merge the ASP with the Arab Ba'ath Party then led by party founders and ideologues Michel Aflaq and Salah al-Din al-Bitar (it was this unified party, renamed the Arab Ba'ath Socialist Party, that was disbanded by the UAR in 1958).

Despite the merging of the two parties, the plural landscape had led to the factionalization of politics and of state institutions. The army had begun to factionalize and disagreements between progressive and conservative politics led to state paralysis. It was in this context that many political leaders, including those of the Ba'ath Party, had begun to openly advocate for political union with Egypt as a means of stabilizing the country. Egyptian President Gamal Abdel Nasser had reluctantly accepted the union but only under terms that would effectively circumscribe Syrian political mobilization and thwart radicalization. To this end, Nasser had imposed harsh demands on Syria, including the dissolution of political parties and the concentration of all constitutional power in his presidency. Moreover, Egyptian officials had imposed on Syria a radical nationalization plan that made the state directly responsible for capital accumulation while restructuring private commercial and industrial sectors (Heydemann, 1999, p. 106). This followed a series of restrictions on Syria's business elite that were intended to disrupt the social and economic networks underpinning their power. Nasser's political and economic restructuring of Syria during this period would have profound impacts on the development of the Syrian state.

The new United Arab Republic (UAR) was declared in 1958 in an attempt to consolidate Syria's political institutions and end instability. Ba'athist leaders were actually given high positions in the new entity but many army officers had been transferred to Egypt and replaced with Egyptian personnel. Abdel Nasser had viewed the Ba'ath with great suspicion and had actively tried to subordinate its leadership to his rule, despite the Ba'ath's insistence on shared governance of the Syrian region of the UAR. Pressures from Abdel Nasser and from within Syria had slowly weakened the Ba'ath Party and led to the migration of many supporters to other blocs.

Other parties had experienced similar fates as Abdel Nasser had gutted the political system and put in place a Cairo-based bureaucracy. The UAR was never successful in incorporating the social backgrounds and basis of the major Syrian political parties into the new system. It thus lacked its own social basis from which to rule. Despite this, the UAR initiated radical reforms in Syria, especially land reform, that gave land holdings to peasants, a blow to the landed elite. A further legacy of the UAR was the authoritarian institutions and structures that were put in place and carried throughout the post-1961 era (Heydemann, 1999). The state transformation that occurred during the UAR period was not reversed afterward but actually was reinforced, right through to the Ba'ath Party coup in 1963.

1963 and the rise of the Ba'ath Party

The failure of the UAR initiated a major transformation within the Ba'ath Party, including shifts in its ideological orientation and the social and sectarian composition of its supporters. When Nasser dissolved all political parties in 1958 as a prerequisite for the creation of the UAR, the provincial and national networks linking Ba'ath leaders and activists collapsed. After 1961, Ba'ath leaders were forced to reestablish the party's structures, as well as dealing with the political and ideological fallout of the failed unification. However, reestablishing the party's networks proved difficult in a climate in which Ba'ath supporters were largely split over the question of whether to seek re-union with Egypt or not. On the one hand, many Ba'athists, including co-founder Michel Aflaq, had supported re-union with Egypt in a federal model. The pro-unionists believed very strongly in Arab union and attributed the failure of the UAR to its undemocratic structure and not to the ideals of pan-Arabism and unity. The unionists were largely members of the urban Sunni middle classes who had supported Ba'athism as the champions of Arab nationalism. They had ideological affinities with Nasserism and remained loyal to the Nasserist ideals of Arab unity and nationalism after the collapse of the UAR. They were joined by other segments of the middle and lower classes that had similarly supported Ba'athism for its pan-Arab ideals and leadership but had abandoned the party after its dissolution or had questioned Ba'athist stewardship of Arab unity after the collapse of the UAR. The pro-unionists were more committed to the ideals of nationalism than to the party itself. On the other hand, the anti-unionists, while still committed to Arab nationalism, remained committed to the party and to reestablishing the pre-1958 Ba'ath networks. These activists were largely from rural areas, especially in Dar'a, Deir ez-Zor, and Latakia, and were organized around the party's provincial branches. In addition, some Ba'athist military officers who were discharged after the formation of the UAR and who were overwhelmingly from

Syria's minority Alawi, Druze, and Ismaili communities, similarly adopted opposition stances toward re-union. A "military committee" consisting of Mohammed Omran, Hafiz al-Assad, Abd al-Karim al-Jundi, and Salah Jedid was formed in order to transform the party and increase the political role of the military. Together with the rural activists, the military committee and other anti-unionist officers shared a rejection of the traditional Ba'ath Party model and the pre-UAR leadership, which they blamed for the dissolution of the party and the failure of union.

Two other major transformations occurred during this period that would have enormous consequences for the party and the future of Syria. First, the anti-unionists had drifted away ideologically from the traditional Ba'ath opposition to class struggle; they moved toward Marxism. Some Ba'ath leaders began openly to espouse socialism, which began a process of radicalizing the party and further distinguishing it from its pro-union elements. Moreover, the emergence of a new generation of Marxist-inspired activists led to the rejection of formal union as the vehicle for Arab unity; rather, mass political mobilization and social revolution were seen as the goal. For them, Arab nationalism was secondary and subordinate to the goals of socialism. Arab unity could only be achieved through mass socialist revolution and not through the conservative, reformist approach adopted by Aflaq and other pro-unionists within the party. Second, occurring parallel to the radicalization of the Ba'ath Party was the emergence of a minoritarian leadership. In the provinces and among the military officers, the new, younger generation of Ba'ath activists were overwhelmingly from Syria's many minority communities, especially the Alawi community. Moreover, the socioeconomic background of these activists was predominantly rural, thus making the reconstituted leadership of the Ba'ath Party predominantly rural and minoritarian in composition.

On the eve of the 1963 coup there was no ideological coherency or consistency to the Ba'ath Party leadership. Rather, the party was splintering along social and ideological lines, with pro-unionists being largely drawn from the

Sunni middle classes who had adopted more conservative, reformist positions, and the anti-unionists, who were increasingly radicalized and adopting socialism, drawn from the rural and minority segments of Syrian society. Under these circumstances of party fragmentation, Hinnebusch rightly states that "it is hard to imagine a more inauspicious juncture for a party to take power" (1990, p. 166). Nevertheless, fragmentation at the ideological and party level did not prevent military officers from organizing themselves to take power. Entirely divorced from the party's grass roots and lacking any sort of national character or mass social mobilization, military officers seized power in a bloodless coup on 8 March 1963. Circumstances prior to the coup had propelled an alliance of mistrust between party officials and Ba'athist military officers who were otherwise on opposite sides of the re-union question. The seizure of power by the Ba'ath in Iraq in February 1963 was a major catalyst, but a general climate of political stalemate and regime paralysis contributed as well. Almost immediately after the coup, internal fighting among the new Ba'athist regime occurred, and the new regime was characterized more by factionalism than coherence. Factionalization and infighting contributed to a climate of political confusion and disarray. Eventually, however, after a few months, the Ba'ath regime was purged of most of its Nasserist elements, and its leadership represented a core of rural and minoritarian officers.

The rural-minoritarian character would fundamentally shape the structure and character of the Ba'ath regime for decades (Batatu, 1999). The Party's revised form of pan-Arabism believed that the road to unity could not be achieved through formal union; rather, Arab unity would come from mass political mobilization and social revolution. Together, rural activists and military officers had reconstituted the party, committed to radical socialism and to overcoming the political embarrassment of the dissolution of the UAR. What occurred during this period was a process Batatu (1999, p. 144) called the "ruralization" of the army, Ba'ath Party, and state bureaucracy.

The assumption of power by the Ba'ath Party in 1963 in a bloodless coup by its military committee on 8 March would eventually bring about a period of relative political stability in Syria. The turmoil and chaos of the immediate postcolonial period had given way to the Ba'athist model of authoritarianism-populism, which sought to "establish the authority of a strong state autonomous of dominant classes and external powers and to launch national economic development aimed at easing dependence and subordinating capitalist forces to populist goals" (Hinnebusch, 1990, p. 2). The Ba'athist regime had, in its early years, pursued a policy of radical social transformation that was to be brought about by the confrontation with, and suppression of, social forces that underpinned the previous social order. The Ba'athists thus derived their legitimacy in part from their ability to organize and mobilize the peripheral classes, such as peasants, and to incorporate them into a political program aimed at destroying the vestiges of the old political order and establishing a new, broad base of social support for the new political order (Batatu, 1999). For the Ba'ath regime, then, the origins of its social base and the social forces that were incorporated into Ba'athist politics are central to understanding the rise and consolidation of the regime and the strategies it employed to remain in power.

By the time that the Ba'ath Party had taken control of Syria in 1963 it was a radically different party than it had been in the Mandate era. The UAR period had initiated ideological shifts in the party and had reorganized its social base. The party had emerged from UAR with varying ideological strands competing for control. Eventually, the more radical strands won out and created a blueprint for Syrian society that was rooted in particular ideas about socialism—which was more important for the new leadership than pan-Arabism as a governing ideology.

The Ba'athist coup

After coming to power, the radical Ba'ath officers had purged the army of Nasserist officers and had taken full control of the party. This began a slow purge of party members who did not share their radical vision for the social transformation of society or who were loyal to other branches of the Ba'ath. In addition to internal conflict, the Ba'ath had to absorb dissent from within Syrian society, especially the remnants of the conservative parties that strongly opposed its radical socialist politics. The challenge for the Ba'athist leaders at the time was how to consolidate political power. As time would tell, however, there was an internal challenge that would also have to be resolved before power could be consolidated.

The initial years after the coup were thus a period of relative instability. The Ba'ath was able to survive in power because of the fragmentation of the opposition and the relative weakness of its conservative foes. The Ba'ath had to reinvigorate its relationship with its main social base in the rural areas to insulate itself from opposition and to enact its socialist revolution. By the mid-1960s, Ba'athist power had begun to consolidate, as opponents were purged from key offices and the army and state apparatus were under the full control of the party. Meanwhile, the government began a period of radical economic reforms through nationalizations of industry and finance and through continued land reforms that diffused land rights to peasants and agricultural workers. Public planning would supersede the market as the main distributive mechanism and the public sector became the main engine of economic development. Private enterprise was severely curtailed and economic relations with the West rolled back. Such policies provided the material basis of Ba'athist rule and allowed them to consolidate a social basis of support outside of the urban areas, which had served as the traditional power centers from the Ottoman period on.

The corrective revolution and the consolidated state

The consolidation of the post-UAR Syrian state was occurring amidst battles internal to the Ba'ath Party. In 1970, Hafiz al-Assad led a "corrective revolution" that was motivated by the 1967 defeat in the Arab-Israeli war and the desire to end domestic conflict. Hafiz al-Assad led an ideological revision of the party while maintaining the cross-sectarian, civilian-military composition of the existing regime. This new "corrective movement" would maintain a commitment to socialism but would reorient the state toward the liberation of the territories occupied in 1967. This entailed a reorientation of Syria's foreign relations and domestic policy to oppose antagonistic social forces. Rapprochement with the oil monarchies in the Arab Gulf would provide financial resources for al-Assad's efforts in exchange for Syria's ceasing to export socialist revolution to Arab countries; economic policy would be slowly liberalized to provide some opportunities for the private sector.

According to Patrick Seale (1990, p. 172), Assad had two ideas about how to govern Syria after the corrective revolution: the first was that there was to be no challenge to his rule, that it would be absolute, and the second was that he would cultivate wide popular support for his policies. The corrective movement thus broadened the social basis of the new regime by placating and incorporating some elements of the traditionally hostile conservative social forces, especially the bourgeois. More important, however, was the institutional basis of the spread of these measures to expand Ba'ath Party reach and incorporate antagonistic social forces into the state. The first move was to create a parliament that successfully co-opted social forces beyond the regime's core rural constituency. The Ba'ath-dominated National Progressive Front (NPF, a coalition of parliamentary political parties) was created to incorporate socialist and communist parties, while Nasserists were also increasingly willing to cooperate with Ba'ath rule. Although Assad believed in his absolute power to rule Syria, he did so through the existing institutions of the state and party that were at his disposal.

Internal turmoil over the proclamation of a new constitution in 1973 that made the Ba'ath Party the leading party in society was eventually ignored after the beginning of the war with Israel. Although the army was unable to regain lost lands, they had performed better than in 1967, and this won al-Assad a great deal of legitimacy in Syria. Equally important was the oil boom of the 1970s that followed the war. Petrodollars flowing into the Arab Gulf countries began to make their way into Syria in the form of grants to support the state in its war with Israel. Petrodollars allowed al-Assad to oversee the expansion of the state and the distribution of resources—jobs, services, and other economic opportunities—to fulfill the party's socialist goals.

The regime that al-Assad oversaw had four pillars of power (Hinnebusch, 2001, pp. 80–87). The first was the party itself (Seale, 1990, p. 174), which acted as an intermediary between the central state and the governorates and villages, ensuring the diffusion of state policy. The party emerged as the main agent of state policy. Moreover, the party was expanded to incorporate the regime's social base and to link party members to social institutions, such as unions. The second pillar was corporatism, a process by which different social forces are subordinated and incorporated into the regime. The regime had linked social forces by organizing hitherto demobilized groups, such as peasants and students, and incorporating them into state-controlled associations. The regime's control of these associations meant that they lacked any independence or autonomy from the government. In exchange for financial support, the social forces were slowly incorporated into the state apparatus and thus created a large constituency committed to the survival of the state and regime.

The third pillar of al-Assad's rule was the state bureaucracy (Heydemann, 1999). The expansion of the state bureaucracy penetrated all facets of Syrian life, and the socialist policies in the 1970s and 1980s led to a bloating of the bureaucracy, which employed close to 25 percent of Syrians at one point in the 1980s. Finally, the fourth pillar of power in al-Assad's Syria was the army and security apparatus (Seale, 1990; Heydemann, 1999). The loyalty of the army and the security apparatus was ensured by placing regime loyalists, mostly Alawis, in positions of power. The army and security apparatus were effectively incorporated into the regime by the purging of non-Ba'athists and non-loyalists. In the late 1970s and 1980s the low-level civil war between the Muslim

Brotherhood and the regime affirmed the loyalty of the army and the security apparatus, which, even throughout the current uprising, has remained loyal to the regime.

Fiscal crisis and the "liberalization" of political and economic space

The consolidation of the Syrian state under Hafiz al-Assad's rule in the 1970s and 1980s withstood the turbulence of the period, which included regional wars (the 1973 Arab-Israeli war, and the Lebanese civil war that began in 1975) and civil violence between the state and an insurgent Muslim Brotherhood that culminated in the Hama massacre in 1982 and the exile of most of the Brotherhood's leadership. In the mid-1980s another source of turbulence occurred when the state suffered a fiscal crisis wrought by the rapidly declining price of oil. Syria's budget was heavily reliant on oil revenues derived from its own modest production and the recycling of petrodollars from Arab Gulf states. The need to generate revenues beyond oil led the regime toward a slow rapprochement with the private sector, one of its traditional antagonists.

With the exception of a few economic moguls connected to the regime, the 1970s and 1980s was a period of private sector stagnation. Most enterprises had to navigate a complicated and restrictive economic environment that was made even more difficult by the regime's open hostility toward bourgeois interests. By the late 1980s and early 1990s this had changed, as businesspeople started to develop stronger ties with the regime through patronage relations (Haddad, 2012a). These emergent state-business relations grew in the 1990s, and businesspeople were slowly incorporated into the web of political power, gaining seats in Parliament and enjoying increasing access to the political elite.

The reintroduction of business interests into the political sphere was gradual as the regime elite continued to view the private sector with hostility. The main dilemma for the political elite was how to foster private sector economic activity while suppressing their collective demands for access to political power and decision-making. The dilemma was clear: the political elite needed the private sector to stimulate the economy, generate foreign exchange to compensate for lost oil revenues, and to create jobs to alleviate the employment bottlenecks in the public sector. In order to bring this about, the elite had to engage in compromises with the private sector. Thus the Ba'ath Party's historical antagonist— the private sector—was slowly incorporated into the regime.

In the early 1990s, the government had passed an investment law (No. 10) meant to liberalize investment restrictions. In 1992, the state budget included substantial restrictions on social welfare spending and tax incentives for private enterprises (Lawson, 1997). Such measures invited criticism from the General Federation of Workers' Union, which accused the government of supporting private enterprises at the expense of the public sector. These policies, although they were gradual and piecemeal reforms, reflected the slow strategic shift of the regime toward greater liberalization of private capital and a rollback of state spending to compensate for the loss of revenues.

Yet, despite these reforms, the private sector and the state remained antagonistic. The regime had never sanctioned associational activity, thus precluding the collective mobilization or articulation of interests by the private sector. Access to economic power was secured through access to the political elite and state bureaucrats who controlled the economic levers of the state. Patronage and economic networks were important to the cultivation of political networks and to the private sector's access to economic opportunities (Haddad, 2012a; Haddad, 2014). Like most other social forces in Syria, the private sector would not be autonomous from the regime.

During the 1990s, the regime was successful in suppressing private sector political demands and in incorporating the private sector into the ruling coalition. This inclusion was not total, however, as the majority of Syrian private sector enterprises that were family-run, small in size, and had limited production, continued to operate outside of the networks of political power and within a web of complicated regulations, fear of asset seizure, and regime suppression. The benefits of the reforms, then, were only accrued by a select group of businesspeople who had direct access to the regime and were embedded in relationships with the political elite.

Consequently, the regime was only partially able to address the economic dilemma caused by the fiscal crisis of the 1980s. The liberalizations of the 1970s and 1980s had provided the space for private sector expansion but this had only benefitted an economic elite that was drawn from the urban Sunni bourgeois and, increasingly, from the sons and daughters of the political and security elite. The basis for the widespread distribution of wealth did not occur, and the state's finances remained mired in stagnation. In the late 1990s, right before the death of Hafiz al-Assad, the state was facing potential economic crisis: a desperate need for widespread job creation and the alleviation of oil dependence, economic stagnation, and decreasing standards of living and increasing poverty (Perthes, 2001).

Bashar's rise

By the time that Bashar al-Assad assumed power in Syria, the authoritarian populism that shaped the early years of Ba'athist rule in Syria had ceased to exist. Since independence, Syria had pursued forms of statist economic development whereby the state was positioned as the dominant economic actor. Under the rule of Hafiz al-Assad, Ba'athist statism was underpinned by a model of social, economic, and political organization that was marshaled in support of state-building rather than economic development. The statist model placed the corporatist logic of inclusion, stability, and state dependence ahead of economic development. As Hinnebusch rightly argues, this model eventually exhausted itself because it fostered "consumption at the expense of accumulation" (Hinnebusch, 2009, p. 17). The exhaustion of Ba'athist statism forced the regime to engage in a series of economic reforms in the late 1980s and throughout the 1990s, which were accelerated considerably after 2000 when Bashar al-Assad assumed power. Since 2000, economic reforms had aimed at introducing market relations into the economy while gradually rolling back the policies, institutions, and distributional patterns of decades of central planning. These reforms were motivated by neoliberal thinking about the economy and framed under the vague strategy of a "social market economy" that attempted to achieve social welfare through increasingly privatized and marketized mechanisms. As the period of marketization demonstrated, however, the reforms failed to address many of the social demands of Syrians. In attempting to do so, however, the marketization period severely disrupted the relationships between state and society that made material gains and social welfare possible.

The changes wrought in Syria during the 2000s led to the gradual deinstitutionalization of Ba'athism as a social, political, and economic model, and the deinstitutionalization of Ba'athism as a cultural and belief system that was designed to support its institutions (see Hsu, 2007). The story of the social market economy in Syria, as elsewhere in the formerly centrally planned economies, is one of the gradual retreat of the state from its active and hegemonic role within society and the simultaneous dismantling of the institutions linking state and society. What was slowly occurring in Syria during the 2000s was a diffusion of economic authority from the public to the private sector through the transfer of responsibility for social welfare from the state to the market. One of the consequences of the diffusion process is that the transfer of authority from the public to private sector undermines the strength of traditional corporatist actors and the linkages they have developed with the regime and the state (Abboud, 2015). Economic policy then aims at introducing the private sector as the main engine of economic growth and development. The state thus cedes authority to the private sector and rolls back many of its distributive policies that had linked other social actors, such as workers, to the state. Therefore, as a discourse and set of policy choices, the social market economy strategy was an attempt to alter the nature of the state's embeddedness in society relative to various social forces.

The government had failed to provide an explanation for what the social market economy actually was, beyond what goals they hoped to achieve through market reforms (Abboud, 2015). The basic structure of the policies was to rebalance public/private sector authority and to encourage private business interests to play a larger role in the economy. The state would adopt a more interventionist role to address market deficiencies, while public-sector assets would be preserved in their current form. Private business interests would be addressed through the creation of new private-sector investment opportunities, and not through the sale of public-sector assets. This method of dual-track liberalization was intended to create parallel and competing public and private sector actors in the economy, whether in finance, insurance, or service provision, such as schools and health care, and to shift Syria's fiscal dependence away from oil revenues, which formed nearly half of all budgetary revenues in the 1990s.

Some of the key policies of the 2000s reflect the regime's strategy of dual-track liberalization and the shift toward a more marketized economy. Public-sector monopolies were slowly broken and new private-sector investments in banking, insurance, education, and other sectors appeared. Meanwhile, the government's vast subsidy system was dismantled and price ceilings on everything from basic foods to housing prices were lifted. The economic volatility caused by the marketization of prices led to tremendous economic uncertainty among many households and businesses. The basic thrust of the reforms was to slowly remove obstacles to market activity and to subject prices to the market, all while maintaining Syria's authoritarian political structures. Investment policy, so central to generating revenues for development projects, was severely limited and tailored to meet the interests of elites connected to the regime (Matar, 2016). The balance between the need for economic reform and regime stability was the main driver of the marketization period.

However, marketization did not broaden the basis of accumulation in Syria. Only very narrow private interests embedded in the regime's power circles benefitted from privatization. To be sure, many in the business community did reap peripheral benefits of marketization but the overwhelming majority (more than 96 percent) of Syrian business enterprises were small (less than ten employees) and were on the peripheries of the economic gains in the 2000s. Moreover, the marketization period initiated a series of economic shocks in Syria that would have profound impacts on the social and economic well-being of the majority of the population.

Most major socioeconomic indicators reflect a deterioration of living standards during the 2000s and reduced mechanisms of social mobility and social welfare. Unemployment rates continued to increase, wages were well below the increasing costs of living, and price volatility created economic uncertainty for millions of Syrians. While the Ba'athist model of development contained structural flaws, the reforms in the 2000s did not necessarily address these. Instead, they have disrupted the institutions of social mobility, such as the public sector, and reconfigured the social stratification that had taken root under Syrian Ba'athism. In the 1960s and 1970s, for example, redistributive policies had vastly improved the economic lives of peasants and the poor. Policies of nationalization and a robust distributive system that was focused on rural development and the privileging of agricultural production enhanced rural life. Meanwhile, public sector expansion created a massive social basis for the regime, middle class jobs, and a strong state bureaucracy from which to govern the country (Haddad, 2012b). Public-sector employees, urban workers, and rural peasants formed the social basis for the regime and the Ba'athist model of development was intended to shelter them from the market. In doing so, however, the regime adopted a purely distributive position in the economy and was not able, for political and social reasons, to extract wealth from these groups or make them a source of capital accumulation (Dahi and Munif, 2012).

By the 1980s, these mechanisms of rural support and public sector expansion were placed under pressure by the fiscal crisis and the state's distributive role was no longer fiscally sustainable. The regime was forced to begin to reorient the economy away from oil dependence, and its past privileging of agricultural enterprise had to shift toward the non-agricultural sectors of the economy (Hinnebusch, 2010). Very slowly, a process of rural and agricultural neglect set in, a betrayal of the Ba'ath Party's primary social and economic basis of support. Three policies in particular would have substantial impacts on rural communities and their relationship to the regime: first, the rapid decline of agricultural subsidies; second, new land laws that reoriented ownership and usage rights away from the cooperative models of the previous two decades; and third, the government's incentives to produce a few "strategic crops," which encouraged farmers to abandon diverse production of crops and instead concentrate on those that were heavily subsidized (Hinnebusch, 2010). Unsurprisingly, agricultural productivity slowly declined as government attention turned toward the non-agricultural sectors of the economy. In the 1990s and into the 2000s there was a gradual movement of rural migrants into the urban peripheries. Most rural migrants had settled in slums around the major cities. This process was so pronounced that one Syrian economist suggested that around 20 percent of the total Syrian population lived in some sort of slum village by the late 2000s (Seifan, 2010).

In parallel to these policies were a set of neoliberal discursive shifts that redefined the relationship between state, society, and economy. The wholesale destruction of the institutions of the Syrian state or the privatization of public sector assets would have delegitimized decades of Ba'athist development. As a result, the new economic reforms had to be presented in a way that made them compatible with the Ba'athist policies of the 1970–2000 period, or, at the very least, did not discredit the decades of social policies that were the material foundations of Ba'athist rule. The social market economy emerged as a set of public narratives about the economy and allowed average Syrians to make sense of the turbulent economic transformations they were experiencing. These new narratives differed considerably from previous decades of Ba'athist rhetoric about the economy (Sottimano, 2008) and reflected the government's strategic shift toward neoliberal policies by focusing on issues of personal responsibility, the central role of the private sector in economic development, decreasing dependence on the state for social welfare, and the greater integration of Syria into regional and global economies through trade liberalization (Abboud, 2015).

The policies pursued in the 2000s after Bashar al-Assad came to power were not simply representative of a new shift in economic thinking toward services or the urban economy at the expense of the agricultural and rural economy. The reforms introduced after 2000 blended neoliberal and authoritarian modes of governance and in doing so had generated a new kind of politics that married the rhetoric of social welfare and protections with the benefits of liberalization and marketization. The regime had actively pursued economic transformation through a new coalition of the private sector elites and a reinvigorated (but not autonomous) civil society. The old model represented an alliance between the army, peasants, workers, the Ba'ath Party, and the public sector. However, this populist-authoritarian model had exhausted itself by the 2000s and gave way for a new model that instead reflected the economic interests of the urban classes, economic elites, and regime officials.

Bashar al-Assad had presided over not only a reorientation of the Ba'athist model of development but a reorientation of Syria's foreign relations as well. He had inherited from his father a collapsed peace process, hostile relations with Turkey and Iraq, and control over neighboring Lebanon. Syrian forces had been present in Lebanon since the civil war and the Syrian hegemonic role was consecrated in the Ta'if agreement that ended the Lebanese civil war in 1991. Syrian hegemony in Lebanon had bred resentment among many Lebanese while fostering a political elite that was dependent on Syria for political power (el-Husseini, 2012).

The events and aftermath of 11 September, 2001, had radically changed the regional geopolitical situation. U.S.-led wars and occupations in Afghanistan and Iraq had disrupted an increasing rapprochement between Syria and Iraq, the latter having emerged as a major importer of Syrian goods and thus an important element of the government's trade liberalization strategies. The Syrian regime was active in fomenting the armed opposition to the occupation by supplying weapons and allowing the entry of fighters from its territory and had thus entered into indirect confrontation with the United States. Meanwhile, a similar rapprochement had occurred with Turkey. The threat of war in the late 1990s was replaced with "brotherly" relations between the two countries (Bank and Karadag, 2013) and the signing of a free trade agreement that was part of Syria's development strategy to achieve greater economic openness and foster market competition (Abboud, 2009). Syria's deepening ties with Iraq and Turkey contrasted with the collapse of Pax Syriana after the assassination of the former Lebanese Prime Minister on 14 February 2005, which prompted a series of demonstrations in Lebanon that led to the withdrawal of Syrian forces from Lebanon. Finally, Syria had deepened its ties to Hizbollah in Lebanon. Hafiz al-Assad had been keen to keep Hizbollah's power in check by supporting another Shi'a-based party called Amal. Bashar al-Assad, however, had actively deepened ties with Hizbollah and had drawn on their Secretary General's imagery to enhance his legitimacy inside the country.

By 2011, the Syrian state looked considerably different than it had merely a decade prior. There had been a radical reorganization of the country's foreign relations that had paralleled major transformation in the economy and the near abandonment of Ba'athist-era socialist policies. The latter transformation had represented the growing convergence of regime-business interests and had further peripheralized those social forces that were central to the exercise of Ba'athist power and legitimacy from the 1960s, including the rural peasants and workers. Ba'athism had morphed considerably over the 2000s in ways that placed political and social pressures on the Syrian populace for which there was no political outlet to express discontent or mobilize.

Circumscribed civil society

Prior to the uprising, Syria did not have an autonomous civil society. There was very limited space for the expression of political dissent. From the 1960s onwards the only associations that were formed and licensed by the state were charitable organizations that were almost all religious. Political instability in the late 1970s and early 1980s, during the direct confrontation with the Muslim Brotherhood, altered the regime's tolerance of these associations, and, slowly, the licensing process was discontinued and the government no longer sanctioned charitable associations. By the 1990s the government had renewed the licensing system and a number of legal, sanctioned associations began to operate alongside the remnants of the old associations that had remained in operation, albeit informally and without government permission.

Civil society organizations beyond charitable associations became a feature of Syrian political and social life during the marketization period in the 2000s. The opening up of political space for civil society groups to form and operate was, however, severely restricted. The regime had fostered civil society groups to bolster its reformist agenda but also as means of alleviating some of the social hardships caused by marketization. Thus, many of the civil society groups that emerged were focused on social service provision while very few advocacy or issue-based organizations were formed. While some rights groups were formed, these were limited and remained subject to regime repression. Those that were licensed and sanctioned by the government endured tremendous obstacles to legalization. Prior to receiving government approval, an application for license had to be approved by all fifteen intelligence agencies, in addition to the Ministry of Social Affairs and Labour itself. Moreover, once approved, virtually all major projects needed approval from the Ministry. Such obstacles further restricted associational life.

Civil society groups that were licensed were never entirely autonomous from the regime. In the early 2000s when the Declaration of One Thousand was signed and various political and cultural forums sprang up throughout the country, the regime was initially tolerant. Many of these forums actually planted the seeds for more organized expressions of associational activity later in the decade, including human rights and charitable organizations. In the early part of the 2000s, the most important forum was the Forum for National Dialogue started by Riad el-Seif, a parliamentarian. The success of the forum and the authorities' apparent sanctioning of its meetings led el-Seif to announce the establishment of a political party called the Movement for Social Peace. Riad el-Seif and his followers had overstepped the regime's limits with this declaration and el-Seif was stripped of his parliamentary immunity and convicted of bogus corruption charges. The attempt to create a new unsanctioned political party also led the regime to close all the remaining forums (except for one) in the country, effectively circumscribing the budding civil society movement.

After this very few spaces existed for political and social discussion among Syrian elites. The Jamal Atassi Forum was never given a license to operate but remained active even though the remaining forums had been closed down by the regime. A second forum was the Syrian Economic Society (SEC), which held weekly meetings in Damascus where intellectuals, business leaders, and government officials came together to discuss the country's economic situation. The former forum was eventually closed down in 2005, while the SEC continued to offer lectures right up until the uprising.

In this period, Syria's civil society displayed two primary structural characteristics. The first is that it was mostly led by intellectuals and elites. This was especially true of the various forums that were established in the country. These civil society organizations were predominantly elite gatherings and their political activity was confined to the exchange of ideas about reform and the future of the country. There were very few attempts at organization and mobilization of key segments of society around specific identities or issues. The second characteristic is that they were largely informal groupings with no established organizational structures, funding streams, or legal relationship to the state. The groupings were spontaneous to some degree and, aside from charitable organizations, had virtually no organizational precedent under the Ba'ath era.

By the mid-2000s these forums had made a return to the social and political arena and had begun to proliferate throughout the country. The growth of new, now formalized and licensed, civil society organizations occurred within the context of the regime's shift to a social market economy of development (discussed in Chapter One). The shift toward a social market economy entailed a reorganization of the state's relationship to society. In particular, the social market economy model, in practice if not in theory, led to the gradual shifting of power from the state to social groups. For this reason, the regime had slowly begun to devolve power to groups that were hitherto excluded from the main centers of power—mainly, the business community.

Thus, from the mid-2000s onwards, the regime had engaged in a process of authoritarian diffusion that shifted more power to social actors. The state would no longer be the central economic actor in society and would now rely on privatized actors (civil society, the business community) to provide social services, public goods, and economic growth.

Such a shift did not, however, entail a substantial loss of regime power. It instead forced the regime into codependent relations with social groups. For example, in the late 2000s, a major charitable organization called the Jama'at Zayd (Zayd Group) had become one of the largest and most organized charitable organizations in Damascus and operated a charitable network of more than thirty mosques (Pierret and Selvik, 2009).

For Pierret and Selvik, the growth of the Zayd Group represented a coalition of private-sector businesspeople working with local religious leaders to provide social and charitable works, or what has been referred to as the 'ulama'-merchant nexus (Pierret and Selvik, 2009). On the one hand, the regime had historically repressed such activities and thus had viewed the growth of these charitable organizations with extreme suspicion. On the other hand, the charities offered a social safety net to buffer against continued economic stagnation and the social effects of the shift toward a more privatized, marketized economy.

The need to pass social service responsibilities to private actors forced the regime to open up the space for civil society groups. With the shift to a more marketized economy, civil society organizations such as the Zayd Group proliferated. Some were, of course, less politically threatening to the regime than the larger Islamic networks. On the eve of the uprising there were hundreds of smaller charitable organizations that were registered with the Ministry of Social Affairs and Labour and that operated within a legal framework. Charitable organizations were by far the largest segment of civil society in the 2000s. The major sources of funding for these organizations were private donations from Syrians. There was almost no Syrian government or foreign funding available to these organizations. The regime had also created a network of non-governmental organizations that were controlled by the government and did not have any autonomy from the state. These Government Non-Governmental Organizations (GONGOs) were largely active in social issues, such as women's and children's rights, and in development issues. The GONGOs operated under the organizational umbrella of the Syrian Trust for Development and included different educational, social rights, and development organizations and were all organized under the patronage of First Lady Asma Assad, which gave the Trust protection from the authorities and a degree of social legitimacy to operate throughout Syria. The Syrian Trust was also the largest recipient of both government and foreign government funds, especially from the European Union. Perhaps not surprisingly, government efforts to engage civil society in the policy and development process were only inclusive of GONGOs.

In addition to the charitable organizations and the GONGOs, cultural and human rights organizations were established in the 2000s. While Syria has a long history of cultural forums dating back to the 1800s, many of these organizations disappeared after the Ba'ath Party took power in the 1960s. However, by the 2000s, they had begun to reappear in Syria but were mostly focused on music and art and had largely stayed away from engaging in political activity. Similarly, women's rights organizations were largely at arm's length from the government and were confined to focusing specifically on women's and children's issues. While some of the more prominent organizations, such as the Syrian Association for Women's Role in Development and the Syrian Women Observatory had engaged in activism around women's and children's issues, they were never treated as threatening by the regime because their activism never threatened the structure of power.

These civil society organizations were largely tolerated by the regime (and in the case of the GONGOs, actively encouraged) in order to expand social service provision or to provide a small, circumscribed, and tolerated space for activism. In the 2000s, human rights organizations were also established that directly challenged the regime's repeated human rights abuses and engaged in activism for prisoners' rights and greater political freedoms for Syrians. A number of organizations existed in the 2000s, including the Syrian Observatory for Human Rights (SOHR) and the Syrian Human Rights Committee (SHRC), which had operated an extensive network of activists in the country up until the uprising. The human rights organizations, however, suffered from a number of problems that limited their political impact within Syria. First, many were underfunded and had failed to develop strong organizational capacities. Second, many of the organizations had attempted, but failed, to pool resources and form larger associations to foster greater cooperation and activism. Unfortunately, personal rivalries between many of the activists led to splits between these organizations and a failure to coordinate activities. Most important, however, was the constant threat of repression, imprisonment, and closure from regime security forces, who viewed their work with hostility. Many of the key players in the human rights organizations in the 2000s spent time in prison, thus discouraging other activists and stunting the growth and efficacy of the organizations.

By 2011 the Syrian regime had undergone dramatic change in its social base and its economic orientation. Civil society organizations, especially GONGOs, were a small but important element of this reorientation as they were incorporated into the state as social welfare providers and as alternatives to public sector provision of goods and services. The most important shift had occurred through the slow, gradual abandonment by the Ba'ath Party of its traditional rural constituency and the incorporation of the business community and the bourgeois into the new ruling bargain. While the business community did not represent civil society as such, the networks many of the urban business elite formed with the Syrian *ulama* connected them deeply to associational life in pre-uprising Syria (Pierret, 2013).

Thus on the eve of the uprising Syrians had very few associations that they could organize around in order to make demands against the regime. The associations that did exist reflected elite rather than mass politics, and had largely failed to give political voice to Syrians or to help alleviate Syrians' dire socioeconomic conditions, which were increasingly worsening over the decade. All of this occurred within a context of continued repression and a seemingly stable regime, buoyed by its regional position and the absence of a formidable political movement that sought its overthrow.

Conclusion

The Ba'ath Party has profoundly shaped Syria's post-Mandate history. Having emerged out of a period of social discontent and popular mobilization, the Ba'ath Party had overseen the radical transformation of Syrian society and the dismantling of a political and economic system that favored landed notables. The seismic shifts in Syria's evolution from Ottoman province to French Mandate and through the independence period have at different times included and excluded various social forces whose antagonism with the state shaped politics. For much of the Ba'ath Party's control of power from the 1970s onwards, social discontent was dealt with through repression. The apparent stability of the Ba'ath period and the economic growth of the 1970s and into the 1980s was underpinned by a highly repressive and brutal security apparatus that ensured that political discontent would be suppressed. Such reliance on the security apparatus exposed the main structural flaw of Ba'athism that was masked by corporatism. The incorporation of social forces into the state did not occur organically or through popular acceptance and adherence to Ba'athist ideology, but rather through some combination of corporatism and repression.

While none of this historical discussion necessarily portends an uprising in Syria, it certainly suggests that the rapid social transformations and reorientation of the state's domestic and foreign policies had a profound impact on the Ba'ath Party's pillars of power and its ability to exercise control over society and suppress discontent. While there is no single identifiable cause behind the decision of millions of Syrians to engage in protest and mobilization against the regime after March 2011, the changing nature of state-society relations, socioeconomic decline, and the suppression of political and associational life were all extremely important factors, alongside others such as climate change and the contagion effect of the Arab uprisings. While the Syrian uprising occurred within this larger context of the Arab uprisings, it has taken on a unique character and has evolved in radically different ways than those in Tunisia, Egypt, Bahrain, and elsewhere.

Any inquiry into the nature, structure, and drivers of the Syrian uprising has to account for the uniqueness of the country and the specificity of its political, social, and economic landscape. The Syrian uprising was shaped by the historical suppression of party politics. The absence of pre-existing institutions that could mobilize society gave the Syrian uprising the unique feature of being highly decentralized and uncoordinated. The absence of coordinating bodies gave rise to the need for greater organization among the protesters, which subsequently led to the creation of various groups both inside and outside of the country who attempted to organize and speak in the name of the uprising. Similarly, as Joshua Stacher (2012) has argued in the Syrian case, the regime's power and decision-making was decentralized, thus creating multiple centers of power in which the Presidency served as an arbiter of power, rather than an absolute power. This decentralization fueled the regime's violent response, with no center of political gravity able to contain or direct violence. Thus, from the very beginning of the uprising, the historical suppression of the political opposition and the decentralized nature of the regime would shape the limits and possibilities of the protesters and force them to create new structures from which to organize and mobilize against the regime.

Political dissent had been effectively contained by the Syrian regime through a combination of repression and limited inclusion of social actors into the state. The corporatist relations that underpinned the Ba'athist model of development had begun to shift, however. In the absence of independent political parties or an autonomous civil society, there were no institutions for the expression and mobilization of political grievances. But socioeconomic decline, political inertia, and the continued state of emergency in Syria that had been in place since the 1960s all provided the basis for the articulation of political grievances and the mobilization of segments of the population within the broader context of the Arab uprisings. The mobilization of the 2011 period was markedly different than previous periods, during which political parties and patronage networks could cultivate and mobilize support around key issues and political demands. Such mobilization along party lines was precluded in Syria, but this did not mean that protesters could not find ways to engage in politics.

This chapter focuses on the first months of the uprising, from March 2011 into the early period of 2012. We will examine the beginnings of the uprising and address how protests were able to sustain themselves in the absence of pre-existing institutions to mobilize the population. Here, the role of the Local Coordination Committees (LCCs) and other civil society groups, in addition to social networks of protesters, was instrumental in giving the protests momentum and allowing them to continue in the face of sustained regime repression. We will also consider the role of the Syrian political opposition in exile and how the relations between opposition groups inside and outside of the country shaped the evolution of the conflict. The formation of the LCCs was vital to sustaining the protests—they took on multiple roles, first as organizers of the protests and as citizen journalists disseminating information about them, and second in relief and governance roles when the regime's forces contracted throughout the country. In many ways, this period reflects the "transgressive contention" conceptualized by Tilly et al. (2001) wherein newly formed and identified political actors employ innovative and novel methods of collective action to make political demands.

The regime's response throughout the first months of the process was to engage in sustained repression of the protesters while passing cosmetic political reforms. Both strategies failed to placate the protesters and the protests quickly evolved into a national movement that was spreading throughout urban and rural Syria alike, giving the early protesters the appearance of being a national phenomenon. Yet despite the national character of the protests, the movement was highly dispersed and decentralized, precluding effective coordination. Moreover, as the uprising continued the exiled opposition formed and attempted to exert its influence, to very little substantial effect, in large part because of its inability to suppress internal cleavages and to marshal material resources for the protesters (and later the armed opposition). As the opposition became more militarized by the summer of 2011 and the exiled opposition fragmented into factions, the uprising had competing leaderships, all of which failed to coordinate and coalesce into a centralized command structure that could have placed military and political pressure on the regime. Regional actors also contributed to this fragmentation by taking up support for the various centers of power within the opposition and encouraging conflict among them. The organizational structure of the nonviolent and armed segments of the opposition was thus never materially, politically, or militarily able to organize in ways that could have overthrown the regime, particularly since regional allies were intent on securing the regime's hold on power. While these issues with the opposition help explain the regime's resiliency throughout this period, the ability of the regime to adapt to the changing circumstances of the protests, cultivate privatized violence, rely on foreign support, and to consolidate its social base in 2011–2012 also helps explain why the regime did not succumb to the protests.

The Syrian opposition

In the forty years of Ba'athist rule the domestic political opposition was severely suppressed. Political parties were essentially forbidden, except for those who accepted the leadership of the Ba'ath Party in the National Progressive Front, a coalition of parties represented in the ineffectual Syrian parliament. The emasculation of these parties and their subservience to the Ba'ath Party precluded the possibility of cultivating a base from which to mobilize against the regime. Political parties such as the Muslim Brotherhood (MB) that did not acquiesce to this order were subject to repression. Simultaneously, the main associational institutions of society, such as unions and syndicates, were corporatized and brought under Ba'athist control, effectively circumscribing political autonomy and eliminating the possibility that they would function as vehicles for sociopolitical mobilization.

In this context, the only opposition to survive in any organizational form was the MB, but it did so outside of the country from the 1980s onwards. The Islamist opposition to Ba'athist rule was motivated by a number of factors, including opposition to Ba'athist secular policies, opposition to nationalization and modernization projects, and a rejection of state domination of the economy (Hinnebusch, 1993, p. 249). The suppression of political activity and the deep cleavages between the regime and the Islamist opposition eventually led to violent confrontation, most dramatically in the attack by regime forces against Hama in 1982 that killed thousands of people. After 1982, the MB leadership was forced into exile and membership in the party remained punishable by death. The party would cease to be a domestic opposition force as its leadership was effectively severed from supporters and constituents. With the elimination of the MB and the exile of its leadership the regime was successful in eliminating any popular threat to its hegemony.

With party life suppressed and the main opposition group in exile and its organizational capacity virtually eliminated, individuals emerged as the main oppositionists to the regime. The regime had effectively prevented the formation of an opposition and instead was left to deal with political opponents, who, as individuals, had no social base from which to mobilize. These individuals were typically academics or political writers who could not organize a popular support base from which to confront the regime. After 2000 and the assumption of power by Bashar al-Assad there was a general feeling among many within Syria that the new President was open to political dissent. Many of these figures began to more openly advocate for political reform. These individuals ranged from academics to businesspeople to existing parliamentarians who may not have shared ideological affinities but were nevertheless committed to some form of political reform within the country. Encouraged by what they believed to be a more open political climate after 2000, these "reformists" began organizing and in January 2001 produced the Declaration of One Thousand: a political document signed by 1,000 activists calling for reform. The increase of political dissent was to be short-lived, however. The Damascus Spring of 2001 was quickly suppressed by the regime, with many of the activists imprisoned, threatened, or subject to physical violence by the *mukhabarat*.

The events of the Damascus Spring highlighted the structural weaknesses and realities of the political opposition. There were no parties to cultivate and mobilize a popular base of support. Politics and political dissent were left to individuals, who were often risking their lives to make basic political demands. The heavy repression experienced by activists, many of whom were prominent figures in their respective professional fields, disincentivized any forms of activism by laypeople, let alone any attempts at organizing into political parties. The existing organizations consisted of small human rights groups and civil society forums, without the capacity to challenge the regime. Human rights groups in particular suffered from a number of challenges that reduced their effectiveness, including the inability to recruit members and raise funds. Civil society forums were mostly meetings for people to come together and discuss social and political issues, leaving no room for collective organization and mobilization. The realities of regime repression and opposition weakness meant that the path to reform could not be taken through mass popular mobilization; only incremental change and sustained demands against the regime, regardless of the risks, were possible. There was thus no serious ideological or class-based opposition movement willing, or able, to confront the regime.

The plurality of the Syrian opposition is another factor that contributed to its overall weakness. Signatories to the Declaration of One Thousand came from all corners of Syrian political life: Islamists, democracy activists, Kurdish figures, nationalists, leftists, social rights activists, and the business community. For Mustafa (2013), this was a major political achievement in the Syrian Kurdish struggle for rights because it represented the first time Kurds had participated in a formal movement with a national character; it fostered anti-secessionist thinking among Syrian Kurdish politicians. Although all parties agreed on the need for reform within Syria there was no institutional expression of their cooperation beyond their collective signatures. Many of the opposition figures remained wary of one another. Such mistrust precluded deeper forms of cooperation between opposition figures and rendered their attempt at making collective demands on the regime impotent and ineffectual.

This situation changed slightly in 2005 after the assassination of Rafik al-Hariri, Lebanon's Prime Minister, and the so-called Cedar Revolution in Lebanon that led to the withdrawal of Syrian armed forces from the country. From Syria's entry into the Lebanese civil war in the 1970s, and especially after the Ta'if Accord that ended Lebanon's civil war in 1990, the regime exercised hegemony over Lebanon. The collapse of Pax Syriana had seemingly weakened the regime and opened up another opportunity for opposition figures to make reform demands. In 2005 many of the opposition figures came together to form joint committees and initiatives that made space for cooperation (Landis and Pace, 2006, p. 54). The Muslim Brotherhood also played a prominent role in the attempts at unifying the Syrian opposition and many ideological adversaries from the secular or leftist political currents made very public overtures to the Brotherhood's leadership.

The move toward creating a broad opposition coalition culminated in the Damascus Declaration, a document envisioning democratic change in Syria. The Declaration expressed commitment to four guiding principles— nonviolence, democracy, oppositional unity, and democratic change—and was signed by five party coalitions, civil society groups, and a number of public figures. Eventually, many other groups and individuals from Syria's plural opposition landscape, including communists, nationalists, and Kurdish nationalists, pledged allegiance to the Declaration. For the first time in the modern history of Syria's opposition, secular and Islamist groups, Kurdish and Arab nationalists, and others from across the political spectrum had legitimized each other and committed to collective change in Syria.

Despite the importance of the coalition, the Declaration signatories were never able to translate their cooperation into sustained pressure against the regime or into an institutional arrangement that could take collective leadership of the opposition. Mistrust persisted to some degree among members and accusations of cooperating with the regime undermined the legitimacy of others. Furthermore, fundamental disagreements over key national questions, particularly as they related to identity and citizenship issues, created schisms between some Arab and Kurdish figures. Perhaps most important, however, was that the coalition was in exile. Many of the parties and figures that supported the Declaration lived outside of Syria and were disconnected from any wide support base. Those inside Syria were subject to heavy repression and increasingly found that exile was a safer and more politically strategic option from which to conduct their activities. It was thus in exile that Syria's opposition would crystallize in the 2000s. In late 2005, former Vice President Abdel Hallim Khaddam had defected to the opposition and formed an alliance with the MB. In 2006, Khaddam and the MB leadership created an opposition coalition called the National Salvation Front (NSF). However, the NSF was unsuccessful in generating public support from groups and figures inside Syria. The NSF was an entirely exile-led coalition that, while novel in bringing together Islamist and liberal currents into a political movement, lacked any wide social or popular base in Syria and was entirely ineffectual in advocating for reform and change within the country. For the most part, then, the regime was able to withstand opposition pressure for political reform. The impotence of the opposition and their lack of a popular base from which to mobilize Syrians ensured that the regime's repression of political activists and cosmetic political reforms would maintain Ba'athist hegemony.

Beginnings of the uprising

There was no single cause of the Syrian uprising. The conflation of social, economic, and political factors alongside the breakdown of a culture of fear in the country all contributed to the protest movement that began in Syria. One Syrian writer, Idris Omar, argues that the entry of the military into power in the 1960s and the militarization of the state created a state in which repression and persecution were the only acceptable means of dealing with the citizenry (Umar, 2016). The regime thus had no other way to respond to demands for reform and openness. Others, such as Kamal Deeb (2013), attribute the causes of the crisis to the broader Arab-Israeli conflict and a political project to weaken Syria because of its anti-Israeli positions. Similarly, Wakim (2012) has argued that the Syrian conflict should be understood geopolitically, especially in Syrian relations to Egypt, Turkey, and Saudi Arabia. It is relations with these countries, and not just Israel, that have contributed to the internationalization of the conflict and have served as its drivers. A collection of essays by prominent Syrian activists, including Yassin Haj al-Saleh and Akram al-Bunni, similarly demonstrates the lack of consensus on the uprising's causes, trajectory, and futures (Cairo Center for Human Rights, 2014).

In the first few weeks, the protests were characterized by spontaneity and a lack of organization. Within months, the protests had spread throughout the country and it became meaningful to speak of a Syrian uprising that had national momentum as protests were occurring throughout the entire country, from rural to urban areas. The lack of a unified or pre-existing Syrian opposition and the absence of a robust, autonomous civil society made organization and mobilization of protesters difficult.

Nevertheless, despite the absence of institutions that could mobilize Syrians, protests continued despite regime repression. This cycle—increasing protests inviting further regime repression—defined the first few months of the uprising prior to the militarization of the opposition later in 2011. The regime's response to the protests was twofold: on the one hand, regime forces engaged in brutal repression of protesters. On the other hand, the regime also rolled out a series of cosmetic political reforms. The rejection of these reforms by the protesters and the exiled political opposition fed into the regime's rhetoric that the protesters only concern was destabilizing Syria and not in political dialogue. In reality, the regime's overtures and reforms failed to placate the protesters because they were hollow and never seriously threatened the regime's grip on power in the country or the impunity in which the security apparatus acted. In the remainder of this section, we explore the first months of the uprising and take a snapshot of key events that occurred in the first few months. The regime's dual response to the protests—reform and repression—simply accelerated the protests and set the stage for the deepening of the conflict.

The Arab uprisings were sparked by protests that began after the self-immolation of Tunisian street vendor Mohammed Bouazizi in December 2010 in the village of Sidi Bouzid. After suffering sustained harassment and humiliation at the hands of local police, Bouazizi ended his life in front of the local governor's office where he had gone to complain about his treatment and had received no commitment from the governor or local government officials to end the harassment. His last words were "How do you expect me to earn a living?" Within hours of his death protests began in Sidi Bouzid and then spread throughout the country. Though sparked by the immediate suicide of Bouazizi, the protests were quickly framed around socioeconomic concerns and the endemic corruption and authoritarian rule of the incumbent regime led by President Zine el Abidine Ben Ali. After weeks of protests and the refusal of the Tunisian army to engage in violence against the protesters, Ben Ali fled the country on 14 January to Saudi Arabia, ceding to protester demands for his removal. The disposal of Ben Ali held promise that Tunisia could embark on a transition away from authoritarian rule and toward a more democratic political system. When similar protests spread throughout the Arab world the hopes of the "Arab Spring" in Tunisia had been projected throughout the region.

Bouazizi's suicide "would change the course of Arab political history" (Sadiki, 2011) as protests gained momentum throughout the entire Arab world. There was not one Arab country that did not experience some form of protest, social mobilization, or political unrest that was motivated by the events in Tunisia. The entire Middle East state system and the geopolitical order on which it was based seemed under attack. In January 2011 Hosni Mubarak, Egypt's long-serving president, stepped down after weeks-long protests throughout the country demanded his resignation, a dismantling of the regime, and a transition toward democratic politics. Although the removal of these "presidents for life" (Owen, 2012) was only the first step in a long process aimed at dismantling the political and security apparatuses that constituted the regimes, the resignations nevertheless were seen as progress toward a transition from authoritarianism. By February 2011, protests had spread to Libya. Although violence, especially state violence, was present throughout the countries experiencing protest, the Libyan case was the first one of the Arab uprisings that descended into what would be considered a civil war. Similarly, protests in Bahrain, in the capital, Manama, led to the mobilization of the Peninsula Shield Force, a Gulf Cooperation Council (GCC) military force, to quell the protests. In Libya, state violence against protesters brought the country to civil war and eventually international intervention by the North Atlantic Treaty Organization (NATO) that led to the removal of President Moammar al-Ghadafi. In Bahrain, the brutal, violent response would quell the protests but not without substantial social and political loss. In all of these cases, regional actors played an important, sometimes decisive, role in the outcome.

The militarization of the Arab uprisings in Libya and Bahrain would portend violence in Syria after protests began in February 2011. In January 2011, Bashar al-Assad gave an interview with the *Wall Street Journal* in which he dismissed the possibility of protests and large-scale violence reaching Syria, claiming, "We [Syria] have more difficult circumstances than most of the Arab countries [in reference to Western pressure and Syria's geopolitical alignments] but in spite of that Syria is stable" (*Wall Street Journal*, 2011). In the interview, he goes on to suggest that the conditions for an uprising in Syria do not exist because of the close ideological links between the government and the people.

Syria, however, was not immune from the contagion effect of the uprisings as protests began in the southern city of Dar'a in February 2011. These protests came in response to the arrest and detention of fifteen middle-school-aged boys who had spray-painted the common Arab slogan of the protests—"the people want the downfall of the regime"—on their school wall. The detention of the young boys sparked immediate protest in Dar'a calling for their release, but eventually morphed from protests demanding their release along with that of other political prisoners into anti-regime protests targeting emergency laws, poor socioeconomic conditions, corruption, police brutality, and arbitrary detention. On 17 February 2011, Dar'a experienced the first protests of the Syrian uprising, labeled the "Day of Anger." By 15 March 2011 a second had taken place. A third, after Friday prayers on 18 March, gave the protesters increasing momentum in the city and put them in direct confrontation with the security forces, who had begun to open fire and use live munitions on protesters. Meanwhile, around the same time in Damascus, hundreds protested and a female-led sit-in around the Ommayed Mosque in Central Damascus occurred, demanding the release of all political prisoners. By mid-March, protests were recorded throughout Syria in Damascus, Aleppo, al-Hassakeh, Dar'a, Deir ez-Zor, and Hama.

Within several weeks, the Syrian protests evolved into a movement that became more organized and which possessed a national momentum, but did not enjoy central coordination. Palestinian writer Salama Kila, who was living in Syria at the time of the uprising and was imprisoned and then deported to Jordan, argues that the term *intifada* (uprising) best describes the specific nature of what was happening in Syria at the time. For Kila (2013) the term *intifada* best describes the nascent, unstructured nature of protests that have not yet developed a clear vision for the future of the country beyond wanting to overthrow the regime. As this was happening, most regional actors had urged caution and restraint, demonstrating a desire not to destabilize the regime. Protests continued throughout the country and a shared language and set of demands emerged among the protesters. The principal demand was for regime change through the dismantling of the security apparatus, the resignation of President al-Assad, and the peripheralization of the political, security, and economic elite from the political sphere; a second demand called for the introduction of political reforms that would repeal emergency laws, lead to an independent judiciary and a new constitution, and create more representative political institutions and laws that were not subject to authoritarian control. Protests were quickly becoming more organized by local groups who emerged to institutionalize the revolutionary energy and mobilize society against the regime. In the early stages of the uprising, these groups were mostly informal and drew on social, familial, and neighborhood ties that protesters had with one another. The first such evidence of institutionalized mobilization against the regime was the declaration of a group called The Youth of March 15 (in reference to the second major protest in Dar'a) who called for the dismantling of the regime, a series of political reforms, the release of political prisoners, and a range of socioeconomic measures to address poverty and inequality in the country. Other local groups reproduced such demands in the first months of the conflict and an uprising that was discursively and politically coalescing around demands for greater political rights was taking shape.

The inability of the regime's forces to quell the protests led to even more repression. The regime began to frame the protests as the work of foreign infiltrators and Islamist groups intent on destabilizing Syria (Ali, 2011). At this point of the uprising, there was no evidence whatsoever that either the Syrian Muslim Brotherhood or any other Islamist movement was even remotely involved in the protests (Leenders, 2012; Leenders and Heydemann, 2012). Regardless, the regime maintained a policy of severe repression and the number of protester deaths increased through April into the summer months. In this period, the international community began to debate the Syrian conflict but the United Nations Security Council (UNSC) failed to adopt a resolution condemning the regime's crackdown. The first signs of a Western-Russian/ Chinese split on the Syrian conflict had revealed themselves in the debates over the proposed resolution. Instead, Western states began imposing sanctions on regime officials in an attempt to place political pressure on regime elites to either defect or end the protests. Key regional actors—Qatar, Saudi Arabia, and Turkey—slowly began to drift away from their policy of appeasement and their public calls for reform. Instead, they began to actively support the goals of the uprising and to provide political support to the emergent opposition in exile. As the conflict evolved, this support eventually found its way into the militarized formations of the uprising.

March and April 2011 were crucial months in the evolution of the uprising. While protesters were becoming more organized and LCCs were emerging to mobilize society, the Syrian regime engaged in a twofold response to the uprising. On the one hand, the regime enacted a series of cosmetic political reforms aimed at placating some of the protesters' political demands. On the other hand, the security apparatus—the army, *mukhabarat* (intelligence services), police, and *shabiha* (thugs)—continued to engage in repression, including collective violence against protesters and against individuals participating in protest activity through arbitrary imprisonment, beatings, torture, kidnapping, and murder. The dual response of reform and repression suggests that the regime decision-makers were themselves divided over how to address the protests and that both security and political solutions to the crisis, no matter how cosmetic the political reforms actually were, had been contemplated by the regime leadership, both as a way to placate protesters and suggest to its supporters and the international community that the regime was capable of change.

Indeed, significant reforms were enacted on paper but these would have little consequences for the repression enacted by the security apparatus. On March 30, 2011, Bashar al-Assad addressed the Syrian Parliament and categorized the protesters into those motivated and fueled by foreign conspirators (a veiled reference to the Arab Gulf states, Israel, and the West) and satellite channels who were fomenting unrest in the country, and those who had serious political demands. Such a framing of the protesters and armed rebels by the regime would persist throughout the conflict. However, the failure of the regime's reforms to bring about an end to protests and violence would be taken as evidence by the regime and its supporters of the unwillingness of protesters to engage in dialogue and reform, and not as a failure of the regime itself. In that same speech, al-Assad dismissed the Cabinet and appointed a new Prime Minister. Later, 200 political prisoners from the notorious Saydnaya prison were released and granted clemency, including many Islamists. On 6 April 2011, citizenship was extended to stateless Kurds and, later that month, the Emergency Law that had been in place since 1963 was repealed, satisfying a key demand of the protesters. The Higher State Security Court, the judicial body that tried cases in secrecy and was responsible for the detention and sentencing of security-related cases, was abolished, and a new law legalizing and regulating certain forms of protest was passed. In practice, however, the security apparatus continued to operate with immunity and these measures proved to have no effect on repression.

The regime's dual strategy of reform and repression would have no demonstrable effect on the momentum of the protests, which continued to increase during the first months of the uprising and which were spread throughout all major population centers of the country as well as throughout rural areas. Nevertheless, the regime continued to enact reforms meant to placate protesters. By the end of April, the weekly Friday protests that were occurring in unison throughout the country had resulted in increasing deaths at the hands of security forces. Meanwhile, activists and anti-regime supporters were arrested, imprisoned, beaten, and subjected to other forms of repression. This did not, however, prevent the regime from establishing a committee in June to discuss the future of Syria—a move intended, yet again, to placate protesters and ostensibly provide a space for the expression of dissent. This occurred in the same week that Internet service was effectively shut down in an attempt to prevent protesters from communicating with one another and the outside world. At no point in the course of these initial months had the security apparatus shown a commitment or adherence to the political track offered by the regime. The confrontation between the regime and activists was quickly spiraling out of control.

By June 2011, the violence in Syria was escalating. Protesters were regularly imprisoned and tortured and a campaign of repression was unleashed by the regime and its proxy security forces against anyone suspected of harboring sympathy with the protesters. Thousands of Syrians were detained in this period and hundreds more killed. Regime violence became more brutal and involved much heavier weaponry, including an aerial campaign in June in the northwest of the country after 120 regime soldiers were killed by armed rebels, inducing the largest wave of refugees into Turkey up until that point. Such large-scale violence would portend the coming months and years for Syrians as more and more people inside and outside Syria took up arms to confront the regime. The brutality of the regime's response to the protests had pushed the uprising rather quickly toward militarization in a sort of self-fulfilling prophecy. In turn, protesters turned to different avenues to confront the regime, including armed violence. This strategy eventually cohered with that of regional actors, such as Turkey, Qatar, and Saudi Arabia, who had begun to calculate that armed insurrection and intervention were the only means by which to overthrow the regime.

A dangerous and violent pattern thus emerged whereby regional actors, either loyal to the regime or to the opposition, began intervening in the Syrian conflict in much more dynamic and militarized ways. With the prospect of reform gone, and the prospects of a peaceful political transition virtually nil, an armed confrontation emerged as the primary means for each of the interested parties, both inside and outside of Syria, to achieve their political goals. The fragmentation that defined the early nonviolent opposition would be mirrored within the regime itself as well as within its international backers. Decision-making within regime circles is opaque and there is no way of knowing how larger strategic decisions are made, especially in a decentralized power structure (Stacher, 2012). What is clear, however, is that there existed different options for regime elites and their regional supporters, mainly Iran and Russia. The calculation that violence and repression was the best way out of the impasse was a clear victory for the more hardline decision-makers at the expense of those who may have been willing to offer some political concessions to stave off protests. From the early stages of the uprising, we saw a division between hardline and accommodationist positions (Valeriano and Marin, 2010) that continues today.

The trajectory of the Syrian uprising from this period onwards would largely be determined by the transformations of the opposition groups (Kila, 2013), the adaptability of the regime to the uprising (Heydemann, 2013), and the central role that regional actors played therein (Phillips, 2016). In the remaining sections of this chapter, I consider both issues by examining the background of the growth of the opposition movement, the problems faced around the organization and mobilization of the protests, and how the regime responded to the new opposition movement. Unlike in previous periods of mass mobilization in Syria, the social and political background of the disaffected was not clearly defined. Syria's social stratification in the decades of Ba'athist rule and the shifts occurring during the 2000s discouraged and prevented the formation of cross-class, regional, or sectarian linkages between different social segments. Indeed, while many different social segments of Syrian society were disaffected and had grievances against the Ba'ath Party, these had never coalesced. As we will see below, the widespread disaffection with the Ba'ath Party may have fostered discontent and led to mobilization, but it was insufficient to generate coherency among the protesters. Moreover, regional actors played a divisive role in pitting different segments of the opposition against one another.

Social and political backgrounds of the protesters

The postcolonial Syrian political landscape was extremely plural, with many political parties and social networks vying for the allegiance of different segments of Syrian society. Syrian society on the eve of the uprising was no less segmented or fragmented than in earlier periods, with one key factor missing: by the 2000s, the Ba'ath Party had been successful in suppressing all forms of organized politics and had rendered all political parties inside of Syria and other associational groups, such as unions, impotent and unable to challenge the Ba'athist monopoly on political power and control of the state apparatus. The absence of formal political institutions in pre-uprising Syria should not be equated with the absence of political discontent; rather, this points to the emasculation of political institutions and the subsequent weak mobilization capacity of Syrian society. Political discontent was prevalent throughout Syria in the 2000s but, unlike in the postcolonial, pre-Ba'ath period, there were no parties or associations that could capture, represent, and mobilize this discontent.

As a result, the protests that began were completely decentered and leaderless, and were not organized by any national associations. They were more, however, than spontaneous demonstrations. From the early stages of the uprisings, demonstrations quickly spread throughout the country and adopted remarkably similar narratives despite the lack of central leadership. The expansion of the protests and the articulation of shared political grievances and aspirations gave the early protests the characteristics of coherent mobilization and not merely sporadic, spontaneous, and fragmented protests. Indeed, for the uprising to have occurred, to have assumed a national character, and to have spread throughout the country, mobilization first had to occur. The key question in the Syrian case is how mobilization occurred in the absence of institutionalized leadership and how was it sustained. Or, in other words, how did the Syrian situation morph from a series of protests in Dar'a, to more coherent mobilization, and then to an uprising with a national character when there were no political parties or associations to lead?

In the early stages of the uprising, Leenders and Heydemann have argued that the social networks of protesters and the "miscibility" of these networks, "or their ability to dissolve easily into one another because of their intense interconnectedness" (2012, p. 140), served as a substitute for formal institutions of mobilization and allowed the mobilization to spread and be sustained. Prior to this, there were significant barriers to collective action beyond the absence of political parties. In particular, widespread repression by the security apparatus had discouraged any form of nonviolent or violent collective action, with even political gatherings of nonviolent activists sometimes leading to long prison terms handed down by Syria's security courts.

There are at least five distinct social groupings (Abbas, 2011) that took part in the early protests and formed the dense social networks that sustained mobilization.

1. *Secular, Educated, Urban Middle Classes.* This group consisted of mostly young people who were professionals or were involved in cultural activities. They were mostly university educated and came from urban or semi-urban centers and had very few political linkages to the exiled opposition or domestic political activists (see below) who made up the pre-uprising opposition. In the early stages of the uprising, this group was heavily involved in media related activities as well as organizing protesters on the ground.

2. *Tribes (Kinship Based Networks).* Al-Ayed (2015, p. 2) has estimated that there are around 7.5 million Syrians (or 30 percent of the total population) of tribal background mostly concentrated in Deir ez-Zor, Raqqa, al-Hasakeh, and Dar'a but also located in the rural peripheries of Aleppo, Idlib, Hama, Homs, and Quneitra. Leenders and Heydemann (2012) have preferred to refer to these kinship networks as "clans" instead of tribes. These tribes were mostly concentrated in socioeconomically deprived areas and had borne the brunt of years of drought and agricultural decline. Tribal leaders were instrumental in recruiting volunteers and protesters in the early stages of the uprising who could mobilize members based on existing socioeconomic grievances and historical exclusion from Ba'ath Party power. There has been no discernible political strategy from the tribes during the uprising, with some pledging allegiance to the opposition and others to the regime. The tribes thus seem more motivated by the specific politics of the moment than any core political program. The geographic concentration of the tribes has meant that they have been forced into conflict or partnerships with the main jihadist groups, the former Jabhat an-Nusra (now Jabhat Fatah al-Sham) and ISIS. In the case of al-Sham, some tribes in the Deir ez-Zor area had been integrated into their command and military

structure, giving the organization a tribal character. In the case of ISIS, many tribes were initially targets of violence and repression and have, as of 2015, largely acquiesced to ISIS's rule in their areas, choosing to find accommodations with the organization.

3. *Political Islamists.* This group can be considered to be adherents of political Islam. Their affiliations and allegiances, however, are very diverse and not confined to the main Syrian Islamist party, the Muslim Brotherhood. As membership in the Brotherhood was punishable by death, many of their activists inside Syria had been forced underground and were largely unable to recruit and organize supporters. Thus, many of the protesters in this group can be considered to support and adhere to some version of political Islam. They were typically supporters of particular religious sheiks who supported the uprising or were compelled to activism and protest by their religious beliefs. In the initial stages of the uprising and throughout there has been no single Islamist party that dominated this group and offered a coherent vision and organizational structure from which to mobilize them. As Jabhat an-Nusra/Fatah al-Sham and ISIS entered the Syrian scene, many of the more militant activists from this grouping have migrated and joined them, while others who took up arms stayed in local, neighborhood groups affiliated with the Free Syrian Army (FSA) or other brigades. Many other Islamist activists have also remained active using nonviolent strategies and have participated in local councils and administrative structures.

4. *Political Activists.* The suppression of formal party politics by the Syrian regime led to the suffocation of political activity in the decades preceding the uprising. Nevertheless, there were many independent, non-affiliated political figures within Syria who had more or less made up the domestic opposition during Ba'ath Party rule. These activists were mostly intellectuals, professionals, or businesspeople. Their main institutional expression came in the early 2000s with the Damascus Declaration and the call for greater political freedoms within Syria, which

only invited heavier repression by the regime and the imprisonment of many of their members. This grouping also consisted of social activists, such as human rights or prisoner rights activists, as well as political activists from leftist and Kurdish groups. Some activists from this group had been active in regime-sanctioned civil society organizations prior to the uprising.

There were, among this group, multiple political divisions that would reveal themselves over time. One of the central divisions was between Arab and Kurdish activities. For some Kurdish observers, such as Mustafa (2013), Syrian oppositionists were trapped in a nationalist thinking that shunned the Kurdish presence and made it impossible for Syrian Kurds to be taken seriously as equals within opposition gatherings. For this reason, Kurdish and Arab activists have often struggled against the same injustices, but in a situation of mistrust. How Kurdish issues and actors were included or excluded from opposition politics was one of the contributing factors to opposition fragmentation.

5. *The Unemployed, Marginalized, and Urban Subalterns* (Ismail, 2013). Unemployment and informality were key features of the Syrian economy before the uprising. The growing numbers of unemployed and under-employed Syrians grew considerably during the decade of marketization when public sector opportunities effectively ceased, agricultural production (a main source of employment) plummeted, and the private sector was unable to provide jobs for the hundreds of thousands of Syrians entering the workforce each year. Informality and under-employment were not only urban phenomena. They affected rural and semi-urban areas as well, leading to a slow migration of many job seekers to the peripheries of Syria's main cities. Many of these migrants lived in informal housing. Many of these people, who were on the outside of economic reforms and had very few job prospects, shared many of the socioeconomic and political grievances of other protesters and were natural participants in the initial protest phases. Paradoxically, many Syrians in this

grouping were also drawn into the *shabiha* and other paramilitary groups.

There was no common demographic (young/old), ethnic (Arab/Kurdish/Turkmen), religious (Sunni/minority or secular/religious), social (urban/rural), or economic (upper/ lower class) background to the protesters. The protesters shared common political and economic grievances against the regime even though they came from all geographic regions of Syria. While these protesters had perhaps dabbled in opposition politics, they were largely not the veterans of Syria's pre-uprising political dissent (as described above) but, rather, newcomers to the political scene who were forced to forge ad hoc organizational structures under conditions of extreme repression and without the organizational, financial, or logistical capacity to do so. The difficulty of organization was compounded by the withdrawal of regime forces from certain areas of the country and the need to maintain and provide food and services to the local populations who had supported their political efforts. The withdrawal of the regime security forces often paralleled the paralysis of state institutions in these areas that no longer functioned, further exacerbating the pressures placed on protesters.

LCCs and the problem of mobilization

Today, the Tansiqiyyat, or Local Coordination Committees (LCCs), have been sidelined by the emergence of armed opposition groups hostile to the presence and functioning of the LCCs, who serve as a political alternative to the rule of the armed groups. Despite their current marginalization, the LCCs were the first formation to emerge during the uprising that sought to organize, mobilize, and speak on behalf of the protesters. The establishment of the LCCs in Syria came as a direct response to the need to organize protesters and to mobilize them against the regime. In the absence of pre-existing structures from which this could occur, the LCCs grew rather spontaneously in the various Syrian locales that were experiencing protest. They initially lacked any form of central organization and for many months remained decentralized and nonhierarchical. This afforded the LCCs some form of shelter from regime repression and gave them flexibility to adapt to the specific circumstances of their areas, free from centralized control. This flexibility was especially important in areas in which regime forces withdrew, leaving the LCCs as the only major body left to govern. Over time, the LCCs developed a much more networked structure that gave them the appearance of a national movement but, even today, much of the LCCs' work is focused on specific villages, towns, or city neighborhoods. This often occurs in parallel with armed groups who have established their own systems of governance, enforced by violence. In their brief history, LCCs' role has shifted and morphed considerably from initially being focused on activism (media outreach and protest organization) and then to providing relief to affected Syrians and eventually into governance.

As protests raged throughout Syria in early 2011, there were no institutional apparatuses (such as political parties, unions, or professional syndicates) which were able to organize and mobilize protesters. The varying social and geographic backgrounds of the protesters made organization between their immediate networks difficult, if not impossible. For the most part, protests were occurring independently of each other and of any central coordinating body, even as they were spreading throughout the country and increasing in their size and momentum. To begin to address the problems of organization the LCCs were created in the first months of the uprising by activists who were seeking greater coordination of protest activity, to increase media visibility of the uprising both inside and outside Syria, and to enhance cooperation with other activists within Syria. In the initial weeks and months after the Dar'a protests, the LCCs were focused on communication and logistical issues. The LCC activists assumed responsibility for setting up sound systems, creating banners, fundraising, distributing information, and agreeing on common slogans for the protests.

The LCCs typically began as small gatherings of one or two dozen activists and then grew in membership well into the hundreds, depending on the locale. They were entirely spontaneous in their formation and born out of the immediate needs of the moment. As they grew, solidarity between activists increased and the roles of the LCCs slowly began to expand. These early efforts created what Doreen Khoury (2013) has called "networks of solidarity" among LCC activists. Activists were similarly bound by their commitment to preserve and continue the uprising while creating a new national narrative that provided an alternative to the regime's own sectarian policy and their labeling of the protesters as sectarian agitators.

The role of the LCCs began to shift as regime power contracted throughout the country. The LCCs had developed in some cases into Local Councils (LCs), which assumed responsibility for governing areas outside of regime control. The LCs had assumed responsibility for providing services, such as health care and education, maintaining the legal system, and attending to administrative issues. A shift was thus under way among the LCCs who were incorporating governance roles into their activities and had begun to morph into administrative actors. The vacuum created by the withdrawal of regime forces and the collapse of state institutions in certain parts of the country was initially filled by the LCs, which had used the opportunity to begin to organize and govern society along revolutionary lines.

There are three central functions that the LCCs and LCs have played in the Syrian uprising. The first is that of activists, organizers, and citizen journalists. The initial protests would not have been sustained without the work of the LCCs and local activists. Citizen journalism was crucial to communicating information about the protests to other Syrians and to the outside world. While maintaining a focus on media efforts and protest organization, the LCCs began to work together to unify their political messages and slogans and to present a unified, cross-sectarian, and national voice from which to counter the regime's accusations that protesters were foreign infiltrators bent on disrupting Syria's stability. In articulating a new national story for Syria, the LCCs were putting forth an alternative vision for the country that could, they hoped, serve as the basis for a new political community free from Ba'athist hegemony (Ismail, 2013). Citizen journalism was essential to legitimizing the revolution for many Syrians as reliable, credible information was communicated from protests throughout the country. The activists had developed a sophisticated system of verification that allowed them to establish and maintain credibility among Syrians and, less important, among international media who were reporting on the conflict.

The second function that they provided was that of relief work. The LCs have consistently focused efforts on providing relief work to Syrians affected by the conflict through a series of civil society organizations created that were devoted to relief efforts. These organizations have been involved with providing medical services, schooling, and housing for displaced Syrians. Finally, the LCs have served a governance function in the non-regime areas. In the absence of functional state institutions, the LCs have served as de facto government in many areas. Unfortunately, the LCCs have not yet been sufficiently integrated into a centralized structure, so much of this governance work is unstructured and unsustainable. In 2014, there were well over 400 LCCs in Syria operating throughout the country. In larger cities, there are often multiple Committees who focus their work on specific neighborhoods or locales. While they often developed more horizontal institutional linkages with other LCCs through the creation of different Majlis Thawar (Revolutionary Councils) that provided a space for LCC activists from different committees to meet and organize, these larger councils never materialized into bodies with national reach.

Notwithstanding the inability of the LCCs to evolve into a centralized structure, the activity of the Committees throughout Syria has been remarkable under the circum-stances. Having evolved from citizen journalists and protest organizers to taking on responsibilities for governance, the LCCs and their supporters were trying to organize a society in revolt in exceptionally violent circumstances. Making this task even more challenging was the absence of a pre-existing network of support or any history of collective activism. The spontaneity of the LCCs' rise and the limited horizontal integration between them has meant that there is no clear institutional structure that is replicated across governorates. There is no hierarchy as such beyond three offices that organize the three main functions of the LCCs: a relief office, a media office, and an executive committee that deals with political and governance activities.

In addition to the LCCs, dozens of Syrian civil society organizations were established during the uprising. These organizations work in multiple fields, including media and relief, and have formed both inside and outside of the country. The uprising has given them the opportunity to grow autonomously from the government. However, the new organizations were all born out of the conflict conditions and of the dire humanitarian situation. As such, they operate in extremely difficult and dangerous environments and largely without sustainable financial and organizational resources. Nevertheless, the LCCs and civil society organizations have formed the backbone of the nonviolent elements of the uprising from 2011 until now and have been caught between regime repression and rebel violence. For many, this has not prevented continued work toward realization of the uprising's goals.

The space between regime and rebel violence has indeed been very narrow for many of the nonviolent activists. In many cases, activists were forced to flee to neighboring countries, where they resumed their political and relief activities. Today, there are hundreds, if not thousands, of Syrian-led organizations that have sprung up since 2011 in direct response to the political and humanitarian needs of the moment. Many of the groups inside Syria lack the political space or material basis from which to mount a serious political threat to the armed groups. The intense pressure from regime and rebel groups has meant that many of these groups have to operate in the shadows or on the periphery to avoid detection and repression. The Aleppo LC, for example, once worked openly in Aleppo City organizing different neighborhoods, but, by the time of the Russian intervention in 2015, had been forced out by armed groups and relegated to holding meetings on the Turkish-Syrian border. Such conditions and circumstances were common among many of the LCs.

A new civil society

The growth of Syrian civil society organizations since the uprising began was necessitated by the demands of the uprising and the opportunities presented by the regime's contraction up until 2013, when a stalemate more or less set in. The geography of the conflict did not radically change until after the Russian intervention in 2015, when regime forces began to extend their authority over parts of Syria that were formerly under rebel control. Despite the contraction of non-regime territory, today, Syrian civil society organizations are active in all fields of social rights, relief and aid services, advocacy, governance, capacity-building, and economic reconstruction. There are also dozens of organizations who operate in neighboring countries to provide relief work for Syrian refugees. Thus, despite the military balance tipping in favor of the regime and its allies since 2015, many Syrian groups that only came into existence after 2011 remain active on various fronts. This has meant, however, that the possibilities for political organization and centralization of activities in the form of a movement or party are severely limited, if existent at all.

Whereas the LCCs focused on media, then relief and governance efforts, civil society groups focused on a range of other services and activities. These groups were engaged in different forms of activism and work. They quickly became embedded in larger networks of activism, such as Nadja Now (Assistance Now) or Mussalaha (Reconciliation) which, respectively, focus on bringing aid to Syria and bringing together community leaders to engage in reconciliatory dialogue. Other networks focus exclusively on aid provision, such as the Union of Syrian Medical Relief Organizations (UOSSM) which operates in the diaspora, or nonviolent civil disobedience, such as Ayyam al-Hourriya (Freedom Days). Given the dire situation, networked activism has become the most effective way for Syrian civil society to affect the humanitarian situation.

The growth of a Syrian civil society during the conflict is a testament to the resiliency of Syrian society in the face of ever-increasing violence and brutality and the persistence of Syrians in their pursuit of a better future. The civil society organizations that have been created since 2011 have faced a number of major challenges during the course of the conflict. The contraction of regime authority and the collapse of state institutions created a dire need for the administration of non-regime areas and for the provision of aid and services to the population. Civil society organizations attempted to fulfill the dual role of administration and aid providers during the conflict. The major obstacle to this role was the deteriorated security situation in the country and the hostility with which most armed groups, from the regime to ISIS, view the civil society organizations. Most armed groups have actually refused to cooperate with many of the civil society groups and have instead established alternative institutions to exercise authority and provide aid. These groups are much better funded than civil society groups or local councils and are thus able to embed themselves in Syrian society more deeply. Today, civil society activists are engaged in a sort of perpetual revolution against the regime and against the armed groups that now dominate areas in which they operate.

In addition to the security situation, civil society groups face the challenge of providing aid and services in wartime. There is a severe shortage of basic necessities in Syria and the armed groups are able to procure goods through the war economy while civil society groups are dependent on them for access to these goods. Such dependence severely compromises the groups' ability to provide relief services and to support Syrian communities. They are thus faced with a dire humanitarian situation which they have very few resources to remedy.

The difficulty of civil society's aid provision was also a function of their limited resources and their reliance on the

Syrian National Council and private Syrian donors for their financial resources. These have been largely insufficient to help support social service provision, especially in major areas such as water, electricity, and communications. The absence of financial and technical resources (such as phones and computers) has impeded the work of civil society organizations. Although financial resources are perhaps the most important challenge facing Syrian civil society, other factors have also made their work extremely difficult, including the challenges of mistrust and corruption, the lack of cooperation between groups, and political and ideological divisions that preclude collective action.

Perhaps the largest challenge facing Syrian civil society today is in finding the space to participate politically and to transform the immense governance and relief work into political momentum that can offer an alternative to militarization. The militarization of the uprising has deflected attention away from civil initiatives and the resiliency of nonviolence in Syria and has rendered much of the work of activists and relief workers invisible or insignificant. The focus on militarization has thus ignored the profound impacts on Syrian society that have occurred in the development and networking of civil society initiatives. The absence of civil society groups from any negotiations, for example, suggests that they are deemed irrelevant to the larger political answers that will decide the evolution of the Syrian crisis.

The Syrian National Council

The Syrian National Council (SNC) was the first coalition of the political opposition formed after the uprising and represented a serious, albeit flawed, attempt at organizing the political energy of the uprising into a coherent voice. Aside from the LCCs, the SNC was composed entirely of parties and political currents outside of Syria and included the Muslim Brotherhood, the Damascus Declaration, the National Bloc, the Kurdish Bloc, the Assyrian Bloc, and independents. The SNC was officially created in October

2011 after a summer of deliberation, when Syria's various exiled political factions came together to form an alternative to the regime. A charter was quickly passed that delineated power-sharing between the parties and created various offices to liaise with the protesters and the international community.

Despite the common goal of removing al-Assad from power, the SNC was fraught with internal divisions from the outset and was never able to develop into a serious and legitimate alternative to the regime. Council members had openly argued with one another and there were repeated threats (some acted upon) by members to resign over key questions of political strategy. In February 2012, for example, twenty SNC members resigned over the SNC's rejection of working with the armed opposition. Such internal division continued to plague the SNC and the various exile political coalitions since the beginning of the uprising.

In 2012, the SNC had decided to join with other opposition groups to form the National Coalition for Syrian Revolutionary and Opposition Forces, or what came to be known as the Syrian National Coalition. The new Coalition was meant to address many of the problems of the SNC and to provide a way for the different opposition groups to speak in one voice. Although the new Coalition was encouraged by the major regional backers of all parties, these same actors actively undermined the Coalition and contributed to its factionalization. The Coalition thus aggravated, rather than alleviated, the problems associated with the first opposition formation, the SNC. By early 2014, the problems within the Coalition had become worse, and the SNC withdrew from the Coalition. While the dispute was ostensibly over the Coalition's decision to participate in the Geneva II peace talks, the problems from within the Coalition had existed well prior to this. This decision isolated the SNC from opposition circles and further exposed their political weakness. Today, although still in existence, the SNC's dream of serving as a government-in-exile has given way to the reality that most regional actors do not wish for it to succeed, the armed groups are actively hostile to its leadership, and the regime refuses to take seriously any negotiations with its members.

Multiple leaderships

Although there is a long and rich history of political opposition in contemporary Syria, for all intents and purposes the opposition that was born out of 2011 was new. The three main networks that emerged in the months after the uprising—the Local Coordination Committees (LCC), Syrian National Coalition (SNC), and the Free Syrian Army (FSA)—were nonexistent prior to the uprising and thus owe their creation to the political opportunity provided by the protests. In 2011 and 2012 especially, there were multiple attempts to unite the political opposition, but these attempts largely failed to bring about coherency or affect political change, leading to a fragmented inside/outside opposition divided over issues of political legitimacy and questions of political strategy. On almost every key political strategy question facing the opposition in the first year of the uprising—whether to engage in dialogue with the regime, support violence or nonviolence, or call for military intervention—the opposition was divided along inside/outside lines (Sayigh, 2012). Activists within Syria (mostly represented by the LCC) were far removed from the politics of the exiled opposition that formed under the SNC.

Mistrust and a lack of coordination between the different opposition groups created the conditions for fragmentation and the emergence of even more opposition groups as the uprising progressed. The multiple opposition groups were not only defined by their lack of horizontal coordination between one another but even a lack of vertical coordination *within* the movements themselves such as that coordination between different LCCs or even within the SNC was not effective. The LCC and the FSA had highly decentralized structures, with each local committee or group operating independently of one another. There was some coordination between different cells but not enough to speak of an organized, linear chain of command. In the case of the FSA, there was no military strategy adhered to by fighters and even less coordination over the distribution of material support.

The opposition movement, then, was more a collection of nodes and networks of opposition than a coherent movement with a clear hierarchical command.

The fragmented and networked structures of the opposition led Hassan Abbas (2011) to refer to this as the problem of a head without a body. The body of the uprising, represented by the demonstrators, has grown apart from the head, represented by the different exiled opposition groups. The opposition in 2011 was thus structurally and politically weak. More important, however, was that the Syrian exile opposition suffered from an early legitimacy deficit that can be traced to two factors (Abboud, 2012). The first is the inability of the exiled opposition to formulate a discourse and narrative of a post-Ba'athist Syria that could resonate across Syria's wide social spectrum. Even in the early stages of the uprising, there were legitimate fears among many Syrians that the sectarianism dynamics of the uprising—a mostly Sunni-led protest movement against a predominantly minority regime—would lead to a bloody civil war and the sectarian fragmentation of the country. The "fear of sectarianism" very early on shaped how the protest movement was constituted (Ismail, 2013). Many Syrians did indeed despise the regime and perhaps wished for it to be overthrown, but their fear of sectarian violence and the division of the country along sectarian lines prevented many from openly supporting the political opposition. Groups such as the LCC engaged in what Ismail (2011) calls "political community making" in which they have publicly taken strong positions against sectarianism and for civil rights for all Syrians regardless of sect. This, however, has failed to resonate throughout Syria and the fears of sectarianism remained strong.

The second factor contributing to the legitimacy deficit was the inability of the exiled opposition to ensure the provision of material support to the demonstrators. For all intents and purposes, the SNC had very little on-the-ground presence in Syria and were not able to provide resources to demonstrators. While the material relationship is important here, the more important factor is that the exiled opposition was made up of oppositionists who were largely unknown to the protesters. They were thus unwilling to politically support the SNC when there was no immediate social basis of support or material benefit for doing so.

All of the early opposition groups were united in their desire for a political transition in Syria. They were not united, however, around questions of political strategy and how to achieve that transition. There were two main questions concerning violence that divided the opposition in the first year of the uprising and which continued to plague the opposition in subsequent years. The first question concerns whether to pursue violence or nonviolence as a political strategy. Virtually all the main opposition groups inside the country, including the LCC, rejected the role of the FSA in militarizing the conflict. The LCC and the National Coordination Body for Democratic Change (NCB) (a Syria-based opposition group) had advocated for nonviolent political strategies to confront the regime. Smaller opposition groups such as the al-Watan coalition and the Building the Syrian State party had similarly criticized militarization. However, the SNC, which initially supported nonviolent strategies, began to shift and openly support arming the opposition and the militarization of the uprising. A second question concerned whether to advocate for military intervention. The case for military intervention was motivated by what oppositionists saw was a successful NATO-led campaign in Libya to oust al-Ghadafi's regime. The LCC, NCB, and other groups inside Syria were initially staunchly against Western intervention while the SNC leadership was increasingly supportive of intervention. Having limited access to the protesters, the SNC resorted to appealing to the international community as a means of affecting political transition. For the SNC, the only substantive strategy they could pursue was to have the Western powers intervene in Syria and collapse the regime.

The multiple leadership problems of the Syrian opposition were compounded by a severe legitimacy deficit and disputes over political strategy. As I discuss in the next chapter, these realities also contributed to the rise and proliferation of armed groups that were actively hostile to both the regime and the original opposition structure—the SNC, FSA, and

LCC. And while these groups were not ideologically or politically coherent themselves, they were powerful and could severely undermine the existing opposition structures. It is thus not entirely surprising, then, that the main opposition structure in 2011 and 2012 had its capacity severely reduced by 2017. In addition to the organizational weaknesses of the opposition, the realities of regime resilience also help explain why the opposition was unsuccessful in bringing about political change. On the one hand, as I discuss below, the regime proved able to adapt to the changing situation on the ground and was successful in drawing on military and financial resources to stave off collapse. On the other hand, the regime's adaptability and resiliency was partially due to deficiencies in the opposition and the inability to provide a stable and sustainable alternative to the regime in liberated areas.

Authoritarian adaptability

What explains the regime's resiliency during the early phases of the conflict? What explains the regime's resiliency during the course of the conflict? There are, broadly, two factors that can answer this question: the first external to the regime, that is, in the deficiencies and weaknesses of the opposition; and, second, in the ability of the regime to adapt to the changing circumstances wrought by the uprising. Indeed, even prior to 2011, the Syrian regime and other Arab authoritarian states had been undergoing transformative processes that were meant to consolidate authoritarian rule. In this period in Syria (as discussed in Chapter One), and throughout the Arab world, significant economic reforms had been undertaken that disrupted the material basis of postcolonial authoritarianism. These shifts had been intended not to destabilize authoritarianism but rather to consolidate and strengthen it. These transformations gave rise to an area of inquiry concerned with authoritarian upgrading (Heydemann, 2007) and how shifting domestic and international political economies were changing patterns of authoritarian rule.

As the outbreak of the Arab uprisings suggests, the authoritarian upgrading project has largely failed, with many states in the region unable to stably balance neoliberal economic policies with authoritarian politics. The new modes of authoritarian governance ushered in during the 1990s and accelerated during the 2000s had the long-term effect of destabilizing the authoritarian states of the region. The Syrian regime's adaptability in the context of the uprising must be understood within the larger trajectory of authoritarian upgrading, with this stage defined by a more militarized, sectarian, and repressive core (Heydemann, 2013a, b, p. 63). For Hinnebusch (2012), authoritarian upgrading had significant costs that, as the uprising demonstrated, could not be contained in Syria. However, this upgrading was unbalanced. While it fostered grievances, it had not led to the withering or contraction of the regime's social base into a specific segment of society. Thus on the eve of the uprising the regime still had a strong social base of support that remained largely loyalist throughout the course of the conflict. The regime's survival is dependent on the support of these social groups, and the support has remained more or less intact throughout the conflict. These groups include the army and security apparatus, the crony capitalists (Hinnebusch, 2012), public sector employees (Haddad, 2012a), religious minority groups, and the middle classes. These social groups have supported the regime because of a combination of sectarian/social, socioeconomic, and security factors (Haddad, 2012a). Perhaps the most important factor contributing to continued regime support has been how the regime has successfully fomented fear of the opposition, portraying them (particularly the militarized opposition) as foreign agents intent on destabilizing Syria. As the conflict evolved, some who may have initially supported the opposition have waned and shifted, increasingly swayed by the narrative that Syria's destruction was not for some democratic end. The regime's narratives about the protesters, moreover, have also been overly sectarian and have played on minority fears of an Islamist takeover of the country. These narratives were seemingly confirmed later on in the conflict when the armed groups were dominated by Salafist-jihadist elements. The fear of a Salafi-jihadist takeover of Syria has frightened both religious minorities and Syrian Sunnis who share fears about what Salafist rule would mean for them. Such fears have been profoundly strong among many Syrians, including those who have supported the uprising.

Yet, the regime's resilience cannot solely be explained by Syrian fears of a Salafist-jihadist takeover of the country. Heydemann has argued that its resilience can be explained through authoritarian adaptation: it adapted to the demands of the uprising while maintaining its own survival (2013). For Heydemann, the regime's adaptation was multifaceted and included a series of institutional and policy transformations while simultaneously maintaining violence against protesters. On the international front, the regime was forced to maneuver around increasing international isolation and restrictive sanctions by relying extensively on its main international supporters, Iran and Russia. Shifts in international alliances and a rapidly transforming geopolitical landscape have been central features of not only the Syrian regime's adaptability but that of other states as well (Aras and Falk, 2015). Domestically, the regime mobilized its social base by appealing to their fears of a broad Islamist takeover of the country. The regime responded to the contraction of the economy by rolling back market reforms and reasserting the state's role in the economy through the reestablishment of subsidies and other forms of economic welfare. This has not stemmed the tide of economic decay but has nevertheless been useful. Finally, the regime reorganized the security apparatus and military to better confront the tactics and strategies of the armed opposition.

The regime's adaptability has thus been structured by many domestic and international factors that have allowed its mutation and transformation in the face of rapid change on the ground. Its ability to navigate the conflict and to remain in control of large parts of the country suggests that regime elements, whether government or security officials or the business elite (Abboud, 2013b), will be positioned to remain key players in the postwar reconstruction of the country. The social transformations wrought by the conflict have contributed to new forms of social stratification in Syria, such as within the business community, that are creating centers of power that are directly benefitting from the conflict (Abboud, 2017). While some regime elements will undoubtedly survive into the postconflict period, the regime's longevity or survival is uncertain and indeed even unlikely given the fragmentation of the country and the multiple military, economic, and political pressures on it. Nevertheless, the regime has remained resilient and adaptive as the conflict has grown and transformed. The dynamics of this transformation have varied considerably since 2011.

The strength of the Assad regime's social base, the fear of sectarianism, the cohesion of the security apparatus, and the adaptability to the changes in the opposition movement all contributed to the regime's resilience during the early stages of the conflict. A second factor—the weaknesses of the opposition—also helps explain the government's resilience throughout this period. Opposition weakness should be understood broadly here to refer to the inability of the opposition to bring about regime collapse but also to how the opposition has been unsuccessful in fracturing the regime's social support base or disincentivizing support for the regime. For many Syrians, support for Assad does not arise out of loyalty or commitment or even agreement with the regime's strategies during the war, but rather out of an objective fear of the opposition and mistrust in the opposition's ability to provide a reasonable alternative. The weaknesses of the opposition and the horrors of violence in which all major armed groups are implicated have placed many Syrians in the unenviable position of having to choose between the lesser of two evils. It is unsurprising, then, that so many Syrians have sought to chart a third way, especially in their cultural production about the conflict. This third way (or *ways*, as there are many Syrian experiences during the conflict) represents a political experience and imaginary that is not bound by the linear narratives of regime or opposition loyalists.

Conclusion

This chapter sought to address three questions of direct relevance to understanding the initial period of the Syrian conflict, from 2011 to 2012, during which a nonviolent and later armed opposition took root: what was the social and political composition of the opposition; what were the opposition demands, and why did they fail in achieving them; and how was the regime resilient in the face of widespread protests and an increasingly armed movement trying to overthrow it? The protests that began in Dar'a in March 2011 created and propelled a national movement of protests against the Syrian regime. The regime's response to the protests was to engage in sustained repression while passing cosmetic reforms, both of which failed to placate or stop the protests. Over the course of the Ba'ath Party's rule over Syria, they had been effective in suppressing all forms of associational activity. When the protests began, there were no institutions such as political parties that could organize and mobilize the protesters. This role was left to the newly created LCCs, a network of local activists who had come together to try and organize a society in revolt. However, the continued repression and the challenges of mobilizing under conflict conditions kept the LCCs fragmented and decentralized. The failure of the political opposition in exile to provide material or political support to the protesters on the ground contributed to the weakening of the LCCs and the inability of the opposition inside and outside of the country to coalesce and form a unified movement.

At the same time, the regime demonstrated its resiliency and adaptability during the conflict, which helps explain why the pressure of the protests did not lead to its immediate collapse. The fragmentation of the opposition and its multiple leaderships contributed to the regime's longevity, which can be explained as much by the weaknesses and shortcomings of the opposition as it can by Assad's military or political strength. The regime's resiliency then represents something of a paradox: on the one hand, it lost control of large parts of

Syria by 2013 and no longer had the administrative capacity to govern in areas that it ostensibly controls. And it has remained under tremendous pressure from within its support base from segments of Syrian society that are increasingly fatigued by the war and are demanding its end (Dark, 2014). On the other hand, the inability of the opposition to cohere and form a structured movement that has the political power and legitimacy to overthrow Assad and put forth a feasible transition plan has allowed the regime to maintain control over key areas of the country amid tremendous political and military pressure.

It has become common in most analyses of the Syrian conflict to draw a clear division between the period of popular, nonviolent mobilization and that of militarization. As I have maintained throughout the book, this is a false periodization of the conflict, as both nonviolent mobilization and armed insurrection or regime violence have been present since the outset. However, in the initial months after the uprising when the nonviolent mobilization had proved unable to overthrow the regime and the political pressures brought to bear by the external opposition proved futile, many in Syria chose the path of militarization as the option most likely to bring about the regime's overthrow. This was supported materially and encouraged politically by regional powers intent on destabilizing Syria and expanding the battlefield. Thus, the seeds of militarization were planted in the initial stalemate that defined the conflict during 2011, a period in which the internal and external opposition was still in its infancy and had proved unable to bring about an end to the conflict.

In the next chapter, I explore the dynamics driving the militarization of the conflict, especially after late 2012 when more armed groups began to proliferate throughout the country. In doing so, I am trying to situate the rise of an armed opposition in parallel, rather than in opposition, to the nonviolent, popular mobilization that began in 2011. Syria's conflict has morphed considerably from 2011, and while militarization has contributed to territorial fragmentation and a humanitarian crisis (both discussed below) there has remained an active nonviolent movement that is committed to the initial ideals of the Syrian revolution. Militarization has not meant the collapse of the early mobilizers discussed in this chapter, but has contributed to the expansion of the wider landscape of the Syrian opposition and the expansion of groups operating inside Syria. Whereas many in the nonviolent opposition had more or less consistent goals around regime change and political transitions, as we see below, armed actors inside Syria have wildly contradictory and conflicting goals. Such conflicts between groups have fueled further violence inside Syria and made the possibilities for immediate resolution even more remote. What is of interest here, then, is understanding why and how armed groups proliferated and how this proliferation set the conflict on a radically different trajectory than that envisioned by the early protesters.

3 | Networks of Violence

The fate of the Syrian city of Raqqa perhaps best exemplifies the complicated, violent, and unstable landscape of conflict in Syria. Raqqa was the first city to be liberated from regime forces in early 2013, a major military achievement for the armed opposition at the time. Supporters of the opposition hailed the Free Syrian Army (FSA) as heroes, after they defeated the regime forces and pushed them to the outskirts of the city. Indeed, for many people outside of Syria, the battle of Raqqa was the first major FSA achievement after more than a year of nationwide battles with regime forces in cities and villages alike.

This narrative of an FSA victory that would propel a domino effect of regime retreat and contraction was misleading, and seriously betrayed the realities on the ground. Those realities were that many armed groups, not just those fighting under the FSA banner, contributed to the battles in Raqqa, including more Islamist-oriented fighting groups that were ascendant on Syria's conflict landscape. Lost in the euphoria of Raqqa's "liberation" was looming conflict between armed groups over who was going to govern territory and reap the benefits of military victory. Almost immediately after regime forces withdrew from Raqqa, such realities began to reveal themselves, with inter-rebel fighting between the FSA and other armed groups. By late 2013, barely a year after regime forces began their withdrawal, the

Islamic State of Iraq and as-Sham (ISIS) claimed control of the city, having taken over most of the territory from the FSA and other armed groups. By January 2014, ISIS had secured the entire city and by midsummer they had overrun a regime military base housing the 17th Division of the Syrian Army, thus eliminating a serious military threat to its hold over Raqqa. Not long thereafter, the city was declared the capital of ISIS. This, too, would not last for long. Three years later, a coalition of Syrian Democratic Forces (SDF) and other armed groups, supported by American-led airstrikes, recaptured Raqqa from ISIS. From 2011 to 2017, the residents of Raqqa had seen no less than four different armed groups claiming to control their territory and their lives. What the future of their destroyed city holds is today unclear.

What does the rapid and violent change in authority in Raqqa tell us about the armed opposition and the nature and structure of violence in the Syrian conflict? The aim of this chapter is to begin to address this question while also addressing other questions about why violence has persisted throughout the conflict, who the main groups are that are contributing to the violence, the role of the international community therein, and what the conditions and consequences are of territorial contraction and fragmentation. One way to think of violence in Syria, proposed here, is through the idea of networks of violence. Armed groups are not homogenous, contained units that are neatly bound by identity or ideology. The Syrian conflict landscape is much more complicated than this. Rather, factors such as the war economy also contribute to the proliferation of violence throughout the country, such that the basis of networks is very fluid. Such fluidity is reflected in the formation and contraction of alliances in Syria.

The militarization of the Syrian uprising began in June 2011 when army defectors formed brigades under the banner of the Free Syrian Army (FSA). Over the next few months, the main armed opposition in Syria grew under the FSA umbrella and quickly spread throughout the country with units and brigades emerging in major cities and in the rural peripheries. Much like the LCCs discussed in the previous chapter, this gave the FSA the appearance of having a vertical and horizontal command structure and, most important, a national character. With the creation of the FSA and the presence of an external and internal opposition, the Syrian uprising expanded into political and military wings that had as their ostensible common goal the overthrow of the regime. However, such coherence between the political and military wings of the uprising was a mirage and no substantive forms of cooperation that could affect political change ever emerged.

Since then, violence has proliferated throughout Syria as the FSA failed to overthrow the regime, inducing the formation of armed groups outside of its loose command structure. The conflict has become bloodier and more deadly with thousands of Syrians murdered or displaced each month. In this chapter, we will explore the growth and use of violence in the Syrian conflict by both regime and non-regime forces. The militarization of the uprising—and the subsequent inability of the political and military opposition to overthrow the regime—led to the dramatic expansion of violence, the proliferation of different armed groups, and the territorial fragmentation of the country. The FSA's failure to overthrow the regime paved the way for the emergence of other armed groups, including but not limited to the Islamic Front, the Army of Islam, Jabhat an-Nusra (later Jabhet Fatah al-Sham), and ISIS, all of whom had conflicting agendas and strategies as well as differing ideological leanings. Thus, while they appeared from the outside to be easily grouped as Salafist-jihadist, their actual beliefs, practices, and alliances differed widely. Meanwhile, the Syrian Arab Army (SAA) has withered and the regime has been forced to rely on homegrown armed groups such as the National Defence Forces (NDF) and regional groups, such as Hizbollah and Iraqi and Iranian militiamen, to achieve its military objectives. Kurdish-led forces have emerged as major military actors as well and have proven adept at allying themselves with different domestic and international actors to achieve major military gains.

In this chapter, we will explore this fractured and complicated landscape of violence in Syria as it evolved until around 2015, and see how it produced a political and military stalemate that persisted until the Russian intervention and the eventual fall of Aleppo to regime forces. The question of how a stalemate emerged is explored in relation to who the main actors are, why there is a lack of coordination between rebel forces, why regional states supported opposing sides, and how the diffused violence in Syria not only precluded both military and political solutions to the conflict, but also contributed to a continued stalemate and the slow fragmentation of the country into areas controlled by armed groups. It was not until the fall of Aleppo to regime forces that the military (and thus political) stalemate was broken. This chapter is thus concerned with the period leading up to the fall of Aleppo.

Understanding violence in the Syrian context

The nonviolent nature of the uprising gave rise to a number of studies drawing on Social Movement Theory (SMT) (Droz-Vincent, 2014; Leenders and Heydemann, 2012) to help explain the mobilization of large segments of Syrian society. Such approaches to mobilization and conflict do not sufficiently explain the militarization of the Syrian conflict or the nature of violence since 2011. Indeed, the proliferation of armed groups and the diffusion of violence throughout the country and beyond any central regime or rebel command structure is an important factor in explaining the continuity of the Syrian conflict, the profound violence being inflicted on civilians, and the stalemate that persisted until the Russian intervention began in September 2015. How then can we understand the proliferation and nature of violence in Syria?

Mary Kaldor (1999) has proposed understanding contemporary civil violence through the perspective of "new wars" theory, an approach which argues that contemporary wars have four defining features: (1) they are fought by combinations of state and non-state violent networks; (2) these networks are motivated by identity politics and not ideology; (3) networks attempt to achieve political, rather than physical, control of populations through fear; and (4) violence is financed through predatory measures that perpetuate violence. Kaldor's approach attempts to understand and theorize how we should understand contemporary warfare. Her approach is not without its critics, who argue that there is very little if anything "new" about the kinds of war and violence she explains (see Utas, 2012; Henderson and Singer, 2002). Moreover, the new wars approach has limited explanatory capacity in the Syrian context because of how its proponents downplay the role of geopolitics and ideological factors in perpetuating conflict, instead identifying globalization as the main structuring factor of new wars.

This is not the space to engage in the new wars debates (for a discussion of new wars and Syria see Malantowicz, 2013). Rather, let us see how these debates have provided analytical tools to help us explain the nature of violence in Syria. There are three main analytical tools in particular that can help us understand the proliferation and diffusion of violence, the structure and interrelations of armed groups, and stalemate and the continuity of conflict. The first concerns how war has become increasingly civilianized. The new wars debates have emphasized the civilianization of war, understood as the increasing involvement of civilians, rather than soldiers, in violence and war. This refers not only to civilians as armed actors, but as victims and supporters of violence (Steenkamp, 2014, p. 58). Thus, civilians become instrumental to the proliferation of violence. The civilianization of violence is in part a response to the threats that emerge from outside communities. As we will see throughout this chapter, many of the rebel and regime armed groups formed initially to protect their locales. Today, many of the localized units in non-regime areas are made up of only a few dozen fighters at most and are concentrated in specific geographic spaces with virtually no mobility. The same is true of many pro-regime militias who are not directly connected to any central command. These units, whether in rebel or regime areas, are embedded and entrenched in their communities. In many contemporary wars, including Syria's, civilians, with little or no prior military training, have formed armed units and are connected to other armed groups in an intricate, networked structure that gives violence an organized character.

A second, related analytical tool concerns how the civilianization of war allows for the multiplicity of violence because it expands the social basis of violence (Steenkamp, 2014). Violence is no longer perpetuated by state actors, or even a small number of non-state actors, but by a plethora of fighting units that all have different social backgrounds, strategies, goals, and capacities. New wars, then, are characterized less by soldiers as by independent, autonomous groups such as militias, warlords, jihadists, insurgents, mercenaries, and regular civilians, who have in common their lack of military training. The members of these groups who exercise violence often lack formal military training. The nature of violence is often small-scale, including light weapons, and does not involve heavy artillery or air attacks and, as such, is not conducive to overrunning and defeating military forces. The objective of violence becomes to consolidate and control specific areas and to entrench themselves there.

A third final tool concerns the political economy of war. Maintaining violence and controlling territories require material resources that are not readily available to many armed groups in the absence of state sponsorship or funding. Conflict provides economic opportunities to finance conflict and profit from it. How armed groups finance their violence is central to understanding new wars and to the role of informality and criminality therein. Contemporary wars create the opportunities for networks to emerge that are engaged in both violence and economic profiteering, giving rise to organized structures of exchange, transportation, and consumption that are structured by war and violence. In wars such as Syria's, virtually all armed groups are dependent on war economies and the opportunities afforded by war. With this in mind, the remainder of the chapter identifies the main armed groups fighting in both the rebel and regime camps.

The rise of the Free Syrian Army

The militarization of the Syrian uprising can be attributed to two main factors: first, the sustained and brutal violence inflicted on protesters by the regime and its armed proxies, which encouraged Syrians to take up arms; and second, the failure of the protests to initiate a political transition process, such as that which occurred in Tunisia and Egypt. The initial protesters were strongly committed to nonviolence as a political strategy, but in the months following the uprising this strategy was put under tremendous strain as some in the external opposition began advocating for international intervention and the creation of an armed wing. As these debates were ongoing within opposition circles, groups of army defectors began forming in their respective locales and began confronting regime forces with violence. Eventually, during the summer of 2011, these groups would coalesce under the banner of the Free Syrian Army (FSA) and would form the core of the militarized opposition. In 2012 and 2013, the FSA was heralded by some as an army-in-waiting, as the force that would both topple the regime and secure stability in the aftermath. Regardless of how fantastical these visions were, the FSA was indeed the primary armed actor on the Syrian stage. Today, however, the FSA has lost a tremendous amount of power and influence on the battlefield. This section explores the rise of the FSA in Syria and how its role in the conflict eventually waned.

While some heralded the formation of the FSA as a necessary step toward bringing about political transition, in reality the FSA was fraught with the same contradictions that characterized the political opposition. Even after more than six years of conflict, it is misleading to speak of the FSA as an army as such, with a horizontal command, a vertical communication structure, common command, shared resources, or even any real sense of esprit de corps among its members. The fragmentation of the FSA and the lack of coherency and centralization within its ranks suggest that the brigades form more of a network of violence than an army. An army has a central and hierarchical command, whereas a network of violence can be understood differently: as a decentralized form in which the various nodes of the network operate independently from one another but in relative cooperation. The lack of hierarchy or integration between the nodes makes their relationships precarious and contributes to the constant shifting of alliances. Interestingly, the organizational structure of the FSA was reproduced among other armed groups in Syria.

The FSA was officially declared on 29 July 2011 when a group of defector officers led by Colonel Riad al-Assad declared the group's existence, pledging to support the uprising's goals of overthrowing the regime. The FSA consisted of only a few hundred, perhaps up to thousands, of army defectors who were loosely organized in their respective geographic locales. Defectors from Homs, for example, were predominantly active in and around that city, and their operations were initially focused on protecting protesters and civilian areas from repeated regime attacks. The FSA's weapons were entirely drawn from stockpiles and caches they had confiscated from regime bases or taken with them when they defected. As such, they had very limited offensive capabilities to engage in sustained battles with regime forces in the major cities. In the late summer of 2011 the FSA had concentrated its activities on defensive activities to protect civilians, raids to capture weapons, and limited attacks on regime forces in areas of the country where they were deemed militarily vulnerable, such as in the urban and rural peripheries.

These military limitations paralleled the fragmented organizational structure of the armed opposition after the formation of the FSA. Broadly speaking, two types of armed groups emerged under the FSA umbrella. The first group consisted of highly localized and geographically concentrated armed groups made up largely of civilians and army defectors who were active in their towns, villages, and cities. These localized units are overwhelmingly under-resourced. While they operate independently of central command they are nevertheless ostensibly loyal to the FSA, as they receive some of their material resources through the FSA. At the very least, they pledge support and allegiance to the FSA in order to convey solidarity and cohesion among rebel ranks. The second group consisted of self-proclaimed brigades that were distinguishable from the localized units in many ways.

They tended to be larger and contain many civilians as well as army defectors. Their material resources were drawn from international donors, and these brigades tended to be more ideologically and eventually religiously motivated, serving the interests and political strategies of their patrons, who mostly came from Gulf countries (Hassan, 2013). Perhaps most important is that these brigades were mobile and could conduct activities across much larger areas of the country, especially across provinces. This put many of the brigades in regular conflict with one another as they fought for control over key distribution routes, such as highways, checkpoints, and border crossings, and other strategic areas. Such infighting between brigades ostensibly loyal to the FSA exposed the weaknesses of the FSA structure in commanding and controlling armed groups.

Infighting, resource and material deficiencies, and the geographical diffusion of the FSA units all precluded the unification of the fighters into a hierarchical command. There were major problems with the FSA's leadership from the beginning, with the founding officers, including the Commander Riad al-Assad, establishing themselves in Turkey and not in Syria. This made control over the local units and brigades as well as communication with field commanders much more difficult, if not impossible. The leadership's location in Turkey meant that they were heavily influenced and controlled by the Turkish government and its intelligence apparatus. This influence would be limited, however, as the exiled commanders exercised less and less control of the units and brigades that continued to sprout after July 2011. Over time (as we will see below) the FSA and the political opposition made multiple, failed attempts to unify the command structure of the rebel groups to provide coordinated military strategies and resources. The presence of such hierarchies should not be confused with their functionality, however. To date, the FSA hierarchy remains severely disconnected from events on the ground.

The FSA model, then, was never well suited to its goals of centralizing leadership and military strategy and serving as a political umbrella for the armed groups. In addition to disconnections between the FSA hierarchy and fighters on the ground, the commanders also enjoyed very little support and legitimacy among the fighters within Syria, in large part because of their inability to marshal resources to the front lines or provide sound military strategies. Attacks against regime forces were increasingly uncoordinated between the different FSA brigades and there was no coherent military strategy to speak of. What then occurred almost instantaneously after the creation of the FSA was the rapid spread of violence and the concentration of violence in specific locales.

Despite the FSA's structural weaknesses and military limitations, a year after its founding many of the FSA-affiliated brigades found themselves in control of large areas of northern Syria along the Turkish border where regime forces had retreated. This included a number of important border crossings, such as Bab al-Salameh. Control of the border crossings allowed the fighters access to more direct supply routes to bring in weapons and goods, which facilitated greater international involvement in the arming of rebels. By the summer of 2012, almost all of the rebel support from the international community was flowing from Turkey, where regional states such as Qatar and Saudi Arabia funneled resources and weapons to the rebels. The so-called liberated areas in the north quickly became an experiment in non-regime governance and control.

To this end, the rebel military commanders took advantage of having a direct link to the FSA leadership and secure supply routes to attempt to unify rebel ranks and coordinate command. Although the rebels had taken over large areas of northern Syria, they remained highly fragmented and infighting had threatened to erase many of their territorial gains and undermine the rebel claim to forming a legitimate alternative to the Assad regime. In September 2012 a Joint Command for the Revolution's Military Council was established in order to organize rebel groups inside the country and better link them to the external leadership. The Joint Command proposed an organizational structure to direct all rebel operations, beginning with a five-person General Command that was made up of five Brigadier Generals:

Mithaq al-Bateesh, Abdel Majid Dabis, Zaki Lolu, Ziad Fahd, and Salim Idriss. Below the General Command were fourteen provincial Military Councils that would be responsible for activities in each province and which would report back to the General Command.

Despite the new structure, the General Command was never really able to exert its full control over the rebel groups. Increasingly, rebel groups formed outside of the FSA structure or broke off from it when they were able to secure resources from international patrons or when alliances with other rebel groups broke down, such as over control of key highways, checkpoints, or border crossings. Infighting among the rebel groups paralleled a lack of communication between the Command's leadership and increasingly autonomous decision-making from the provincial councils. This contributed to further fragmentation of the rebel groups and more withdrawal from the General Command. More important, however, was the growth of rebel groups that did not adhere to the FSA's larger strategies, particularly around the inclusion of minorities and their alliances with the external opposition. The increase in violence after the summer of 2012 led to more and more sectarian groups motivated both by an increased religiosity permeating the rebel ranks and a desire to exact revenge for the regime's brutality. Thereafter, more Islamist-leaning commanders came to prominence in the rebel movement. The rise of sectarian and ideological commanders did not in and of itself immediately lead to the collapse of the Command structure, but disagreements over the administration of non-regime areas, particularly around issues of law and governance, as well as disagreements over military strategy, did so as well.

Toward the end of 2012 many of the brigades that were previously under the FSA umbrella began to break off and form independent brigades, further spreading and decentralizing violence and making attempts at consolidation difficult. The political and material relationships with the General Command were increasingly of limited benefit and international patrons were willing to provide resources to brigades outside of the FSA model. This was particularly the case after Saudi Arabia and Qatar were lukewarm about their support for the General Command, with each country accusing the other of exercising undue influence within the Command. Both countries were thus reluctant to provide full political and military support to the Command and found identifying and resourcing particular brigades to be a more fruitful and advantageous strategy. Such a strategy would end up dividing the more powerful brigades and turning them against one another, fostering mistrust among the commanders and between them and the General Command. With Qatar and Saudi Arabia jockeying over control of the appointment of commanders and other leadership positions, fighters on the ground grew disillusioned with the FSA model and began holding alternative, parallel elections for military leadership roles. Many provinces very quickly had more than one military council leader. Rivalries ensued and infighting between rebel groups under the FSA umbrella increased. Splits among the brigades contributed to further defections from the FSA model, but, paradoxically, did not always lead to internal fighting, with some groups choosing to cooperate militarily in certain areas.

Nevertheless, the FSA eventually fell from prominence. By the time the major battles of 2016 occurred, they were on the sidelines and irrelevant to the battlefield dynamics, as JAN, ISIS, NDF, SDF, and others had grown in strength and power. Legrand (2016) argues that the descent into irrelevance was a function of both battlefield losses and the role that foreign backers played in discouraging FSA attacks against the regime. Turkish and Jordanian intelligence, which exercised major influence among the FSA brigades, began supporting FSA operations against other armed groups instead of the regime after 2014 when a stalemate had taken root. With fewer fighters and resources, the strategy was to severely deplete the FSA and force a retreat into the southern provinces in and around Dar'a, where FSA brigades remained strong until after the Russian intervention. Their losses and the reduction of operations against the regime ceded the battlefield to the more radicalized groups like JAN, ISIS, and the other Islamist brigades.

The FSA has thus faded into irrelevance, especially after the breaking of the stalemate. Many Syrian political oppositionists hold on to the fantasy that the FSA will be revived and will overthrow the regime, but its foreign patrons have proven to care more about themselves and their relations with the regime than the strength of the FSA brigades. Today, FSA factions still exist throughout the country but they are very localized and have very little ability to grow. The last stronghold in the South has been effectively wiped out by the Russian intervention, scattering fighters around the country. Local truces negotiated with the regime have similarly disbanded brigades and led to their dispersal. While some may have reappeared with other armed groups, they are no longer fighting under the FSA umbrella. In addition to its battlefield retreat, many no longer consider the FSA an army-in-waiting because of the criminality associated with its fighters, which undermined the FSA's goals and forced Syrians to support other armed groups.

Networked rebel groups

With the defection of larger brigades from the Joint Command, alternative networks of violence began to emerge toward the end of 2012. The facade of rebel coherence and unification was put to rest at this time, with armed groups sprouting throughout the country, particularly in the non-regime areas where territorial, political, and administrative control was contested by competing armed groups. Inter-rebel relations were defined both by cooperation and conflict, depending on the particular situation. What was consistent, however, was that the relations between rebel groups were quickly unraveling and that they failed to cohere. Rather than forming into coherent command structures, armed groups assumed a networked structure that was defined by its insta-bility and fluidity, as constituent elements of what came to be known as Jabhet (Fronts) pledged and withdrew allegiance to them with alarming frequency.

Conventional or popular narratives of the conflict suggest that rebel fragmentation was a cause of ideological distinctions. This has certainly been reinforced by the political debates between which "moderate" rebels to support versus those "radical" ones, criteria for which have never been put forth, let alone defined. Nor do these distinctions capture the variety of ideological leanings of the armed groups despite being subsumed under the label "Islamist" or "Salafist-jihadist." But reducing rebel fragmentation to ideology ignores serious issues of legitimacy and the rebels' social base, leadership, access to military and economic resources, and overall strategy. Indeed, more recently, analysts have been paying much more attention to the role that criminality and economic factors play in the formation of networks and the exercise of violence in Syria. Many armed groups exercised violence for very different reasons. Not all rebel violence was aimed at overthrowing the regime; increasingly it was driven by the need to secure supply routes, impose or break sieges, or reap the economic spoils of war. The motivations and drivers of violence thus expanded as the conflict landscape widened to include more armed actors.

In each governorate, the networks of violence looked and interacted differently. Some FSA brigades were stronger in the south and northwest, while the emergent Islamist groups were powerful in the north and east of the country. In some cases, armed groups were entrenched in the areas they were active in and drew most of their fighters from surrounding villages. This gave them some air of legitimacy. In other cases, armed groups established themselves in villages and governorates through the provision of resources, including food, and the creation of administrative institutions, no matter how precarious. Different armed groups proved incapable of spreading themselves geographically and were ultimately slowly confined to specific territories that they could consolidate. Consolidation required establishing governance structures and embedding social forces into rebel structures to ensure acquiescence. Such efforts proved futile within a widening conflict landscape and contributed to the decentralization of violence, thus making attempts to establish an FSA central command pointless. As time passed, the General Command became more insignificant on the ground and unable to exercise influence over local units and brigades, who were increasingly defined by their networked structure.

It is nearly impossible to determine how many brigades and local units exist in Syria now. In 2013, the Carter Center estimated that there were at least 1,050 brigades and 3,250 battalions or companies (smaller localized units) operating in Syria (Carter Center, 2013, p. 24). These numbers have undoubtedly increased since then. The localized units often consist of a few dozen fighters with limited training and limited resources. The brigades have a few hundred fighters and have slightly more resources. Both the units and brigades are typically associated with larger structures that bring together a network of fighters (networked rebels) versus those outside of any broader structure (independent rebels). Particularly after the collapse of the General Command model, many of these groups are independent of any larger central command, with the preferred association occurring through the creation of various Fronts that serve more as regional conglomerations of fighters than hierarchical commands. Loyalty to the Fronts is often weak, with different brigades pledging and withdrawing allegiance with alarming frequency. The example of Liwa al-Tawhid (Tawhid Brigade) highlights the fluidity of allegiance and coordination among rebel groups. Tawhid was originally formed in and around Aleppo and was made up of thousands of fighters who had initial success on the battlefield. Their original affiliation was with the FSA but, owing to their increasingly Islamist leanings, they broke off from the FSA in 2012 and formed a coalition called the Syrian Islamic Liberation Front (SILF). Within a year, Tawhid, along with two of the other larger and more powerful brigades in the SILF (Jaish al-Islam and Suqoor al-Sham), were withdrawing from the SILF (which subsequently ended all joint operations and dissolved its command structure) to join the Islamic Liberation Front (ILF), a newly formed group of Islamist brigades. By August of 2014, the ILF, with Tawhid still a member, had joined the Majlis Qiyadat al-Thawra al-Surriya (Syrian Revolutionary Command Council), an alliance of more than seventy armed factions from across the geographic and ideological spectrum. However, by late 2014 many of the brigades had disbanded and Tawhid fighters dispersed among a number of different groups in northern Syria. In 2015, former Tawhid commanders and fighters re-emerged in the Levant Front, only to split again a year later when many of the fighters left to join a new movement, Nour al-Din al-Zenki, which was one of the more powerful Fronts in Aleppo and its surrounding areas.

The basic function of the Fronts is to provide leaders a space for coordination and joint decision-making and resource sharing. The Fronts sit as the central node of networks of violence and today include a number of major groups, including the Syrian Democratic Forces (SDF), ISIS, and the Front for the Conquest of the Levant (JFS; formerly JAN), all of which share remarkably similar characteristics in their networked structure. Previous Fronts that were prominent on the battlefield include the Syrian Revolutionaries Front and the Syrian Islamic Front. All of these Fronts are composed of smaller, less mobile fighting units who are active in geographically concentrated areas, and larger brigades of a few hundred members who are more mobile, more active, and have greater power on the battlefield. The alarming frequency of changes in the names and numbers of Fronts in the conflict are reflective of the fluidity and instability of the conflict landscape and the rapid changes within the organizational structure of violence.

The landscape of violence looks very different throughout Syria's governorates and has shifted over time. Smaller, localized units are concentrated in specific areas of each governorate. This could include a neighborhood, village, or town. Often, larger areas will have hundreds of these smaller units that typically consist of fewer than ten individuals with little if any vertical command structure. These smaller units often coalesce and form a brigade, which has more geographic mobility and a more vertical command structure, with a commander usually controlling fighters and strategy. These brigades are often associated with a Front that is directed by a collection of commanders who ostensibly share responsibility for strategy and resource distribution. This gives the appearance of a national character when in reality the coalitions are simply amalgamations of brigades whose allegiance to the Front is quite fluid. The reason for this entrenchment is complicated but mainly due to resource and capacity issues. On the one hand, many brigades are strong enough to defend areas, hold territory, and establish some semblance of an administration there. On the other hand, they are not strong enough to make significant advances across territories because of the presence of other, hostile armed groups and the regime forces. However, because coordination is weak and mistrust among the groups remains very high, the coalitions do not exercise national power and have different capacities across governorates. Thus different brigades exercise power in their specific locales—town, city, village, governorate—rather than on a national level. Such national limitations have largely driven coalition-making in the Syrian conflict: the inability to make larger military advances coupled with the demands of administering and governing held territory have fostered coalition building.

The fragmentation of the militarized opposition and its effects can best be seen in the city of Aleppo prior to the takeover of the city in late 2016 by regime forces. All of the major coalitions were present in Aleppo prior to this, as the city and its surrounding areas are the most strategic regions of Syria. Aleppo is key to the Turkish supply routes, which were essential to the survival of the armed groups. This is why many of these armed groups engaged in conflict to control highways, routes, checkpoints, and border crossings. Such geographic control allowed these groups to reap the benefits of the war economy and maintain their military entrenchment in Aleppo. The FSA's Command was strong in Aleppo but shared control of the non-regime areas with the SILF, SRF, PYD, and Jabhat an-Nusra, as well as a number of other smaller brigades and fronts. Relations between these groups were rarely cooperative. They were mostly engaged in conflict with one another as they attempted to expand their geographic and military control. While the outer boundaries of Aleppo remained relatively stable from 2013 to 2016, armed groups inside Aleppo fought amongst each other for control of specific territory. On the other side of Aleppo's conflict divide were regime forces, including the SAA, NDF, and militia groups. The city remained divided by these groups until the Russian intervention forced the last remaining rebel fighters out of the city.

While the case of Aleppo is perhaps unique, it was indicative of the larger fragmentation and division of the militarized opposition. The city and its countryside are home to thousands of fighters, all of whom have fluid affiliations with larger units and brigades. The many fighters divided into smaller groupings have never coalesced into a larger unit capable of coordinating and overtaking regime forces. Rather, the opposite has occurred. Most fighters turned against each other and allowed the regime forces to remain entrenched in the parts of the city under their control. All of these coalitions alternated between conflict and cooperation but ultimately vied for as much control of the city as possible. Not unsurprisingly, then, the penetration of regime forces, aided by Russian aerial intervention, into Aleppo was significantly easier in the context of conflict between armed groups.

But these coalitions are very rarely coherent in terms of their ideological leanings and often contain brigades that have different loyalties. An excellent example of this is the Jaish al-Mujahideen (Mujahideen Army) that was formed in early 2014 and is concentrated in the strategic corridor between Aleppo and the Turkish border. This coalition of Islamist-leaning brigades largely grew out of the FSA command structure but contains brigades that were created and operated outside of the General Command. The main reason for coming together was geography.

By early 2015 the FSA was a patchwork of armed brigades and local units that were scattered throughout the country but had begun to concentrate in the southern parts of Syria where they controlled large areas of Dar'a, Quneitra, and Suweida. By 2017, in the aftermath of the Russian intervention, FSA brigades had been scattered throughout the country, no longer capable of mounting a serious military challenge to regime-aligned forces, the SDF, or any of the other armed Fronts.

Such realities were a reflection of the inability of the FSA to overthrow the regime and the losses of its affiliated brigades on the battlefield opened the space for the entry of larger, more powerful competing networks of violence to emerge. Moreover, as the FSA brigades began to lose legitimacy among Syrians, who were increasingly weary of the FSA's own brutality and criminality, many groups were able to step in and fill a void. In addition, the arrival of newly formed armed groups, who were often better equipped and more disciplined than the FSA, led to the migration of fighters to these groups. While the FSA formed a distinct network of violence, the movement among different brigades and across networks would become a common feature of the composition of the armed groups. Thus, factors beyond ideological coherence, such as resources access, criminal opportunities, and battlefield prowess, shape networks of violence.

Jabhat al-Nusra and other Islamist fighters

The landscape of Salafist-jihadist violence in Syria is large, with dozens of fighting units and brigades that adhere to Salafist-jihadist ideals. At the pinnacle of this large network of violence is the al-Qaeda–affiliated Jabhat al-Nusra, which is the largest and most organized Salafist-jihadist group in Syria. Although these groups share ideological affinities and cooperate with one another in military and administrative activities, they have not coalesced into a larger structure and still operate independently of one another. Many Salafist-jihadist groups are concentrated in the southern parts of the country as well as the northwest, but are active in and around Damascus and in the eastern areas where they have engaged in repeated battles with YPG and ISIS fighters. Thus, the Salafist-jihadist networks of violence are spread throughout the country but exercise a great deal of power in the northwest and southern parts of Syria.

Relations between the Salafist-jihadist groups vary depending on the geographic area. The lack of a centralized leadership and the failure of the groups to coalesce into a larger unit reflect the mistrust that continues to plague intra-rebel relations. Cooperation and joint administration by the groups, on the other hand, demonstrate their pragmatism and a recognition that the diffusion of power in their geographic areas means that governance and administration must be cooperative and shared.

Although JAN is the largest and most powerful brigade and has engaged in many battles with ISIS, YPG, FSA, and regime forces, they have pursued largely cooperative relations with other brigades that share their ideological commitments and who are sympathetic to the basic tenets of al-Qaeda's ideology. These larger brigades, such as Ahrar al-Sham (who are part of the Islamic Front), enjoy friendly, strategic relations with JAN that have led to military and administrative cooperation. Infighting between these groups over territorial control has not occurred on a wide scale (see Chapter Five); violence between them has been rejected in favor of shared governance of areas under their control. Thus the larger brigades have not attempted to subordinate others but have instead worked together to achieve common goals.

There are other Islamist groups who may not share JAN's ideological affinities but who are nevertheless embedded in shared governance models and who engage in military battles together. These are Islamist groups that are largely part of the Islamic Front (IF) and the SIF before it, such as Suqour al-Sham. In Aleppo and Dar'a where Shari'a Committees have been established, JAN shares membership with multiple groups, including those Islamist brigades that do not necessarily adhere to Salafist-jihadist ideology but who are nevertheless sympathetic to JAN. There are smaller fighting units outside of the IF structure that JAN similarly coordinates with on the battlefield, but these relations have not translated into their integration into JAN or IF, on the one hand, or the Shari'a Committees in Aleppo or Dar'a. Relations among these Islamist groups are confined to coordinating military activities. Many of the smaller

Islamist fighting units are locally based and do not have the fighters or resources to expand beyond their specific locales. Cooperating with JAN and IF in local battles shores up their military strength.

Generally cooperative relations between the major Islamist brigades contrast with the fluidity of relations with the FSA and other armed groups. The four major networks of violence—JAN, ISIS, FSA, and YPG—are in regular conflict with one another. However, the FSA has, depending on geographic area, entered into associations with both JAN and the YPG. This reflects the weaknesses of both networks but also the desire of groups such as JAN to incorporate opposition activities into their own. In many parts of the country, JAN operates side-by-side with FSA brigades such as the Hazm Movement and different brigades under the SRF umbrella (although relations between the SRF shift between conflict and cooperation quite regularly). The main difference between Islamist-FSA relations is that they are largely mutually beneficial and strategic and have not evolved into any administrative structures. Groups such as JAN and the IF may share resources, ensure the security of supplies, and exchange intelligence, but, beyond this, cooperation is nonexistent.

While the majority of Islamist groups beyond ISIS have proved remarkably flexible in entering into military cooperation with each other and with other armed groups, this has largely been a necessary by-product of their battlefield and administrative weaknesses. Intra-rebel relations are extremely complicated and cooperation should not be confused with solidarity, cohesion, or centralization of command. The relations between JAN and other networks of violence are mutually beneficial and are prone to changes based on the evolution of the conflict. For example, JAN's largest and most powerful ally is Ahrar al-Sham. The ideological backgrounds of both groups have facilitated cooperation and thus both have interest in shared governance and the establishment of Shari'a courts. Militarily speaking, they support each other's activities and coordinate across multiple battlefronts. The majority of groups that JAN has good relations with are

Salafist-jihadist groups, as shared ideology facilitates cooperation on military, social, and legal matters. Throughout
Syria, there are many networks of Salafist-jihadist violence
that coordinate closely with JAN, including Ansar al-Din, a
coalition of smaller Salafist groups, and then smaller fighting
units in different parts of the country.

Ideological affinities and military coordination notwithstanding, these alliances are not concrete and therefore do
not necessarily represent JAN's overall strength vis-à-vis
other rebel groups. In March 2015, Ahrar al-Sham leaders
began carving out boundaries of influence between them and
JAN (Ali, 2015). Prior to this, Ahrar al-Sham had entered
into an informal agreement to cooperate and coordinate
with the YPG, who have been in regular battles with JAN.
It appears, then, that JAN's closest military and ideological
ally is slowly shifting away from its orbit of influence. A
severing or reduction of relations between JAN and Ahrar
al-Sham would have substantial consequences for JAN's
military capacities and their administrative influence within
non-regime areas. Currently, areas in the northwest and
south in which JAN is active are considered to be very fluid
and subject to multiple authorities' control, as evidenced
by the cooperation around social service provision and
courts. However, the severance of the relations that form the
network of violence and authority could radically reshape
non-regime areas and contribute to further fragmentation, as
groups such as JAN and Ahrar al-Sham lay claim to specific
territories and exclude other groups from their administrative
structures. Further splits between JAN and other groups have
been revealed on the battlefield, as battles between them
and Hazm Movement and the SRF have dampened JAN's
relations with other groups, exposing the fragility of their
relations.

By 2015, JAN's influence and strength in Syria was
based on its military capacities and its ability to provide
social services. By entering into cooperative relations with
other armed groups, JAN was able to extend its influence
throughout the non-regime areas. However, the fragility of
these relations has been recently exposed, and JAN's alliances

are shifting quite rapidly. This pattern is highly consistent with rebel relations throughout the conflict, with certain brigades' strength rising and waning based on the power of their alliances. JAN is no different.

The PYD and the Kurdish political landscape

Syria's Kurdish population had long suffered the denial of basic rights in Syria, including the denial of citizenship and thus forced statelessness for hundreds of thousands of Kurds (Tejel, 2008; Allsopp, 2015). The Kurdish population has historically been concentrated in the north and northeastern parts of the country but the major cities, including Damascus and Aleppo, have sizable Kurdish populations. Kurdish participation in opposition politics prior to the uprising was traditionally very limited, as many Kurdish oppositionists and political parties had closer ties to the regime and were also skeptical of opposition politics. The complicated relations between Kurds and their Arab compatriots continued in the first stages of the uprising.

Despite their collective frustrations with the regime, many Kurds and political parties that represented them attempted to steer a neutral path in the first stages of the Syrian conflict. Although many Kurds did participate in protests and were included in opposition structures, the political parties purposely steered clear of formally joining the opposition while simultaneously maintaining some political distance from the regime. The largest and most powerful Kurdish political party, the Democratic Union Party (PYD), is an offshoot of the Turkish-based Kurdistan Workers Party (PKK), and was initially very reluctant to confront the regime throughout the conflict (International Crisis Group, 2013). The dynamics of PYD–regime relations have been in flux, however, after the Russian intervention, as PYD-led forces have made major military advances that have provoked increasing Turkish military intervention into Syria (see following chapters). There are other parties in the Syrian Kurdish areas that also exercise some influence among the population. Many of these parties operate under the larger umbrella of the Kurdish National Council (KNC). Although under the KNC umbrella, they are an ideologically diverse group, with different social bases of support and different external patrons. The dominant parties within the KNC, the Kurdish Democratic Party of Syria (an offshoot of the Iraqi party of the same name), and the Kurdish Democratic Progressive Party of Syria (an offshoot of the Iraqi Patriotic Union of Kurdistan), are heavily influenced by their Iraqi Kurdish patrons. The KNC and the PYD are the main political competitors within the Syrian Kurdish population and are outgrowths of the two competing versions of Kurdish nationalism espoused by their regional patrons in Turkey and Iraq. All Kurdish parties control some armed elements and are embedded in various networks of violence throughout the Syrian conflict landscape.

Syrian Kurds have also supported different factions of the opposition during the conflict and have joined the ranks of FSA- and JAN-affiliated brigades, although, generally speaking, many of the armed and political opposition groups have not been inclusive of Kurdish political interests. Intra-Kurdish competition and coordination, then, has been an important determinant in Kurdish participation in the Syrian conflict. While the PYD is the stronger of the political parties and has taken the administrative and military leadership of the Kurdish regions, their strong ties to the PKK have made the Turkish authorities reluctant to accept their increasing autonomy within Syria. As PYD-led forces made advances to create contiguous territory after 2015, Turkish intervention increased to prevent territorial consolidation. Conversely, the KNC, while not enjoying the same level of domestic support among Syria's Kurds, has stronger ties to both Turkey and the Iraqi Kurdish groups. Massoud Barzani, leader of the Kurdish Democratic Party (KDP) in Iraq, brokered a deal between the two factions in 2012 called the Erbil Declaration, which created a Supreme Kurdish Council (SKC) consisting of members of both the PYD and KNC, and including a power-sharing agreement meant to avoid continued conflict between the factions.

Barzani's intervention into Syrian Kurdish politics also sought to balance PYD military power as well. The PYD had, in 2012, repatriated many of its fighters from Turkey and had begun to engage in active combat in Kurdish areas. The PYD was the primary military force within the Kurdish areas when, in July 2012, Barzani announced that the Kurdish Regional Government (KRG) in Iraq would train and equip Syrian Kurdish fighters. This military force has never swelled to the point of seriously competing with the PYD forces but is nevertheless present in the Syrian Kurdish areas and under the control and influence of the Iraqi Kurdish groups. While there has been some evidence of military cooperation with the PYD, the two armed groups have generally operated independently of one another. The PYD consolidated its hegemonic position in Syrian Kurdish politics a year after the creation of the SKC, when it unilaterally broke away from the Council and created its own Movement for a Democratic Society (TEV-DEM), which would dominate administration in the Syrian Kurdish areas.

The PYD has established a rather sophisticated military apparatus in the northeast that paralleled its administrative power. Local People's Protection Committees (PPC) serve as a surrogate police force in Kurdish areas to maintain order. The PYD also has a militia that predates the uprising called the People's Defense Corps (YPG), which currently functions as the armed wing of the PYD and the de facto army of the Syrian Kurds. The YPG is deployed throughout the Kurdish areas; they are concentrated in the boundary areas where fighting with ISIS and other armed groups is most intense.

Despite the lack of military coordination among Kurdish groups and the persistence of mistrust among them, the PYD has actually been highly successful in creating an administrative structure that is exercising autonomy beyond the state. The Rojava (meaning Western Kurdistan) Project has not been fully supported by all of the Kurdish parties but is nevertheless an ambitious project to provide administration to the Kurdish-dominated areas. This has strengthened the PYD and the YPG's strength in those areas even though there has been a lack of consensus among Kurdish parties with regard to the authority and legitimacy of the Rojava administration (now the Democratic Federation of Northern Syria, DFNS). The PYD's strength within the Kurdish community, however, has allowed it to pursue the project despite opposition among some groups. Although this opposition has been politically relevant and has led to the collapse of intra-Kurdish projects aimed at unifying the Kurdish parties, such as the SKC, it has not descended into sustained violence between opposing Kurdish factions. The YPG's military strength relative to that of the other parties has largely discouraged such violence. Within this context of PYD strength, relations between the Syrian regime and the Kurdish parties are extremely complicated, and vacillate from direct conflict to the pursuit of mutual interests. On the one hand, the YPG has been very successful militarily in battles with ISIS and has prevented the expansion of ISIS-held territories in the northeast. Such battles have placed military pressure on ISIS and other armed groups and in some cases have directly affected their access to supplies. On the other hand, the PYD has taken over many of the government buildings in the northeast, and through the DFNS the Kurdish parties are governing the territory as the de facto authorities. It is unclear why the regime would have allowed the emergence of an autonomous Kurdish region without any political or military action whatsoever. However, the accusations that the PYD is working closely with the regime may provide some insight into a secret alliance between the two.

Such accusations of covert Kurdish–regime alliances are not entirely plausible, given both the history of the regime's treatment of Syrian Kurds and the legacy of mistrust this has bred. The withering of the regime's security apparatus has likely led to the calculation that security forces cannot engage Kurdish YPG fighters, as this would deflect from other, more strategic areas of the country. The inability to engage militarily with the YPG should not be confused with the regime's tacit acceptance of Kurdish moves toward autonomy. Moreover, for the moment, the regime and the PYD have a common enemy in ISIS, and this has fostered cooperation. In this way, the same factors that shape intra-rebel conflict and cooperation—pragmatism, capacity, and the need for military alliances—have shaped Kurdish–regime relations through 2015. The regime, however, is unlikely to allow the unchecked growth of the PYD and the YPG without some form of intervention into Kurdish affairs. For now, the regime tolerates the Rojava Project out of political necessity, and not out of some commitment to Kurdish autonomy or larger political calculation in favor of decentralizing power to the governorates in the postconflict phase. Such Kurdish advances are as much a product of the PYD's ability to organize Kurdish areas in the context of the uprising, relatively unabated by the Assad regime, which has been militarily and politically focused on developments in other parts of the country. The convenience of a common enemy in ISIS has given the appearance of Kurdish-regime coherence, when this is in fact much more precarious than it appears, and subject to changing conditions on the ground.

One reflection of the changing battlefield dynamics is the rise to prominence of the Syrian Democratic Forces (SDF), a coalition of different Kurdish, Sunni, and Christian Arab fighters. The SDF is essentially a PYD proxy working under a different umbrella, as the YPG is the most dominant military element in the network. In 2014, as the SDF encircled ISIS in the battle of Kobane around the Turkish-Syrian border, U.S. forces provided aerial support. Thus was born a U.S.–PYD partnership to defeat ISIS. From then on, the Obama administration provided limited military support to SDF brigades and increasingly called on them in the fight against ISIS.

Complicating matters is Turkey's belief—rightly—that the SDF was a proxy of the PKK and that its advances against ISIS were merely excuses to create contiguous Kurdish territory in northern Syria as a prelude to a declaration of independence. As such, Turkey, a U.S. ally, has repeatedly intervened to prevent advances and territorial consolidation of the SDF, a temporary U.S. ally. The SDF has proven to be the only local force willing to directly confront ISIS and, as such, as has received extensive U.S. support. This has translated into the politicization of the SDF as well, which has formed the Democratic Syrian Assembly (DSA). Although this contains non-Kurdish elements—its co-President is well-known Syrian dissident Haytham al-Manna—this body is heavily dominated by the PYD and TEV-DEM movements. Today, after the fall of Aleppo, the SDF is perhaps the strongest Syrian-led Front operating in the battlefield.

The Islamic State of Iraq and as-Sham (ISIS)

The roots of the ISIS phenomenon in Iraq and Syria lie in the collapse of the Iraqi state, the subsequent U.S.-led occupation, the rise of extremist movements in Iraq as a response both to occupation and political exclusion, and the rise and fall of the Sahwa (Awakening) movements in Iraq. The latter factor was central to ISIS's constellation in the late 2000s. The Sahwa movement began around 2006–2007 and was a central component of the U.S.'s surge strategy in Iraq. The strategy relied on cultivating Iraqi Sunni tribal leaders, initially in the al-Anbar province, to take up arms against al-Qaeda fighters in Iraq. In September 2006, Arab tribes from Ramadi formed an alliance called the Majlis inqadh al-Anbar (al-Anbar Salvation Council) in cooperation with occupation troops to force al-Qaeda fighters out of the province. At the time, tribal leaders had become weary of al-Qaeda's presence and had opposed their ambitions in Iraq. Initial success of the al-Anbar Council led to its replication in other parts of the country and the creation of other Salvation Councils. Many Arab Sunni fighters had flocked to the councils for many reasons: tribal affiliation, a genuine desire to remove al-Qaeda from Iraq, or financial reasons. Regardless, the mobilization of fighters under the banner of the Salvation Councils proved militarily successful and by late 2007 many of the areas where al-Qaeda forces had been embedded were effectively pacified.

By 2009, however, al-Qaeda fighters had returned to areas such as Ramadi and began to wage attacks against Sahwa members and leaders. Although this occurred scarcely two years after the initial Sahwa mobilization, the counterattack forced the collapse of the movement, as members were not as quick to organize and take up arms, for a number of reasons. First, many had believed that the mobilization would have enhanced Sunni participation in the political system—but this proved not to be the case. Second, the drawback of U.S. forces left Sahwa leaders without direct access to resources and funding with which to maintain a counter-offensive against al-Qaeda. Third, the economic grievances that drove Sahwa mobilization—frustration over the loss of key economic resources and reconstruction contracts—were never fully addressed after 2007. The movement to expel al-Qaeda was largely motivated by economic needs and desires to capture both reconstruction contracts and the benefits of illicit activity rampant in the tribal areas, such as smuggling. By mid-2000, many tribes had ceded authority in the illicit economy to al-Qaeda and had used the Sahwa movement to regain it (Benraad, 2011). Furthermore, Sahwa fighters had been promised opportunities in the formal economy such as jobs in the public sector and security services, but the central state failed to deliver and left many of the fighters out of work. Under such conditions the former Sahwa fighters were not capable of reorganizing and mobilizing against the al-Qaeda attacks in the late 2000s, nor did many desire to. Finally, the central Iraqi state led by Nouri al-Maliki had opposed Sahwa from the beginning. The major Arab Sunni parliamentary bloc, the Iraq Accord Front, similarly bore hostility toward the movement for fear that it could grow to rival the Front's authority within the Arab Sunni community (Benraad, 2011). Such fears meant that the government failed to integrate the movement into the state and continued to deprive the movement and its core areas of economic resources.

The weakening of the Sahwa provided the opportunity for the reemergence of al-Qaeda fighters in Iraq. In the mid-2000s, as the Sahwa were organizing, al-Qaeda and other insurgent groups had been forming alliances out of which ISIS grew. In 2006, al-Qaeda in Iraq (AQI) declared a merger with five other groups to form the Majlis Shura al-Mujahideen (MSM). Later in 2006 amid the Sahwa movement the MSM announced the creation of the Islamic State in Iraq (ISI), an altogether new movement that was intended to be subordinate to the main al-Qaeda leadership. The ISI model and its supporters survived the period of the Sahwa and had begun a resurgence in the late 2000s, a period in which Abu Mohammed al-Julani, the current leader of JAN in Syria, assumed a leadership role within the organization. Despite the Sahwa effect and the death or capture of many of its top leaders, ISI survived in Iraq and was able to maintain local support for their operations because of widespread frustration with the failures of the central Iraqi government. By the time the Syrian conflict began, ISI was embroiled in continued battles with the Iraqi army. The conflict provided an opportunity for expansion.

In early 2012, less than a year after the uprising began, Jabhat an-Nusra (JAN), led by al-Julani, declared its presence in Syria and quickly became one of the strongest brigades, successfully engaging in battles with regime forces in both the northern and southern battlefields. By the end of the year, JAN was widely considered to be one of the most effective brigades in Syria. The expansion of JAN and its success in Syria prompted the leader of ISI, abu Bakr al-Baghdadi, to publicly reaffirm JAN's relationship with ISI and its subordination under the newly formed organization, the Islamic State in Iraq and as-Sham (ISIS). The attempt to subordinate JAN to the new ISIS structure led to a power struggle between the two groups that resulted in the fracturing of JAN into two factions: mostly Syrian fighters remained in the JAN structure while the foreign fighters largely defected to ISIS. Moreover, the split between the groups and the subsequent refusal of ISIS leaders to accept subordination to al-Qaeda's central leadership prompted al-Qaeda leader Ayman Zawahiri to publicly denounce ISIS and declare them outside of the organizational structure of al-Qaeda. Henceforth, ISIS would be an independent entity operating in both Iraq and Syria.

The advances of ISIS in Syria and Iraq have fundamentally changed the course of the Syrian conflict and the international response to the crisis (discussed in the next chapter), inviting U.S. intervention and fundamentally reshaping the international perception of the Syrian conflict. At the beginning of 2014 ISIS controlled large swathes of Syrian and Iraqi territory stretching from Anbar in Iraq to the regions immediately east of Aleppo in Syria. By June of 2014, ISIS took control of Mosul in Iraq: the largest city under its control up to that time. Since then, ISIS advances have been limited but the territory under their control has not contracted, despite U.S.-led coalition air strikes, anti-ISIS coalitions in Syria consisting of various rebel groups, and operations by the Iraqi army and Kurdish and Shi'a militias against ISIS positions.

In addition to ISIS's ability to maintain multiple active fronts, they have demonstrated an ability to engage in counteroffensives. Repeated attacks in Syrian Kurdish areas, and the group's expansion against regime and rebel forces in the central parts of the country, serve not only to expand ISIS's territory but to increase their control over the economic levers of conflict. Much attention has been paid to ISIS control of oil and gas fields (Macias and Bender, 2014) but their control of supply routes and major corridors linking rebel reinforcement routes has also been a major economic and military gain for ISIS. As territorial expansion is the raison d'être of ISIS and is a main source of its own legitimacy, the group has developed sophisticated military capabilities without which expansion and territorial control would have been impossible.

While ISIS shares many of the networked characteristics of other armed groups, they are distinct in their transnational character, their rejection of sovereign borders, and the almost entirely foreign composition of their leadership and fighters. ISIS thus stands out in distinct ways from the other networks of violence. The Assad regime's networks of violence, on the other hand, share some features with the rebel groups. The growth of different armed groups operating independently of each other, the presence of foreign fighters, and the absence of a central command structure are all features of the regime's network of violence, as well as of the rebel groups.

The proliferation of armed groups on all sides of Syria's conflict divide contributed to a military stalemate. As new groups entered the conflict, they failed to coalesce and instead engaged in military combat against each other, complicating the battlefield even further. This was certainly the case up until the breaking of the Aleppo stalemate, where networks of violence remained strong enough to maintain a presence on the battlefield and reap the benefits of Syria's war economies. However, as the trajectory of the conflict demonstrates, different groups exercised more or less power at different times. Whereas the FSA once dominated the rebel landscape, they play a more peripheral role today as JAN, ISIS, and other Islamist groups dominate. Similarly, the NDF played a major role in the regime's counter insurgency strategy early in the conflict. Today, however, the regime is heavily reliant on Hizbollah, regional fighters, and the Syrian Democratic Forces (SDF) on the battlefield.

Regime violence: local and regional actors

Independent armed actors have played an increasingly prominent role in perpetuating violence to further the Assad regime's strategic political and military objectives. The regime's reliance on these actors poses a serious dilemma: on the one hand, these actors, especially Lebanon's Hizbollah, have played a central role in preventing a military defeat of the Syrian Arab Army (SAA) while also inflicting terror and violence on communities outside of the SAA's reach, such as in the rural areas. On the other hand, reliance on these privatized actors moves strategic decision-making concerning military and battlefield issues more and more outside of the control of any centralized regime leadership. As such, the regime's leadership and the SAA itself is becoming increasingly peripheral to the execution of violence. Thus, while these independent groups are certainly fighting alongside the regime and in pursuit of their objectives, they are not doing so through coordinated leadership or planning. Regime violence, much like the violence of the rebel groups, is privatized, decentralized, and increasingly civilianized.

By 2015 it was difficult to determine exactly how much territory was under regime control or, because of internal displacement and refugee flows, what percentage of the Syrian population was located in these areas. The regime had consolidated its control over key corridors of Syria, mainly the Damascus-Homs-Aleppo axis as well as Hama, the coastal areas of Tartous and Latakia, and even some areas in the northeast that remain outside of ISIS or PYD control. The contiguous areas under regime control stretching from Damascus up to the north and west of the country to the Mediterranean contain the largest population concentrations in the country. Paradoxically, the SAA was largely absent from these areas, with local and regional militias largely responsible for security and control of checkpoints and the main highways. Thus, while the regime retained nominal control over large areas of the country and the majority of the remaining population, the networks of violence that maintained this control were largely outside of the regime's traditional security apparatuses—the army and the security service—and are instead reliant on privatized, civilianized forms of violence.

Aron Lund has called the process that brought this about "militiafication," to describe the evolution of the regime's reliance on militia groups for violence and security. From the beginning of the protests, the regime relied on the SAA, and not local police forces, to attack protesters. The SAA was aided by small groups of armed individuals known as the shabiha (thugs) who used knives, bats, guns, and other light weapons to attack protesters. The shabiha were quickly organized in lijan shaabiyya (popular committees) who assumed the dual role of providing violence in support of the regime and securing their neighborhoods from opposition violence. Despite this security role, they became feared within Syria, as they acted with impunity and enjoyed the support and sponsorship of the intelligence apparatus and key business leaders who funded them and provided salaries. Early on in the uprising, it was largely assumed that the shabiha consisted exclusively of poor Alawite men. This was not the case. Instead the shabiha should be understood as a genuine expression of regime support from different segments of Syrian society. While many of the members of the popular committees may have been Alawite, membership was by no means exclusive to the sect. Rather, the fostering of the shabiha by the regime should be understood as a means of militarizing civilian support for the regime on a cross-sectarian basis.

The cross-sectarian roots of the popular committees did not prevent their evolution into more institutionalized forms of civilianized violence. Shabiha recruits came from all corners of Syria's social mosaic—Ba'athists, Sunni tribes, religious minorities, and semi-urban dwellers—who had more commonalities in their socioeconomic backgrounds than they did in their religious affiliations. The main determining factor in the participation of youth with the popular committees was their geographic locale, as groups were composed of people from the same neighborhood or region and were not united by sect. In Jaramana, for example, popular committees were made up overwhelmingly of Druze members, while in Wadi al-Nasara they were predominantly Christian. In Aleppo, most of the popular committees were composed of Sunnis, while those in Homs and Latakia were mainly Alawites (Khaddour, 2014).

Although they began as informal, armed groups that sought to quell protesters, they quickly rose in importance, as the SAA contracted and the regime was forced to rely on privatized violence as the opposition become more militarized. The militarization of the opposition eventually led to the institutionalization and formalization of the shabiha. The popular committees morphed and grew into what is now the National Defense Forces (NDF). The NDF originally appeared in Homs and was involved in fighting alongside the SAA. Rather quickly, the NDF model spread throughout the country and different units fought alongside the SAA. Their loyalty to the regime has never seriously been in question, despite the cross-sectarian membership of NDF fighters. By early 2013, the NDF had emerged as a potential alternative center of power within Syria and a possible threat to the regime's power.

Such fears hastened the institutionalization of the NDF and their slow incorporation into the regime's security apparatus to guarantee their loyalty and codependence on the regime. In early 2013, the NDF had been granted government buildings for its leadership, was offered training facilities, an official government stamp and logo, standardized uniforms, and monthly government salaries (Khaddour, 2014). Most NDF leaders and many fighters have received extensive training and financial support from Iran and have developed strong military ties with non-Syrian militias and other localized fighting units. Yet, despite their institutionalization and their importance to the regime's war strategy, the NDF remains a largely autonomous network of local units very loosely organized under central command from Damascus. Much like the localized rebel units, the NDF units were created in specific neighborhoods in which they remain entrenched. Coordination between NDF units is limited and, while the network has a hierarchy with provincial commanders that report to Damascus, any forms of integration between the units across provinces is limited. Consequently, many of the NDF units operate with a high degree of autonomy and are less cohesive than their institutionalization would suggest. Their role, however, is central to the regime's military strategy as they serve as local counter-insurgency forces.

The NDF are by far the most sophisticated and powerful pro-regime Syrian militias, but there are many other units operating throughout the country that perform similar military functions (Khaddour, 2014). The Ba'ath Battalions are the official armed wing of the Ba'ath Party and are the only other militia in Syria with national structure and reach. They have branches in Aleppo, Damascus, Latakia, Tartous, and other parts of the country. The remaining pro-government militias are mostly local groups concentrated in particular areas of the country. For example, the Jerusalem Brigade consists of Palestinian fighters from the Neirab refugee camp in northwest Syria; it is active in Aleppo fighting alongside other pro-regime militias. Other militias are more sectarian, including Syrian Resistance, which is made up almost exclusively of Alawite fighters, and a militia controlled by the Syrian Social Nationalist Party (SSNP), an armed wing of the SSNP political party which operates mainly in Christian areas around Homs.

The social and religious backgrounds of the pro-regime militias vary considerably. There are other Palestinian factions as well as more sectarian militias active in specific locales. Syrian Sunni tribal militias are active in the Qamishli and Hassakeh region while there are known to be multiple secular militias operating under the title of the Arab Nationalist Guards. Beyond these groups, there are also other smaller conglomerations of fighters that have no official or formal affiliation but who are organized into small units and who receive weapons and resources from the regime. The most prominent of these auxiliary forces were the Local Defence Forces (LDF), who are active in and around Aleppo. The LDF consists of a small number of brigades of fighters from the surrounding areas and works closely with regime, Hizbollah, and Iranian forces on the ground. Their role in breaking the Aleppo stalemate has translated into moderate political influence, with LDF forces said to be negotiating truces between Syrian communities as well as supporting independent candidates in the Syrian parliamentary elections. They, like the NDF, are thus grounded in Syrian society and have a social base from which to exercise military and political influence.

The local Syrian militias have played a pivotal role during the conflict. Although they operate with relative autonomy from the regime their participation in fighting rebel units has reduced the burden on the increasingly emasculated SAA. Indeed, four years after the conflict began, it is clear that the regime would not have survived and maintained control over large parts of the country without the active participation of militias. Yet the presence and reliance on militias obfuscates the regime's actual control over the country. The presence of militias throughout the country and the absence of rebel groups in those territories actually reflects the regime's weaknesses, for its reliance on decentralized, privatized violence has dispersed decision-making power to centers potentially outside of the regime's control.

As the SAA contracts further the army is forced to engage in military attacks alongside local and regional militias. Such reliance on militias that are outside of the immediate command and control of the regime implies a withering and not a strengthening of the regime. In addition to the NDF, local militias include the Public Support and Security Forces, the Syrian Jazeera Shield, National Shield, Eastern Lions, Desert Hawks, Imam Mehdi Army, and Qalamoun Shield Forces brigades. These are among the more powerful of the dozens of Syrian armed groups fighting on the regime's behalf.

While the local militias have been central to the regime's defensive strategies and its ability to withstand rebel advances in key areas, Hizbollah's participation in the Syrian conflict has been the decisive battlefield factor allowing the regime to regain control of territory and key transportation routes. There is no doubt that the regime's forces would not have been able to regain territory and make military advances against rebel groups without Hizbollah's participation in the conflict. The participation of Hizbollah's forces in Syria on such a large scale was not due to sectarian calculations, as some have argued (Phillips, 2015), but rather to the threat posed by the disruption of the arms pipeline from Iran. Rebel control of key distribution routes, especially along the borderlands between Syria and Lebanon, seriously compromised Hizbollah's ability to maintain the steady weapons flow from Iran and Syria. Any interference of this distribution network could have serious consequences for Hizbollah's military capacity to withstand future Israeli attacks.

Hizbollah's combat involvement in Syria was thus motivated more by concerns over access to material resources than it was for sectarian considerations. This is not to suggest that sectarianism was not an important factor motivating Hizbollah to enter Syria. By 2013, more radical Sunni jihadist groups had entered the Syrian arena and a series of car bombs in areas populated predominantly by Shi'a in Lebanon raised the threat of a spillover of the Syrian conflict into Lebanon. Although it was believed that Hizbollah operatives were active in Syria in some capacity from the onset of the uprising, it was not until May 2013 that Hizbollah's involvement expanded significantly in the form of a ground assault on the Syrian town of al-Qusayr, a small town close to the Lebanese border that was controlled by rebel groups. Hizbollah forces were directly responsible for retaking the town and had done so with involvement of the SAA and other regime-affiliated militias. Al-Qusayr was strategically important for Hizbollah because it cut through their communication and distribution networks. If these had been disrupted the group's military readiness in the event of an Israeli attack on Lebanon would have been compromised. The assault on al-Qusayr began in mid-May and lasted only a few weeks before rebel forces retreated and then eventually withdrew entirely from the town. Less than a month after the al-Qusayr battle began, it was over.

Hizbollah's participation was not restricted to al-Qusayr. In fact, the success of the al-Qusayr operation led to a major commitment on the part of Hizbollah's leadership to preserving the Syrian regime, something that had been previously absent from their public comments about the Syrian conflict. Initially, at the outset of the conflict, Hizbollah's leadership was committed to not intervening in the Syrian conflict despite its strong relationship with the Syrian regime. This was motivated by many factors, among them a desire not to upset the delicate sectarian balance in Lebanon and anger other, mainly Sunni, religious communities, as well as a desire to avoid accusations of sectarianism. Thus, Sayyed Hassan Nasrallah, Hizbollah's Secretary-General, conducted many interviews in the first months of the conflict laying out the party's position toward the Syrian protests. Distinguishing the Syrian regime from the "stale" regimes being overthrown in Egypt and elsewhere during the Arab uprisings, Sayyed Nasrallah argued that, unlike them, the Syrian regime was capable of reform and of initiating a process of political dialogue and negotiation with nonviolent protesters (Abboud and Muller, 2012). Hizbollah's desire to steer clear of direct, large-scale involvement in the Syrian conflict was untenable, however, as the regime's hold on territory contracted and threatened Hizbollah's strategic interests.

The victory at al-Qusayr thus also involved a shift in the leadership's framing of the Syrian conflict and its involvement therein. The hesitancy exhibited in the early months was quickly gone and Hizbollah's leadership adopted a policy of regime preservation, effectively committing itself to securing the Syrian regime. Subsequently, Hizbollah's participation in Syria increased beyond al-Qusayr and the border areas that were of immediate strategic interest to include fighting in major areas around Homs and Aleppo, particularly around key strategic highways and routes that effectively cut off rebel groups from supplies. Over the next few months, Hizbollah's participation in combat operations proved crucial to the regime's offensive strategies. While battles in Aleppo did not allow the SAA to retake the city from rebel groups, they made significant enough advances to force rebel retreats and to strangle many of their supply lines. Battles in and around Homs and Damascus had similar outcomes. Contrary to what some believed after the quick victory in al-Qusayr, Hizbollah's participation in combat with the SAA, NDF, and other militia groups did not decisively tip the military balance in favor of the regime, although it did allow for more offensive combat operations.

It is impossible to determine how many Hizbollah fighters are active in Syria or the extent to which their participation in the conflict has depleted their human and material capacities to engage Israel in the event of an attack on Lebanon. What is known, however, is that Hizbollah fighters have been active throughout the major combat zones in Syria, including the northern areas, borderlands between Syria and Lebanon, Damascus, and even in the southern parts of the country. The size and importance of the units fighting in these areas varies widely. In the Lebanese borderlands, Hizbollah fighters assume the lead in combat operations while in other parts of the country they may play an advisory or complementary role on the battlefield.

In mid-2017, Hizbollah's military operations into Arsal in Lebanon effectively sealed off the Syrian/Lebanese borderlands from any armed groups' presence. The events in Arsal demonstrate the complicated Syrian battlefield like no other example. After having ceded borderlands to groups such as JAN, ISIS, and others, Hizbollah's main operations after 2015 focused on the border areas. In Arsal, home to many Syrian refugees as well as smugglers and foreign fighters slipping in and out of Syria to engage in combat, the Lebanese army had imposed a broad siege aimed at controlling movement from Arsal into the rest of Lebanon. It is widely believed that many of the car and suicide bombings that have occurred in Lebanon were planned and prepared in Arsal. By July, 2017, many of these armed groups had been cornered in Arsal. Some had accepted mediation and surrender to Hizbollah, others rejected it. The ensuing battle for Arsal lasted barely three days, with Hizbollah forces fighting inside Arsal, supported by Syrian aerial bombardment, while the Lebanese army controlled the periphery, ensuring that no fighters could exit.

The increasing importance of Hizbollah's combat operations in the conflict demonstrates the regime's weakness and increasing dependence on external armed groups for military gains. As the conflict has dragged on, Hizbollah and Iranian leaders have taken on greater roles on the battlefield and while they may coordinate with Syrian commanders, tactical and strategic decisions are increasingly out of the hands of Syrians. Moreover, Hizbollah is not the only non-Syrian armed group operating in Syria on the side of the regime. Militias from Iraq and Afghanistan, as well as fighters from other regional countries, have flocked to Syria and are also fighting alongside the SAA, NDF, and Hizbollah.

Iraqi militia fighters are extremely active in Syria and have entered the country in larger numbers after the ISIS threat. Many of these militia groups have military ties to the Iranian Revolutionary Guards and, in some cases, are under their indirect control. Indeed, many of the units that are participating in Syria, such as Asaib ahl al-Haq (League of the Righteous), were formed as militias by Iranian authorities after the U.S.-led invasion of Iraq in 2003. Other groups, such as Kataib Hizbollah (Hizbollah Forces) were also active in fighting U.S. occupation forces and have now moved many fighters into Syria to counter ISIS (Slavin, 2015). Other larger groups include the al Nujba Movement and Badr Corps. Together, there are dozens of organized Iraqi brigades in Syria as well as hundreds, if not thousands, of unaffiliated Iraqi fighters.

Other non-Syrian fighters fighting alongside the regime have flocked to Syria for largely sectarian reasons. Many Shi'a fighters have joined the battlefield from around the world for reasons that include the defense of religious shrines and as a counterweight to the growth of ISIS and spread of Sunni radicalism. These groups are organized from many countries within the region: Afghani fighters have formed the Afghani Hizballah and the Fatamiyoun Brigade, Pakistani fighters are organized in the Zeynabioun Brigade, Bahrainis in the Saraya al Mukhtar, and Yemenis in the Ansar al-Allah Brigade. It is nearly impossible to determine how many foreign Shi'a fighters are active in Syria or to evaluate their impact on the battlefield. What is known, however, is that they are quite active fighting alongside Syrian and Hizbollah fighters throughout the country. Foreign fighters have not concentrated in specific areas but are rather distributed throughout the country and are engaged in active battles on the side of the regime.

The Syrian regime has been forced to rely on privatized and civilianized forms of violence to maintain its military capabilities and its ability to hold contested territory. The SAA has been gutted of personnel, with defections rampant and many Syrians avoiding being conscripted at all costs. During the conflict, more than 40,000 SAA fighters are believed to have lost their lives and many regime loyalists from across Syria's sectarian mosaic have begun to openly question and challenge the utility of sending soldiers to their deaths. Such discord among loyalists has been a sensitive issue in Syria and has placed tremendous pressure on the regime. The combination of low military morale, rampant defections, loyalist discord about rising deaths, disintegration within its ranks, and mistrust among SAA soldiers have all forced the regime to turn to civilian or non-Syrian violent actors. Without the involvement of fighters from outside of the SAA, the regime would likely have been unable to maintain control over large swathes of Syrian territory.

As the conflict drags on and the militias become more central to the regime's survival they are exercising more autonomy from any central regime command. Throughout Syria, the NDF elite are emerging as a conglomeration of warlords with their own agendas and interests that may not coincide with those of the Assad regime in the future. Similarly, non-Syrian and Syrian militias active in the country are deeply embedded in the war economy and are especially active in looting and extortion. Such activities not only breed fear among Syrians, but also are a source of potential instability in the future. As regime violence has become more widespread, groups such as the NDF and regional militias are gaining a stake in the continuity of conflict. Warlords are benefitting handsomely from the persistence of violence and conflict and thus can serve as obstacles to any potential political solution. The phenomenon of warlords is not exclusive to non-regime areas. These warlords have benefitted from the opportunities of war and have established entrenched economic interests that may be difficult to break. The emergence of warlords and this particular architecture of violence in Syria have contributed to the regime's withering and their loss of decision-making power during the course of the conflict. This has complicated not only the battlefield but the prospects for future resolution of the conflict as well.

Conclusion

By 2015 Syria was slowly fragmenting into four distinct regions: areas controlled by the Assad regime (from Damascus and then northwest to the coastal areas), areas controlled by the PYD (northeastern Syria around al-Hassakeh and Qamishli), areas controlled by ISIS (eastern Syria around al-Raqqa and Deir ez-Zor), and areas controlled by FSA-affiliated factions (in southern Syria around Dar'a and Sweida). The control of these territories, however, was precarious and constantly shifting until the Russian intervention rolled back rebel advances and brought more territory under regime control. In April 2015, for example, Idlib had fallen to JAN fighters and most of Dar'a to FSA-affiliated brigades. The capture of these major cities was an important development in the conflict but a temporary one, as all armed groups have had difficulty holding territory and Dar'a soon fell again in 2016. In the course of the Syrian conflict, armed groups have proven strong enough to make limited advances and hold some territory but have not been strong enough to expand and control larger areas. Such is the ebb and flow of violence and territorial control in Syria.

As I discuss in subsequent chapters, violence and the military stalemate is contributing to the slow fragmentation of the country into different administrative centers of power. Yet these centers of power were never consolidated. The contraction of regime authority has not led to the growth of alternative or coherent state institutions but rather to a patchwork of administrative authorities that are backed up by violent networks. None of these networks are fixed. Fluidity and the constant shifting of alliances means that violence is widespread and will be extremely difficult to contain. As this chapter has demonstrated, the emergence of networks of violence that are often in competition with each other has been determined by many factors, including ideology, military strategy, and pragmatic calculations around the utility of alliances that serve economic and military interests in a particular moment. As these factors are not stable, neither are the networks of violence that make up the militarized landscape of the Syrian opposition.

With this in mind, it is easy to conclude that there is nothing resembling central control of the armed groups. The nodes and networks of violence in Syria are present in both regime and non-regime areas. The regime has been forced to rely on actors outside of the SAA and the security apparatus for military support. These privatized actors include regional militias, unorganized armed supporters, the NDF, and Hizbollah among others, who are exercising power and violence in regime-dominated areas. The exercise of this power is largely decentralized and outside of central regime control. The institutionalization of the NDF, for example, was meant to curb this power, but the continued growth and strength of the NDF and other militias has meant that they exercise authority and make decisions outside of central regime control. These militias, like the armed groups fighting against the regime, have the ability to perpetuate violence even in the event of a peace agreement.

A central factor explaining the proliferation of armed groups inside of Syria is the role of the international community, which is the focus of the next chapter. Throughout the conflict regional states have played an essential role in the cultivation, financing, and support of different armed groups in Syria. This is especially true of the main regional players: Iran, Saudi Arabia, Qatar, and Turkey. In many ways, the proliferation of armed groups and their division into competing networks of violence is a function of the role of the international community and the desire of regional states to assume control and stewardship of the militarized opposition. Regional conflicts over influence among the armed groups have certainly played a large role in the conflict but this not the only way in which the international community has intervened (or not) in the Syrian conflict. As I discuss in the following chapter, the tensions and competing interests among the different regional actors have played a profound role in shaping the Syrian conflict. The absence of an international consensus on how to solve the Syrian conflict, and the lack of a political process that all parties are committed to, has fostered a situation in which most states have rejected international mechanisms and institutions as channels to end the conflict. With the exception of the American and Russian agreement over the dismantling of Syria's chemical weapons program, most international attempts at solving the conflict have failed. There is also a lack of international consensus about how to deal with key questions, such as whether and which armed groups to support, whether or not to intervene, and what a political transition process should entail. This lack of consensus has meant that regional and Western states have adopted radically different policies toward the Syrian conflict. The intervention of these states into the Syrian conflict has not, however, helped to de-escalate the violence or move the country toward a resolution. Instead intervention has propelled violence, solidified the stalemate, and embedded the Syrian conflict into wider regional geopolitics. In this context, the Syrian conflict has taken on an ever more important international dimension that will determine the prospects for de-escalation and the long-term resolution of the conflict.

4 | Before Aleppo: Stalemate and Fragmentation

The internationalization of the Syrian conflict was an almost immediate aftereffect of the inability of regime forces to quell protests in 2011. The continued spread of protests and the repeated violence inflicted on protesters by regime forces had forced the international community to pursue different forms of diplomatic and military intervention to halt the violence. International concern with Syria increased, as the uprising became more militarized and regional actors adopted radically different and opposing solutions to the conflict. On the one hand, powerful regional states, such as Qatar, Turkey, and Saudi Arabia, adopted a policy of regime change after initially pursuing diplomatic efforts and have marshaled considerable resources in support of opposition groups. On the other hand, the regime's allies, mainly Iran, Russia, and Hizbollah, have adopted a policy of regime preservation at all costs. As the conflict has progressed, the role of international actors in militarily, financially, and politically backing their respective allies in Syria is perhaps the single largest factor explaining the continuity of the conflict, the proliferation of armed groups, territorial fragmentation, and the failure of reconciliation efforts. Together, these patterns of the Syrian conflict produced a political and military stalemate that defined the conflict for years. That is, until after the Russian intervention began in September 2015 that eventually led to the retaking of the city of Aleppo by regime-aligned forces, a key turning point in the Syrian conflict.

In this chapter, we seek to explore how a political and military stalemate emerged in the conflict and how the conflict landscape was shaped by two parallel and reinforcing developments: first, the increased intervention of regional states into the conflict, and, second, the territorial fragmentation of the country and the emergence of alternative and competing models of governance that accelerated Syria's political and social fragmentation. The aim of the chapter is thus to answer the question of how a stalemate emerged with reference to the balancing roles that international actors played prior to the Russian intervention, and to the ways in which Syria was increasingly becoming fragmented and divided up into competing centers of power among various armed groups.

The chapter is divided into two main sections. The first highlights and outlines the differing regional actors' positions on the Syrian conflict and how this contributed to stalemate. For example, although states such as Qatar and Saudi Arabia share a common goal of regime change, they have pursued this policy often in conflict with one another and at great detriment to the political opposition. The second section identifies and explores the consequences of regime contraction and territorial fragmentation by identifying different patterns of armed groups' governance in non-regime areas during the conflict. The chapter concludes with a reflection on how the role of international actors and fragmentation shaped stalemate leading up to the Russian intervention in September 2015.

When the world wades in

There is no doubt that the Syrian conflict began as a domestic crisis brought about by a protracted protest movement that was met by regime violence. The protest movement and its demands were certainly domestic in nature and reflected the long-standing political concerns of many Syrians. However, as soon as the protest movement became more militarized and the political positions of regional actors began to shift— many states, including Turkey, Qatar, and Saudi Arabia, initially called for reforms and supported the regime's efforts to do so before supporting the nascent armed opposition— the Syrian conflict took on wider regional dynamics. These various intervening states and regional organizations all contributed to shaping the trajectory of the conflict.

The Arab world

The response of Arab states to the Syrian conflict must be understood within the overlapping contexts of the Arab uprisings sweeping through the region and the geopolitical rivalries between Iran and Saudi Arabia and their respective regional allies. Both contexts have shaped Arab states' response to the Syrian conflict. In the initial phases of the uprising, Arab states adopted a largely conciliatory and diplomatic approach to the conflict and attempted through League of Arab States (LAS) diplomatic efforts to bring about a resolution in the summer of 2011. The failure of LAS efforts and the lack of an Arab consensus on how to deal with Syria forced divergent policy paths among Arab states, especially Gulf states, and Syria's immediate geographic neighbors.

In October 2011 the LAS adopted a resolution condemning violence in Syria and advocating for immediate dialogue. This was on the heels of the Arab League's successful foray into the Libyan war, which resulted in a NATO-led intervention to topple Gaddafi, who had ruled Libya from 1969 until 2011. Egypt, traditionally a major actor in Arab affairs, could not contribute to Syrian diplomatic efforts due to its own internal political transition. This left Saudi Arabia and Qatar to lead diplomatic efforts in Syria.

Both states initially worked through the LAS on diplomatic efforts when there existed general consensus that the solution to the conflict lay in political dialogue. At the behest of Saudi Arabia and Qatar, LAS officials made overtures to the newly formed Syrian National Coalition and effectively legitimized the body as a participant in any political talks. The Syrian regime was unwilling to support the LAS-led talks or abide by the terms of a peace plan, which was put forth by the LAS in early November 2011 and was initially accepted by the regime. The plan consisted of the following main points: the withdrawal of the army from cities and towns, political dialogue with the SNC, the release of political prisoners, and the entry of an observer mission to Syria to monitor the regime's compliance. Within days of the proposed peace plan, the regime had not withdrawn the army from the conflict areas. Army attacks against protesters continued despite LAS threats.

The regime had signaled its unwillingness to accept the LAS plan. Nevertheless, a new peace plan was agreed upon the following month that was identical to the one agreed upon a month earlier. The regime's strategy in this period was simply to buy time and attempt to pacify the protests in the process. After the agreement on the second plan, however, an observer mission was allowed entry into Syria in late December 2011. The presence of the observer mission had no effect on regime violence and the lack of cooperation among government officials made it very clear that the observer mission was going to be unable to perform any of its mandated tasks or to have any impact in resolving the conflict. By late January 2012, the LAS suspended its observer mission, thus acknowledging the failure of its efforts to resolve the Syrian conflict through diplomatic measures.

The lack of cooperation led the LAS to take two important decisions: first, to suspend Syria's membership from the LAS in November 2011, and, second, to impose economic sanctions against Syria, including a freezing of government assets. The first decision was highly symbolic and isolated the Syrian regime from the regional arena. The second decision to impose sanctions would contribute to the slow collapse of the Syrian economy and the emergence of illicit wartime economic activity. The majority of Syria's non-oil trade was with Gulf countries and the closure of these markets would have a destructive effect on Syrian enterprises that were reliant on Gulf markets. The sanctions stipulated that contracts would be honored but could not be renewed; thus over a few months no new agreements were signed between Syrian and Gulf businesses, effectively destroying many Syrian businesses, especially in textiles (Abboud, 2013a). The economic effect of the sanctions was lessened to some degree by the refusal of Iraq and Lebanon, two other key trading partners, to honor the sanctions. Nevertheless, the closure of the Gulf markets was a major blow to Syrian enterprises. In addition, all Gulf investments in Syria ceased and billions of dollars were withdrawn from the country. The withdrawal of Gulf funding led to the closure of many public and private investment projects, including key projects in infrastructure and public services. In the absence of public funds to complete the projects, many of them remained unfinished.

Such measures did not represent a consensus among Arab states. There were disagreements between states as some, such as Algeria and Iraq, were wary of increasing LAS involvement in Syria and of military intervention in the country. Moreover, Arab states were divided over the legitimacy of the Syrian political opposition, whose officials had actually advocated for military intervention over the LAS peace plan in late 2011. Such disputes among the LAS and the futile attempts at a diplomatic solution through the organization quickly foreclosed the possibility of a regionally negotiated solution or any substantial role for the LAS in the Syrian conflict. Henceforth, the LAS would not play any significant role in Syria: diplomatic efforts were now pursued by the UN and Arab states began to pursue separate policies toward Syria (see Chapter Five). Out of the rubble of the LAS efforts emerged Qatar and Saudi Arabia, the two most important Arab actors in the Syrian conflict.

Qatar has been an extremely important regional actor during the conflict, particularly in the formation of the political opposition and in the financing of key armed groups. Qatar's policy has shifted considerably since 2011. Its then leader, Hamad bin Khalifa al-Thani, charted a policy that began as accommodating and reconciliatory toward the Syrian regime and then quickly shifted toward confrontation. In 2013, power was handed over to his son Tamim bin Hamad al-Thani, who has since slowly moved Qatar to a more neutral and less direct role in the conflict. Nevertheless, by 2017, tensions between Qatar and Saudi Arabia reached a very serious level, as the latter led a movement of Arab Gulf states to isolate Qatar for its perceived pro-Iranian political stances. Thus, divisions among Qatar and Saudi Arabia on the Syrian conflict morphed into much larger divisions that further threatened regional stability.

Although both are Sunni-dominated Arab Gulf monarchies, Qatar and Saudi Arabia have adopted divergent policies regarding the Arab uprisings that have put the two countries in regular conflict. Qatar's policies have often clashed with those of Saudi Arabia, leading to a war by proxy in Egypt, Libya, and Syria, among other states. These proxy wars have occurred in both the military and political arenas, with Qatari and Saudi interests supporting rival armed and political factions throughout the Arab world. In Egypt, for example, Qatar had supported the Muslim Brotherhood after Hosni Mubarak's resignation in January 2012, while the Saudis had supported the military officers and remnants of Mubarak's regime. The first presidential elections after Mubarak's resignation brought Mohammed Morsi to power, a Brotherhood official supported by Qatar, who defeated Ahmad Shafik, Mubarak's previous Prime Minister who was supported by Saudi Arabia. The Qatari–Saudi dispute in Egypt continued thereafter, with Saudi Arabia supporting a military coup d'etat against Morsi's presidency, leading to the assumption of power by the Saudi-supported Field Marshall Abdel Fattah al-Sisi.

Similar jockeying for political influence in the aftermath of the Arab uprisings would shape Qatari and Saudi involvement in the Syrian conflict. Qatar's leadership was initially keen on positioning the country at the forefront of the uprisings by supporting the overthrow of regimes. Although pursuing a diplomatic approach through the LAS at first, Qatar quickly shifted toward a more confrontational policy with the regime. Qatari officials began cultivating stronger relationships with different factions of the Syrian National Coalition (SNC), especially the Muslim Brotherhood, in an attempt to exert influence over the direction of the SNC. Similar efforts by Saudi Arabia have effectively split the SNC into Qatari, Saudi, and nonaligned factions that are in regular conflict with one another over policy and political strategy. Moreover, while the Saudis and Qataris have been keen to meddle in the SNC's affairs and cultivate conflict and mistrust among members, they have failed to sufficiently legitimize the body, in part out of fear of the other state exerting undue influence and control. For example, despite supporting efforts to remove Syria from the LAS, both Qatar and Saudi Arabia resisted requests from the SNC to hand over the seat to the opposition. The political weaknesses and fragmentation of the SNC and the political opposition in general is in some measure the outcome of the Qatari–Saudi dispute over policy on the Syrian conflict.

As the two countries were cultivating their respective factions in the SNC, Qatar was simultaneously, in mid-2012, shipping light weapons to the militarized opposition which were acquired from Libya and Eastern Europe, flown to Turkey, and then distributed by Turkish and Qatari intelligence officers to the armed groups (Wezeman, 2013). The slow arming of rebels in 2012 brought about coherence in Saudi and Qatari policies. The largest and most effective brigades at the time, including Liwa at-Tawhid, were believed to have received light arms from both states. The policy on arming rebel groups at the time was characterized by confusion. Qatar, Saudi Arabia, and Turkey facilitated the inflow of light weapons that were dispersed to multiple armed groups, preventing the concentration of weapons in any particular group. Such strategies contributed to the proliferation of violent groups but also ensured that there would be military balance among them. This environment was not conducive to cultivating cohesion or solidarity among the armed groups; instead, it fostered mistrust and competition between them over scarce resources.

The factionalization of the opposition mirrored that of the Supreme Military Command (SMC) under General Salim Idriss. A demand of Western states was the formation of the SMC to coordinate opposition military and political activities. However, while publicly supporting the formation of the SMC, Qatar and Saudi Arabia renewed their competition over the appointment of key Provincial Military Council leaders and, much to the detriment of the SMC's legitimacy, bypassed SMC structures to provide resources to armed groups. Rather than coordinating policies through the SMC structure, both countries actively undermined the SMC and pursued parallel policies that delinked brigades from the broader SMC structure and made them more dependent on foreign patronage than on the SMC leadership.

Russia

Russia has been the Syrian regime's most ardent supporter in the international community, having blocked efforts at the UNSC to place political pressure on the regime to initiate a political transition or to pass UN-supported sanctions. Moreover, Russia has been a major arms supplier to the Assad regime and continued to trade with Syria amid blockades and sanctions imposed by other states. Clearly, the most important way in which Russia supported the regime was through intervention in September 2015 (explored in Chapter Five). Russia's support, however, has very little to do with any shared affinity with the Syrian regime or any ideological or political commitment to the survival of Ba'athism. Nor is Russian support determined by a reactionary impulse to "protect" an ally or its arms market (Strategic Comments, 2012). Instead, Russian support of the Syrian regime has been determined by the interplay of geopolitical, domestic, and economic factors. The major drivers of Russian policy toward Syria include skepticism and concern over the threat of Western military intervention, particularly after the NATO-led intervention into Libya; the threat posed by the spread of Salafist-jihadist extremism in the region and the Caucasus in particular; and wider domestic and geopolitical interests.

Russian concern with Western intervention predates the Arab uprisings and goes far back into the early 2000s during the colored revolutions in Georgia, Ukraine, and Kyrgyzstan. At the time, the Russian political establishment largely viewed the revolutions as Western-led uprisings to promote regime change (Strategic Comments, 2012), a strategy that might eventually be exported to Russia itself. Such fears of foreign-led attempts at regime change through ostensibly grassroots national movements would shape Russian framings of the Arab uprisings only a few years later. By the time that the Syrian conflict had evolved into a crisis that would warrant international attention and give rise to discussions of intervention, Western interventions had already taken place in Afghanistan (2002), Iraq (2003), and Libya (2011), in addition to the unrest in the former Soviet bloc that was viewed by the Russian political establishment as being Western-led. Such interventions were extremely threatening to the Russian establishment, which viewed the continued instability wrought by interventions as a threat to both the international system and to their own geopolitical interests and to stability in their former spheres of influence (Charap, 2013).

The Russian political establishment was particularly shocked and alarmed by the Libyan intervention. In March 2011 the UNSC adopted Resolution 1973 authorizing a no-fly zone over Libya. Although Russia abstained from the vote, its representatives were active in articulating concerns over the meaning of the mandate and the potential use of military force for humanitarian reasons. Almost immediately after the passing of the resolution, Russia's position became critical of the implementation of Resolution 1973 as it became increasingly clear that the coalition was using the mandate not only to enforce a no-fly zone but to use force to overthrow the Libyan regime (Allison, 2013). The Russian establishment was jolted (Aras and Falk, 2015) not only because of the manipulation of the resolution by the coalition to engage in direct military intervention in the conflict on the side of one party, but also by the unilateral expansion of the mandate with UNSC approval and the implicit judgment of Western states about the political legitimacy of the Libyan regime (Aras and Falk, 2015).

The Libyan intervention would thus have profound effects on Russia's shielding of the Syrian regime. This, along with unrest in the 2000s leading up to and after the Arab uprisings, has decidedly shaped Russian views on the Syrian conflict. Russian skepticism concerning Western intentions and deep mistrust of any Western efforts to resolve the Syrian conflict, whether through military or political means, has been the most decisive factor in explaining Russia's intransigence toward any international efforts to resolve the crisis. Informing the Russian mistrust of international efforts are the ongoing rivalries with the United States over key regional issues, including the Iranian nuclear issue. As Russia increasingly views the regional developments through the prism of its own simmering conflict with the United States, Russian policymakers have adopted positions in direct contradiction to the U.S. Such is the reason behind the continued use of the Russian veto at the UNSC to block any efforts to impose economic sanctions against the Syrian regime. In all three cases of the use of Russian veto to date, they have framed their opposition in terms of the principle of non-intervention into the sovereign affairs of Syria (Strategic Comments, 2012), a principle that reflects both the belief in the threat of continued intervention and their skepticism about Western intentions.

Dannreuther (2015) has argued that there has emerged a distinctively "Russian idea" about the nature of political order that is grounded in a critique of Western interventions to promote democracy in non-Western countries. While the immediate Russian concern has been with Western intervention into neighboring states, this idea has been extended to the Russian establishment's framing of the Arab uprisings. The Libyan case has merely affirmed Russian perceptions that Western states would use humanitarian motives to impose regime change. The Russian position on shielding Syria from diplomatic or international intervention efforts must be understood within this larger context.

Other geopolitical factors are important as well, including Russia's relations with Iran, Syria's major regional ally. Both countries border the Caspian Sea and have common interests in maintaining their naval superiority there as well as opposing the construction of oil and gas pipelines on the Caspian Sea bed (Strategic Comments, 2012). Iran is also a major purchaser of Russian arms and has relied extensively on Russian support for the development of its nuclear technologies. Finally, both states share a common fear of the spread of Salafist-jihadist fighters throughout the region and into the Caucasus. The spread of such fighters could be severely destabilizing for both states. For now, common economic and geopolitical interests have shaped the convergence of Russian and Iranian perspectives on the Syrian conflict. Such convergence is also exemplified in the cooling of Russian relations with Gulf countries, who have used the Russian stance on Syria as an impetus toward realignment away from Russia. This movement has included the canceling of lucrative economic agreements between both countries. In contrast, despite Turkish and Russian divergence on the Syrian conflict and the insistence by the Turkish leadership that Russia is partly to blame for the resiliency of the regime, there have been no noticeable negative economic effects of the conflict on Russian–Turkish relations (Dannreuther, 2015). Trade between the two countries has remained stable and, unlike relations with Arab Gulf states, economic agreements have not been threatened by their political disagreements over the Syrian conflict.

Finally, there are domestic reasons for Russia's support for the Syrian regime, including an arms market, a naval base in Tartous, and economic investments and commercial trade deals with which Russian companies are involved. Although it is impossible to determine the exact amount, it is estimated that Syria has around $4 billion in unpaid military contracts with Russian military companies (O'Toole, 2012). Russian companies have also made extensive investments throughout the economy, especially in oil and gas exploration (Gorenburg, 2012). Russian manufacturing firms have also been active in Syria, with many contracts signed in the late 2000s and in the early stages of the uprising for the creation of joint Syrian–Russian projects or for the Russian provision of goods. While many of these contracts have been affected by the conflict, Russian traders and the establishments are concerned that any regime change would mean a loss of existing contracts and their peripheralization in any postconflict reconstruction. The arms establishment is particularly concerned that the Libyan scenario could be repeated. In that country, more than $2 billion in contracts that were agreed upon by the Gaddafi regime were invalidated after the new government took over. The new government subsequently signed weapons agreements with French military companies, effectively closing off a once robust market for the Russian arms establishment.

The interplay of these geopolitical, domestic, and economic factors has made it difficult for the Russian political establishment to abandon the Syrian regime. While support for the regime is clearly not based on any ideological considerations or commitments, there are very strong reasons behind Russian support of the regime. Geopolitical fears of Western intervention, coupled with the threat of Salafist-jihadist expansion into Russian spheres of influence, as well as a wide range of interests, have all contributed to the sustained Russian support of the Syrian regime.

Iran

Iran has the largest geopolitical stake in the survival of the Syrian regime. Iran has exercised a tremendous amount of control over regime decision-making up until this point, and is likely to continue to do so, as the regime is financially and militarily dependent on Iran for its survival. However, its staunch support of the regime has brought the country into proxy conflict with Saudi Arabia and has inflamed sectarian tensions in the region. For the time being, Iran seems willing to assume the short- and long-term burden of its support of the Syrian regime.

There is a long history of strong Syrian–Iranian relations that predates the uprising and goes well back into the 1970s (Goodarzi, 2009; von Maltzhan, 2013). For the Iranian establishment, the survival of the Syrian regime is not merely a necessity born out of this historical relationship however, but a policy goal that is viewed within a larger regional and geopolitical context. One of the central prisms through which the conflict is refracted is the regional conflict with Saudi

Arabia and other Arab states. While it has become common-place and convenient to frame this as a Sunni–Shi'a rivalry with the two states at opposite poles, this is simplistic. It ignores how political ambitions and interests, and not merely amorphous sectarian expansionary goals, shape geopolitical rivalries (Hokayem, 2013). With this in mind, it is difficult to unravel Iran's role in the Syrian conflict without reference to its regional geopolitical situation.

Iran has had to balance its regional rivalry with Saudi Arabia and its support of the Syrian regime alongside the negotiations over its nuclear program, which culmi-nated in 2015 with a long-term deal called the Joint Comprehensive Plan of Action. The effect of sanctions on Iran and the decline in oil prices had been major drivers of the Iranian desire to break its international isolation and submit its nuclear program to international inspection. Prior to the deal negotiated between Iran, the United States, Russia, China, France, the United Kingdom, and Germany, there was a belief that any nuclear deal should be embedded into a larger regional bargain that would also contain agreements concerning Iran's role in Syria. However, such a grand bargain does not seem to have been achieved. All indicators are that the negotiations occurred independently of any reference to Iran's role in the Syrian conflict. There were suggestions that any nuclear deal would involve pressuring Iran to lessen its support of the Syrian regime and its other allies, including Hizbollah, but the nuclear deal is unlikely to yield a shift in Iran's regional alliances.

Primary to Iran's regional alliances is its relationship with Hizbollah in Lebanon. This relation has evolved since the 1980s when Hizbollah was first formed (Shaery-Eisenlohr, 2008; Abboud and Muller, 2012; Alagha, 2006). Today, Hizbollah cannot be said to be in a subservient relationship with the Iranian regime, whereby the latter dictates the former's goals, interests, and policy choices. The Iranian leadership does not control Hizbollah; rather, there is an alliance and relationship based on mutual interests and coordination within the region (el-Hokayem, 2007). Thus,

Iran's involvement in the Syrian conflict goes well beyond what some commentators suggest is the control of Hizbollah and the use of Hizbollah's weapons to serve Iranian interests (Daoud, 2014).

While Hizbollah has indeed been active in the Syrian arena, Iranian involvement has gone well beyond this. Iran has provided military supplies to the Syrian regime and training to thousands of shabiha who eventually formed the core membership of the NDF. Iranian military officials and fighters have been active in Syria and some Iranian strategists have died in fighting between regime and rebel forces (Evans and Karouny, 2013). Moreover, Iran has likely financially supported the movement of Iraqi and Afghani militias into Syria and provided them with training. Thus Iran's military involvement in Syria is extensive, so much so that it is believed that Iranian officials are making key battlefield decisions in place of Syrian officials (Hashem, 2015).

Although Iranian support for the Syrian regime has been sustained and unyielding, there is no reason to believe that Iran wants a continuation of the conflict. Over the long term, the Syrian conflict directly threatens Iranian interests in the region (Goodarzi, 2013). The stalemate has forced readjustment of the Iranian strategy and what appears to be a gradual move away from a military solution to the conflict. For example, Iran has played a large role in the local ceasefires and the leadership is believed to have floated the idea that a deal for a political transition could be reached if key Iranian conditions were met. At this point, the Iranian calculation may be to contain the damage of the conflict and attempt to reach a gradual solution, as the instability wrought by the conflict directly affects the Iraqi government and Hizbollah, both key Iranian allies (Goodarzi, 2013). In addition to this, the military and financial dependence of the Syrian regime on Iran is unsustainable over the long term (Sadjadpour, 2013). With sanctions and low international oil prices crippling the Iranian economy, it is likely that the Iranian establishment will eventually question its support for the Syrian regime.

Turkey

Turkey plays a major role in the Syrian conflict, first as a supporter of the opposition and as facilitator of the flow of weapons and fighters into Syria, and second, as a host of hundreds of thousands of Syrian refugees and as the main corridor for humanitarian aid work. After initially urging President Bashar al-Assad to enact meaningful political reforms, Turkey abandoned its Syrian ally and declared the overthrow of the President to be its foreign policy objective. Today, Turkey's leadership has again begun to shift its Syria strategy in response to two major developments: the rise of the Kurdish-dominated SDF and the recapture of territory by the regime after the Russian intervention. The Turkish position on the Syrian conflict has thus evolved considerably over the last few years but one constant has been a commitment to removing Assad from power. Under this broader policy objective of removing al-Assad, Turkey faces a number of challenges regarding the Syrian conflict which have shaped its policies.

Turkey had initially adopted a nonconfrontational policy toward the Syrian regime in early stages of the conflict, advocating for reform and seeing the protests as an opportunity to push for the inclusion of marginalized Syrian political forces. When this strategy failed, Turkey adopted a three-pronged policy toward the conflict (Stein, 2015). First, the Turkish government allowed for the transit of army defectors who would later form the nucleus of the FSA. They were given shelter by Turkey and permitted to operate from inside Turkey. Second, Turkey worked to organize the external opposition and to legitimize the opposition as the representative of the Syrian uprising. Finally, Turkey adopted a policy of advocating intervention in Syria and the creation of a no-fly zone in the northern parts of the country. The goal of this strategy was to organize an opposition and provide them a geographic base from which to conduct operations and govern Syria.

By 2012 this strategy was in tatters and the consolidation of rebel groups under the command of an external opposition never materialized. This forced a rethinking of Turkish strategy and a partial abandonment of its earlier allies. Increasingly, Turkish intelligence had provided covert and overt support to other armed groups, including Jabhat an-Nusra, which had been making substantial military gains against the regime. The Turkish government tried to reorganize the external opposition and to rally the international community into supporting it through the creation of the Friends of Syria initiative, a coalition of states supporting the Syrian uprising. These policies have had a major impact on the course of the conflict and the shaping of both the political and military opposition.

One explanation for the failure of Turkish policy to bring about regime change is that policy has occurred largely within the context of multiple balancing acts between Turkey and regional powers. On the one hand, Turkey's regional relations have stunted Turkish ambitions and interests vis-à-vis the conflict. Turkish policies have placed the country in direct confrontation with Iraq, Iran, and Russia, all important political and economic partners prior to the uprising. While there has been minimal economic fallout from the conflict on relations between Turkey and these countries, the threat of regional tensions or, at worst, conflict, has likely tempered Turkish activities in Syria. Not all that dissimilar are Turkey's relations with erstwhile allies Qatar and Saudi Arabia. As I have detailed throughout the book, disagreements between the three states over which armed groups to support and how to structure the external political opposition have been important factors in explaining the rebel and opposition weaknesses during the conflict. On the other hand, the Turkish government's policies in Syria do not enjoy the full support of Turkish citizens. Indeed, Turkish policies in Syria have caused considerable national discord.

The Turkish government's need to balance its regional alliances alongside domestic opposition to the conflict is further compounded by the challenges posed by the conflict itself. The first challenge concerns the threat of civil violence and the spillover effects of the war. There have been a number of bombings and attacks in the southern borderlands that have led to dozens of Turkish deaths. The second challenge concerns Turkey's military involvement in the Syrian conflict. In 2015, Turkish forces, working in coordination with the YPG, entered Syria to remove the tomb of Süleyman Şah (the grandfather of Osman I, the founder of the Ottoman Empire). This was the first direct Turkish troop intervention into the Syrian conflict despite multiple border clashes and the downing of two Turkish planes by Syrian forces in 2012. As the conflict worsens and spillover occurs there is the potential for deeper Turkish military intervention. The third challenge is represented by the presence of Salafist-jihadists in the opposition's ranks and the concern that some groups, especially ISIS, could begin to target Turkey if the government adopts restrictive policies on the movement of fighters and supplies. Fourth, there is the challenge of ensuring humanitarian assistance for the increasing number of refugees in the country.

The West

Western states have not adopted similar positions and strategies toward the Syrian conflict. The lack of a Western consensus on Syria, coupled with Russian obstruction of UNSC intervention, has meant that many Western states have adopted largely ineffectual and insignificant policies in relation to the conflict. From the conflict's outset, Western states were unanimous in imposing sanctions against the Syrian regime and state institutions in an attempt to induce high-level defections and paralyze the regime into a political compromise. However, as the conflict developed and there was paralysis within the UNSC, the range of policy options available to Western states shrank. This has led to the perception of Western inaction and ambivalence on Syria. In reality, most Western states began to see the Syrian conflict through the perspective of two perceived threats: the influx of massive numbers of refugees and the infiltration of ISIS into Europe.

From the perspective of many Syrians who had pinned hopes on Western political or military intervention, the

European Union's policy toward Syria has appeared inconsistent and ambiguous (Trombetta, 2014). Indeed, such
sentiments reflect a major problem of Western policy toward
Syria in general: mainly, that disconnect between actual
policy and official positions has not translated into any
meaningful policies to effect change. Across the EU, North
America, Australia, and New Zealand, Western states have
been unanimous in their condemnation of the Syrian regime
and their expressed desire for regime change and a political
transition. Yet very few political resources have been brought
to bear to realize this. Russian obstruction of UNSC efforts
has been met largely with head-scratching in Western capitals
while the failure of sanctions to bring about regime change
has simply led to more extensive and deeper sanctions that
are having profound effects on average Syrians (Moret,
2015).

For the European Union, sanctions have been the main
policy tool. Seeberg (2014) has identified four phases of
sanctions imposed by the EU on Syrian officials and state
institutions. The first three phases were between 2011 and
early 2013 and were defined by the imposition and extension
of sanctions. This included sanctions against a range of
officials, state institutions, and trade, such as the banning
of all Syrian oil exports (this was significant because the
European Union was the main market for Syrian oil). The
fourth phase, which began around April 2013, represented a
shift in European Union policy toward the conflict and was
defined by the easing of some sanctions with the intention
of supporting the political and military opposition by, for
example, allowing them to sell oil from non-regime areas.
This easing suggested a reinvigorated policy toward Syria,
which has never materialized. Since 2013, there have been
few sanctions and the European Union has even shifted
positions on the major issue of whether the Syrian regime can
be a party to any political negotiations.

What explains the European Union's sanctions regime
and the shift toward acceptance of the Syrian regime as
a negotiating partner? One explanation is that European
Union officials had come to the realization that sanctions

were mostly ineffective (Seeberg, 2014, p. 10). The sanctions had not induced defections of the political or economic elite or led to a collapse of the security apparatus. Moreover, the failure of the political opposition to marshal European sanctions toward regime change forced a rethinking of the role of sanctions as a strategy and as a tool to support the opposition. Most important, however, were the disagreements among European Union states about how to deal with the situation (Trombetta, 2014). The divisions between member states manifested in multiple ways, including disagreements over the oil embargo (which threatened certain domestic interests) and a general unwillingness to use the weight and power of the Union in a conflict concerning which many member states were on the periphery. Such disagreements and ambivalence mirrored the ineffectiveness of European Union institutions in coordinating a response to the humanitarian crisis caused by the conflict. Four years into the conflict, there has been very little coordination between European institutions around it and many member states have retreated into policies that privilege their domestic interests over those of the larger regional body (Trombetta, 2014).

Similarly, within the United States there has been little agreement over how to deal with the Syrian conflict. On the one hand, the Obama administration can rightly be accused of saying one thing on Syria and doing another. Much like the European Union, the Obama administration has not been willing to marshal political resources and capital toward achieving its stated goals of regime change and a political transition. On the other hand, the administration's hands have been tied by the lack of an international, let alone Western, consensus on Syria, Russian and Chinese blocking of UNSC efforts, and internal disagreements over what policies the administration should adopt, including whether to intervene militarily or not. Without a doubt, the Obama administration's calculations have been shaped by the legacies and fatigue of the Afghanistan and Iraq wars that have reduced American and Western appetites for long-term commitments to overseas military occupations.

The Trump administration, with its alleged ties to Russian interests, has more or less accelerated Obama's policy of noncommitment in Syria and ceded to Russian designs for Syria. This has included providing material and military support to the SDF and removing support for other armed groups that were directly engaging in combat with regime forces. They have coordinated with Russian forces in Syria to the latter's benefit and have eased the public rhetoric about the need for Bashar al-Assad to step down. As in the case with the Obama administration's selective engagement on Syria to combat ISIS and ignore the regime, the Trump administration has similarly taken measures that shore up the regime and enforce Russian designs for Syria. Strikingly, there is no parallel U.S.-supported political process to end the conflict in Syria, as the administration has effectively ceded this ground to Russia and the Astana process.

For the most part, Western policy toward the Syrian conflict has been reactionary, with the European Union and United States exercising much less influence than the other regional states involved in the conflict, such as Turkey, Iran, Qatar, and Saudi Arabia. In many instances (elaborated throughout the book), Western allies in the region adopted policies that directly contradicted or undermined stated Western goals. In such cases, Western states have not been able, or willing, to adopt policies that radically alter the course of the conflict.

Western disunity and disagreement about how to deal with the Syrian regime has perhaps best been highlighted by the response to the rise of ISIS in Syria. The presence of ISIS has actually initiated a slow retreat in Western capitals toward a position of greater neutrality to the regime and to the larger conflict. Increasingly, discourse in Western states is presenting the problem as one of the regime or ISIS. Such framing of the conflict has given the regime allies within Western states who believe that the regime should be supported in order to eliminate the ISIS threat (Dreyfuss, 2014). Such framing of the conflict presents false choices, however, as the battle is not between the regime and ISIS.

In any case, the ISIS threat has begun to shape Western thinking on the conflict and is leading to a relegitimization of the Syrian regime as a proxy partner in the fight against ISIS. The Western shift on the regime brought about by the presence of ISIS highlights Western paralysis around Syria. As the next section will detail, disagreements among Western states on key issues persist despite agreement on the need to confront ISIS.

Major dividing issues: Arming the rebels and intervention

The previous section highlighted how different states approached the Syrian conflict, and how these approaches were often contradictory, thus contributing to the political and military stalemate that defined the conflict until late 2015. In this section, I explore how two major issues raised by the conflict—on whether to arm the rebels and on whether the West should militarily intervene—further contributed to stalemate, as major actors failed to resolve these issues and instead pursued parallel policies that exacerbated conflict and violence.

Arming the rebels

Syrian armed groups have received weapons from three main sources: weapons provided by regional patrons, weapons captured from government supplies, and the black market trade in light weapons, mainly from Iraq and Lebanon. These weapons have been insufficient, and their supply inconsistent enough to preclude larger military gains against regime forces. As a result, one of the key demands of the political opposition and the armed groups inside of Syria has been to provide weapons for the armed groups. However, there is no consensus in the international community and the Friends of Syria Group—a coalition of more than seventy countries that support a political transition in Syria—has failed to develop a common policy on arming rebel groups. Qatar, Saudi

Arabia, and Turkey (discussed below) have taken the lead in providing weapons to armed groups but have largely avoided providing heavier weaponry such as anti-aircraft equipment. Western states, on the other hand, have been less willing to provide weapons to rebel groups. The Obama administration in particular has been hesitant to provide anything other than nonlethal equipment to armed groups. France and Britain have advocated for a more active EU policy involving direct arming of the rebels but have thus far been rebuked by most other EU states.

The question of whether to arm rebels has been in the West a question of ensuring that weapons are controlled by "moderate" rather than "extremist" forces. Yet, as the rebel landscape beyond ISIS demonstrates, such distinctions are false ones and do not accurately reflect realities and the fluidity of alliances on the ground and the levels of cooperation between rebel groups. The dispersed and fragmented structure of the armed opposition is such that no brigades or units exercise autonomy from one another. Groups are deeply interconnected, whether through alliances or battles over territorial control. Confusion and misunderstanding in the West concerning the fluidity of the rebel landscape has complicated the question of arming rebel groups. At various times in the conflict, different Fronts, brigades, and units that are Islamist have either pledged allegiance, fought alongside, or maintained some affiliation with the FSA. In 2012, for example, the Islamic Front for the Liberation of Syria fought alongside FSA brigades and had closely cooperated with them. Later iterations of different Islamist Fronts, such as the morphing of the Syrian Islamic Front into the Islamic Front (IF), have complicated alliances on the ground. The IF, for example, has rejected the SNC and is largely funded by private donors (more below), but has also cooperated with FSA brigades on the battlefield. One of the principal brigades of the IF, Liwa at-Tawhid, had once been a part of a broader Islamist Front under the FSA umbrella but had removed itself and eventually joined the IF.

For Qatar and Saudi Arabia, the calculations have been quite different and have been informed by more pragmatic calculations and a different understanding of the rebel landscape. Distinctions between "moderate" and "extremist" groups were not major factors in the calculations except in reference to specific jihadist groups believed to be affiliated with al-Qaeda. Instead, three major approaches were adopted concerning arming the rebels. First, the rebel groups that were strongest and were believed to have made the most substantial gains were provided with resources. Qatar and Saudi Arabia were very interested in supporting those who were successful and had battlefield momentum. This approach had the effect of drowning out many of the smaller brigades and units and eventually forcing their absorption into larger networks of violence. The intervening variable here is that Saudi Arabia had eschewed support of many Islamist, especially Salafist, brigades and had thrown most of their support behind FSA-affiliated groups. Qatar, on the other hand, had no reservations about supporting Islamist groups. However, as discussed below, many of the more hardline groups have received their support from private donors. Second, the rivalries between the two states for control of the opposition manifested on the battlefield with both states arming rival brigades (Byman, 2014, p. 91). This was especially the case after the creation of the Supreme Military Command, as different provincial councils were wholly supported by one state or another. Differing international alliances among the provincial military councils led to sustained conflict between them, mistrust, and a failure to share resources. Thus, Qatar and Saudi Arabia (and by extension Turkey, which largely facilitated the transfer of weapons to rebels) made radically different calculations in approaching the question of whether to arm the rebels. For these states, playing out their regional rivalry and supporting the most militarily successful groups took precedence over ideological calculations.

In addition to the differences between Arab and Turkish and Western approaches to the question of arming the rebels, the role of private donors needs to be sufficiently understood. In 2012, the majority of financing directed at more radical, jihadist groups had been provided by private donors from Gulf countries, including Syrian exiles (Windrem, 2014). The private financing of these jihadist groups gave them superior military resources and allowed them to make significant battlefield gains at the expense of FSA brigades. Moreover, the flow of private donations allowed the jihadist groups to avoid the criminality and illegality that was rampant in FSA brigades who were increasingly infiltrated by opportunists and criminals hoping to gain economically from violence.

In sum, then, there has been no consensus between Arab and Western states over the question of arming rebels. Moreover, private donors from mostly Gulf countries have played an instrumental role in arming the more radical, extremist elements of the rebels, much to the frustration of both Saudi Arabia and Western states who have actively attempted to prevent the growth of more extremist groups.

On intervention and non-intervention

The NATO-led intervention in Libya during that country's civil conflict brought hope for some that Western countries would similarly intervene in Syria to aid the opposition in overthrowing the regime. Given the military stalemate, many supporters of intervention argued that Western involvement could tip the balance in favor of the rebels (Kleinfeld, 2013) and lead to the collapse of the al-Assad regime. In this view, intervention would be a definitive solution to the stalemate and would allow the rebels to take Damascus.

To date, there has been very little Western appetite for intervention in the country. Similarly, Arab states have not directly intervened against regime forces, relying instead on proxies. Nevertheless, there has been outside military intervention in Syria by Israel, Turkey, and a U.S.-led coalition of Arab states, all of which occurred for very different geopolitical reasons. Israel has intervened a number of times during the conflict by bombing key regime sites and transport convoys believed to be delivering weapons to Syria. Turkey's military intervened in 2015 to rescue a mausoleum but then quickly retreated back into Turkey, while the U.S.-led coalition began aerial bombing of ISIS targets in Syria in August 2014. In all three cases, outside military intervention targeted specific targets and did not directly engage regime forces. Outside powers have proven willing to directly intervene when there are specific reasons and have shied away from pursuing policies of intervention aimed at regime change.

Fragmentation

Conflicts over policy toward Syria between and among the West, Arab states, and regional actors such as Turkey, Iran, and Russia, contributed to producing the conflict stalemate up until late 2015. Another major factor that contributed to stalemate was the internal fragmentation of the country that prevented the rise of a single, alternative power to the regime. Instead, the Syrian conflict evolved in such a way as to fragment—territorially, politically, economically, and socially—the country into competing centers of power. In this section, we explore the various drivers and consequences of fragmentation through the perspective of governance strategies of armed groups. In particular, three radically different models have emerged: one that lays claim to statehood (ISIS); one that establishes the basis for either federalism or independence (DFNS); and ad-hoc, localized modes of governance (first, local councils, and now primarily Islamist armed groups).

Until late 2015, the country was very loosely divided among four large, identifiable areas that are militarily and politically dominated by different groups: areas controlled by the regime (between Damascus and the coastal areas); areas controlled by the PYD in northeastern Syria near the Turkish-Syrian and Syrian-Iraqi borders; areas controlled by ISIS in eastern Syria, mainly Raqqa; and southern and north-western areas controlled by various rebel factions. There was no monopolization of violence or authority in these areas, as intra-rebel infighting, regime bombardment, and international intervention rendered different authorities' control over areas tenuous at best. Thus while Syria fragmented no single alternative to the regime emerged. Instead, outside the regime areas the country divided into a patchwork of administrative structures with competing politico-military groups vying for power throughout the country, and these competing administrative structures contributed to the fragmentation of the country.

What happened in Syria, then, was the emergence of new political authorities whose military power was translated into different political-administrative structures: a rapid decentralization of authority into multiple, often competing networks of violence and power structures. Decentralization and dispersal of administrative authority gave the Syrian conflict two features that are contributing to its longevity. First, authorities are highly decentralized and lack vertical (with central or external authorities) and horizontal (with other administrative structures) integration. Administrative models differ radically. In the Kurdish areas, for example, the grounds are being laid for autonomous government in a post-conflict Syrian state while in ISIS areas there is a radical social engineering project under way to reimagine those territories as part of a new Caliphate. Second, the lack of integration between the authorities has led to the parallelization of administrative institutions and has prevented the monopolization of power and the establishment of alternative state institutions.

The normative view of conflicts suggests that the contraction of state authority leads to sovereign gaps, creating lawless and ungovernable spaces. Such a view is too simplistic, however, and fails to capture the organizational structure of violence and how armed groups do more than just commit violence but also attempt to govern and administer territory. In Syria, a form of alternative governance (Carpenter et al., 2013) is emerging. "Alternative governance" here refers to forms of governance in which constellations of actors exist in an architecture whose functionality is inconsistent and temporary. These are organized and administered by "non-state complexes" (Podder, 2014) whose power and agency in a conflict is constantly shifting and contested by other groups.

In this view, there can exist governance without sovereign government. This is precisely what has emerged in Syria, as different, competing projects of territorial control have led to the rise of different administrative models. Because of the constantly changing geography of the conflict and the fluidity of alliances, these administrative models were unstable and unsustainable over the long term. While they have not proven resilient in the face of Russian intervention, they nevertheless had a major impact on the course of conflict and have influenced what a postconflict Syrian state may look like.

Rojava/DFNS

In mid-2013 the PYD had declared its intention to carve out an autonomous region in Kurdish-populated areas in the northeast of Syria. Later that year, the PYD announced that an interim government would soon be formed that would include KNC parties and be inclusive of most Kurdish political currents in Syria. This led to the establishment of an Assembly that declared the three regions of Efrin, Cizre (Jazeera in Arabic), and Kobani (Ayn al-Arab in Arabic) as three autonomous administrative units linked to a central administration. By January 2014 the three cantons had declared their autonomy and began establishing a new administrative authority officially called the Canton Based Democratic Autonomy of Rojava (CBDAR). Militarily, the YPG has focused on securing the Rojava areas and in creating contiguous territory under Syrian Kurdish administration.

The emergence of the Rojava administration during the course of the conflict is remarkable given the history of Syrian Kurds' relationship with the central state and the regime. After the breakup of the Ottoman Empire, Syria's Kurds found themselves separated from social and familial networks in Turkey and Iraq. The borders drawn by the French authorities in the Kurdish populated areas had imposed on

Syria's Kurds new forms of identity and belonging that had hitherto been nonexistent. In the population movements and political upheavals of the late Ottoman period, many Kurds had migrated back and forth across what would become the Syrian-Turkish border. The French authorities' creation of a border, and a state apparatus to enforce authority within that border, meant that many Kurds found themselves locked in a political community that was ethnically, linguistically, and socially new. The development of the new Syrian state's bureaucracy and its institutions were to service an Arabic-speaking population. The demands of Syria's political elites at the time for an Arabized state reflect their ideological gravitation toward Arab nationalism. As such, the Arabization of the Syrian state and the strength of the Arab nationalist movement had created the discursive and political conditions to define the Kurdish population as a minority community—despite many being co-religionists with the majority Sunni Arab population (White, 2012, p. 112).

French authorities in this period recognized how potentially destabilizing Kurdish unrest in the new Syrian state could be for both Syria and Turkey, the latter of whom had placed pressure on French authorities to restrict Kurdish autonomy and political power in Syria. For this reason, the carving out of an autonomous, or even separate, Kurdish political entity was never taken too seriously by the French authorities, who instead sought to integrate the Kurds into the new Syrian state. The Kurdish community's differential incorporation into both the new Turkish and Syrian states, and the new post-Ottoman regional order in general, bred political resentment and hostility to the colonial and state authorities.

Subsequently, the threat of armed activities by Kurds in Turkey and Syria remained strong, and the urban Kurdish notables in Damascus had begun agitating for deeper Kurdish integration into the Syrian state (White, 2012, pp. 112–16). Such agitation on behalf of the Kurds in the northeast was simultaneously a reaction to emergent forms of Kurdish nationalism and a means of resurrecting patronage networks between the urban notables and rural communities, shoring up community support for notables' power (White, 2012, p. 116). The assertion of Kurdish minority rights and demands by notables for greater access to the state was met with hostility from Arab nationalists who rejected the Kurdish claim to a separate identity within Syria and autonomy in the northeast. In the clash of identities and identity politics at the time, Syrian Kurdish interests ultimately were subordinated to the larger Arab nationalist interests.

The differential and unequal incorporation of Syria's Kurds into the Syrian state would be a key feature of Syrian politics up until the uprising. In the 1960s right before the Ba'athist coup, the state conducted a census that was then used to strip more than 100,000 Kurds of their Syrian citizenship and to effectively render them stateless. They have no rights to work, own property, travel, or benefit from social services, except through registration as foreign residents in the country. From the 1950s onwards, the Kurdish language was banned in all educational institutions in an attempt to eliminate its use in Syria. Simultaneously, Kurdish place names were increasingly Arabized.

The Syrian Kurdish population has been spread throughout Syria, with large numbers of Syrian Kurds in Damascus and Aleppo. The Rojava areas are themselves not ethnically homogeneous; they have large non-Kurdish populations, including Yazidis, Sunni Arabs, Armenians, and Turkmen. The diversity of Kurdish areas and the dispersion of Syrian Kurds has contributed to their relative political quietism during the Ba'ath period. The most important factor, however, has been Ba'athist cooptation of Kurdish parties and the suppression of all forms of political activity. Syria's regime had fostered strong relations with the PKK in the 1990s and had even harbored its leader Abdullah Öcalan. In 1998, Turkey had threatened to wage war against Syria over the issue. Succumbing to this threat, the Syrian regime forced Öcalan to leave the country. While the regime was willing to support Kurdish political and military activity in neighboring countries, the same was not tolerated in Syria. Instead, the Syrian Kurds lived under severe discrimination, with tens of thousands deprived of Syrian citizenship and basic rights.

When the uprising began, then, the Syrian Kurdish community was balancing regime cooptation, which afforded the areas certain benefits, and political quietism, which had been the result of decades of exclusion from access to the Syrian state. Indeed, the precariousness of Syrian Kurdish politics was evident in the first months and year of the uprising. Many Kurds joined the protests and participated as activists and organizers. Yet many others were pacified by the regime's extension of citizenship to stateless Kurds and the release of some political prisoners. Major parties refused to throw their support behind the regime or the opposition, playing a waiting game that was as much about political expediency and strategy as it was about genuine distaste for both camps. While the opposition worked to court Kurdish officials into its ranks, the regime largely left the Kurdish areas alone militarily, despite some protests in these areas, in order to avoid opening another battlefront. Regime security forces had gradually redeployed during the uprising, creating an opportunity for the PYD to assert its authority in the northeast. Eventually, by 2012, with regime security forces largely absent from the area, the YPG removed government officials from state buildings and took them over, lowering the Syrian state flag and replacing it with PYD flags. The process of asserting Kurdish control and authority over the Rojava areas had begun.

Despite the conflicts between Kurdish political parties and factions, especially the KNC and PYD, the northeast has come under the administrative control of the Rojava administration. The Rojava administration is not an ethnic-based authority but rather a body that has assumed responsibility for the administration of a particular geographic area. The distinction between an administrative versus an ethnic project is important; the basis of the Rojava claim to authority is not based on the name and interests of the Kurdish community. Kurds form a numerical minority in Rojava, and officials have been keen on including non-Kurds in the administration and in using the Kurdish, Arabic, and Syriac languages in all administrative proceedings. The de-emphasis on Kurdish identity and interests in the administration is further reflected in the Charter of the Social Contract of

Democratic Autonomy: a sort of constitution governing the structure and work of the Rojava administration. In it, all ethnicities of the region are recognized as equal partners and the commitment to autonomous decision-making within a centralized state structure, not separatism and the creation of an entirely new state, is affirmed.

The central idea behind the administration is that of Democratic Autonomy, a notion developed by PKK leader Abdullah Öcalan to refer to the rejection of a separate Kurdish state and the desire to seek integration and participation into existing state structures, including respecting current borders and state authorities. Moreover, any ethnic identification is removed from the notion of Democratic Autonomy and instead "unity in diversity" is stressed. The multilingual, multi-ethnic, and multi-religious milieus in which Syrian Kurds reside are assumed as the basis of communal unity, rather than ethnicity.

Such public proclamations should not necessarily be taken at face value, however. The possibility of Kurdish separatism remains real. First, any declaration of independence by the Rojava administration would have radically altered the strategic calculations of all neighboring states and the regime itself. Demands for an autonomous administration within Syria remain politically unpalatable to most regional actors. Second, there is no monopoly on political authority in the region; intra-Kurdish disputes often lead to violence between different groups and consensus around major issues such as negotiations with the regime and relations with the political opposition is lacking. Such rivalry threatens to paralyze or even collapse the Rojava administrative project. Third, continued military threats from ISIS, HTS, and of course Turkey threaten the security monopoly that the YPG currently enjoys. In an environment of fluid strategic relationships and constantly shifting battlefield dynamics, the relative calm in Rojava areas remains precarious.

Nevertheless, the Charter of the Social Contract has established a sophisticated network of administrative institutions that have assumed the role of the contracted Syrian state. The three cantons are divided as follows (Kurdistan National Congress, 2014):

Table 4.1 Cantons of the Rojava Administration

Canton	Capital	Official Languages	Official Religions	Population
Cezire	Amude	Kurdish, Arabic, Syriac	Islam, Christianity, Yezidi	1.5 million
Kobane	Kobane	Kurdish	Islam	1 million
Erfin	Erfin	Kurdish	Islam, Alawi, Yezidi	1.3 million

The structure of the Cezire Canton sheds some insight into the institutional architecture of the autonomous region. There are four main councils. The Legislative Council consists of 101 members (at least 40 percent women), a President, and two Deputies. The Legislative Council works directly with the main Executive Council, which serves as the central government for the canton. This body has twenty-two ministries, including environment, external relations, defense (YPG), and education, and is presided over by a Kurdish President and one Arab and one Syriac Deputy. The Judicial Council (composed of at least 40 percent women) constructs and regulates the application of the law. Finally, the Local Administration Council is the main body representing the ten cities within the Cezire Canton. A seven-person (at least 40 percent women) Constitutional Court oversees the application of law while the eighteen-member (at least 40 percent women) High Commission of Elections regulates electoral procedures. Below this larger structure are a series of other institutions, such as a police force, civil society groups, and neighborhood councils. Even the YPG units have begun to institutionalize through the establishment of a higher military council and military academies to recruit and train a new generation of fighters. Finally, the PYD established an umbrella organization called the Rojava Democratic Society Movement (TEV-DEM) that coordinates all aspects of political and social life in the areas. Technically speaking, the PYD is one sub-entity among many of the TEV-DEM.

The administrative structure of the cantons and their relationship to a centralized provincial government is not without problems. First, the territory under Rojava administrative authority is not contiguous, making relations between the cantons and the authorities extremely difficult. Second, the basic mechanisms of population management, such as a census, are unavailable to the administration. Third, the institutional architecture within and between the cantons is subject to PYD influence and control. Notwithstanding the official and public rhetoric of diversity and cohabitation among all, the PYD exercises tremendous influence within the administration. Local councils, for example, have very little decision-making authority and have been relegated to carrying out PYD directives. Other bodies are largely powerless and the theoretical responsibility of governance and administration that lies in the different integrated units actually lies with the PYD, who largely make major decisions outside of the administrative structure. Another problem is not necessarily administrative, but political. The Rojava project is essentially an entirely PYD project as the KNC, the major political alternative to the PYD, withdrew its support for the project before its inception. The split between the PYD and KNC was largely about which group has the authority to speak and act on Kurdish political interests, but it also reflected the rivalries between the PYD and KNC's patrons and their desire to similarly exercise leadership in regional Kurdish politics. The creation of the Supreme Kurdish Committee aimed at creating committees made up of PYD and KNC members, but the agreement has never materialized into any concrete cooperation. Finally, there are serious battlefield issues facing the Syrian Kurdish project. On the one hand, the Turkish military has repeatedly intervened to prevent the conjoining of territory under Kurdish administration and has continued to threaten to do so in the future. Nothing in the Astana process restricts this right. On the other hand, the Kurdish project has been based on the ethnic cleansing of many border areas. While the SDF has the appearance of a multi-ethnic, multi-confessional force, the reality is that many Syrian Arabs have been victimized, displaced, and killed as the Rojava project developed.

In establishing the Rojava administration, Kurdish leaders have taken full advantage of the political opportunity presented by the collapse of the Syrian state and the withering of the regime. Although it is unclear whether collective Kurdish political aspirations will result in a separation from the Syrian state, it is certain that any postconflict Syrian political architecture must absorb or contend with Kurdish autonomous administration and the demands of the leaders and many community members for institutionalizing and recognizing decentralization and Kurdish autonomy. However, the success of the Rojava project and its potential integration into a postconflict Syria will be shaped by many factors moving forward, some of which are intra-Kurdish disputes and radically different visions for how Syrian Kurdish areas should be governed and administered and by whom. Kurdish parties, much like the Syrian opposition and rebel groups, have international patrons who exercise a tremendous amount of influence on them. Thus, the future of Rojava will be subject to regional geopolitics and any grand bargain made by regional actors to resolve the Syrian conflict. The main question moving forward is how a postconflict Syrian authority can incorporate Kurdish autonomy into the larger political body in ways that satisfy Kurdish political demands and entrench Syrian Kurdish rights and aspirations into the political system. In the absence of such recognition and institutionalization of Kurdish autonomy and rights, the likelihood of Kurdish separatist aspirations may increase.

At this stage of the conflict, the Rojava project is an ambitious attempt to organize a segment of society embedded in a larger conflict. The transformation into the DFNS, however, may better reflect its future in a postconflict Syria as one region among many. The ability to establish an administrative structure that will outlive the conflict remains to be seen. The DFNS administration is already being contested by the KNC and, for all intents and purposes, the project remains dominated and controlled by the PYD. Pacifying or co-opting Kurdish competitors and gaining legitimacy among the Kurdish population and diffusing political power throughout the region are major challenges facing the PYD.

ISIS areas

By late 2017, the ISIS project had been declared all but dead. After years of American, Russian, and Syrian regime bombardment, coupled with battlefield defeats at the hands of the SDF in Syria and the Iraqi army in Iraq, ISIS had retreated into a small enclave of territory and has been considered by many observers to be waning in influence on the Syrian and Iraqi battlefields. This was a major blow to a movement that presented itself as a state with the ability to capture, control, and govern territory.

Indeed, central to ISIS's legitimacy among its supporters was its territorial control and expansion over parts of western Iraq and eastern Syria. The control and administration of territory was central to ISIS's claims of representing the new Caliphate and distinguishes the group from all other rebel groups in Syria in that its claim is to function as a state. The projection of ISIS power and authority across these lands represents a dramatic attempt at radical social change. Unlike the other armed movements in Syria, ISIS does not profess or have pretensions toward political integration into a post-conflict Syrian order. Nor does ISIS aspire, as does the PYD through the DFNS, to accept the nation-state system and some form of communal or geographic autonomy institutionalized in the Syrian state. ISIS's control over large swathes of territory that transcends the borders of two states represented an altogether different form of fragmentation. Whereas the DFNS areas are attempting to establish a structure of autonomous government that intends to be incorporated into a larger centralized structure, ISIS's administrative structure and political goals leave no room for such integration into a postconflict order. The ISIS project represents an objective threat to the Syrian state and Syria's territorial contiguity and integrity.

Some caution should be exercised when discussing the goals and structure of ISIS's administrative project in particular because information from these areas is severely limited. The Western world knows very little about daily life in ISIS territory beyond anecdotal stories emerging from individuals who have fled from it. The secrecy of the organization, the lack of adequate reporting from ISIS areas, and the rapid growth of the group within Syria and Iraq have made key questions around its social base of support, economic management, and bureaucratic capacities difficult to answer. What follows, then, is an attempt to outline the broad contours of the administrative structure of ISIS in the areas under its control, the background of its leadership (and to the extent possible, its supporters), and its overall organizational and bureaucratic capacities.

Unlike the Syrian Kurdish project, ISIS's raison d'être is the establishment of a state, or an alternative political authority in the form of the Caliphate, out of lands extracted from Syria and Iraq. The state ISIS purports to govern is headed by Abu Bakr al-Baghdadi, who has recently taken on the title of Caliph. Personal advisors and assistants surround al-Baghdadi, while the larger administrative structure includes deputies, a cabinet, and a military council (these councils are relatively small). While al-Baghdadi has attempted to project legitimacy through his clerical background, many of his deputies and other officers lack any forms of Islamic legitimacy.

Two of al-Baghdadi's known deputies were actually formerly high-ranking officers in the Iraqi military under Saddam Hussein: Abu Ali al-Anbari was a major general in the Army while Abdullah al-Hiyali was a lieutenant colonel in the Iraqi Military Intelligence and a former Iraqi Special Forces officer (Gorman et al., 2014). Below these deputies are hundreds or thousands of military commanders who similarly have no religious training or background but have expertise in bureaucratic and security affairs.

A central factor in explaining the expansion and consolidation of territorial control is ISIS's embeddedness in the Syrian and Iraqi war economies and the ability to generate and distribute wealth in its territory. This income is not generated through productive activities but rather through wartime economic activity—extortion, kidnapping, taxation, resource extraction, and looting—that is not sustainable. Under such conditions, populations develop dependencies on the authorities for the distribution of goods, as jobs and other means of productive economic activity are severely limited, particularly as trade occurs through black markets or smuggling channels. The productive activity that does occur in ISIS areas is limited. There has been a great deal of attention paid to the oil resources controlled by ISIS and the belief that the group accrues handsome profits from the extraction and sale of oil to neighboring countries and to the regime itself (Hubbard et al., 2014). However, many of the figures offered in popular accounts are presumptive and it is more likely that ISIS production is limited and that the revenues are not in the daily millions of dollars. While it may indeed be the case that ISIS was the "richest terrorist group in history," it may also be that their wealth is severely exaggerated. The only other products produced in ISIS territory are agricultural and are mainly distributed within the territories and thus have not generated sufficient income to financially support their administration.

Electricity provision is severely limited and has forced ISIS to enter into barter deals with regime forces to exchange electricity for oil (Taylor, 2015), further limiting the extent to which oil and agricultural production can serve as the financial backbone of the ISIS administration. The issue of electricity provision also highlights the codependence ISIS has on the Syrian regime. After ISIS seized control of dams and gas plants in Syria, agreements were made with the Syrian regime to exchange gas for electricity. Since ISIS does not have the engineering capacity to operate the plants, the Syrian regime also continues to provide salaries for the workers at the dams and plants. The same situation has occurred in Iraqi areas where ISIS controlled key production plants while the employees are paid their salaries from the central Iraqi government. Control of these plants has not meant that ISIS can provide the actual service; it has forced them into agreements with the Syrian and Iraqi states.

Beyond agricultural production and oil extraction, ISIS is economically dependent on illegality and wartime activities for its finances. Extortion is a major source of income and ISIS networks of extortion operate throughout Syria and Iraq.

Transport and customs taxes are regularly imposed on goods traveling between Jordan, Syria, Iraq, and Turkey, reflecting ISIS's control over key transport routes in the region. Finally, the looting and sale of antiquities has provided ISIS with another substantial source of revenue, at the expense of Syrian and Iraqi cultural heritage. It is for this reason that the ISIS project has collapsed so spectacularly in recent years as their main sources of income have receded as the Russian and U.S.-led interventions targeted them from the air and SDF-led forces on the ground.

The control of key economic levers and the ability to acquire finances through wartime economic activities was thus not a sufficient basis for the ISIS administration. Indeed, throughout most of its territory, services were virtually nonexistent. This is especially true in the rural areas, where brute force and fear are as important to their ruling strategies as distribution of goods and services. In major cities, such as Raqqa, ISIS developed administrative presence and the residents are provided some limited services, as schools and medical facilities are most developed in the more densely populated areas.

Ultimately, however, the ISIS project in Syria is subject to the same economic logics and restraints of all wartime orders. As discussed in Chapter Three, a conflict war economy is important in structuring how armed groups relate to one another and how they finance their military activities. Despite its claims to statehood and to being a Caliphate, ISIS has not been immune from these logics. Warlords within the ISIS structure operate throughout Syria and Iraq, taxing populations and extracting wealth from them. As the ISIS project collapsed, these warlords have dispersed throughout the conflict landscape. In this way, ISIS operated similarly to other warlords and armed groups in Syria. Like many of these groups as well, ISIS's economic activities and attempt to impose a separate administration on these areas contributed to deepening fragmentation in the Syrian context. ISIS is no longer the main player on the Syrian conflict landscape that it was prior to 2015. Having lost its main area of Mosul in Iraq and an ever-tightening SDF-led siege imposed on Raqqa in Syria, the ISIS has all but lost control of any significant territory. Defections have begun to multiply and there is no clear established leadership from which to revive, let alone guide, the group.

Jabhat an-Nusra and the Salafist-jihadist network of violence

The split between ISIS and JAN in 2013 was an important development in the Syrian conflict, as it diffused Salafi-jihadist loyalties between the two groups, who were already in conflict with other armed Islamist groups on the battlefield. The split between the two reflects the pluralism of the Salafi-jihadist landscape in Syria and demonstrates the ideological and political distinctions among the different groups which have prevented cooperation, despite a presumably shared ideology and worldview. Despite its association with al-Qaeda, JAN's leadership and its fighters had a remarkably Syrian character. The roots of JAN's leadership in Syria's social mosaic are an extremely important factor in explaining their military success and their adoption of particular strategies. Their Syrian rootedness also helps us explain their evolution from JAN into today's Hayat Tahrir al-Sham. This is an important point of distinction between JAN and ISIS: whereas the latter is mostly made up of foreign fighters and leaders who see the Syrian conflict as part of a larger struggle to expand the Caliphate and are thus less focused directly on the overthrow of the Syrian regime, JAN's leaders and fighters have adopted rhetoric and political strategies that are consistent with the original goals of the uprising.

Since its entry into the Syrian conflict in 2011, JAN has become one of the major alliances fighting the regime. Alongside its military activities has grown an administrative apparatus that is quite distinct from that developed in other non-regime areas in Syria. The alliance has acquired a tremendous amount of administrative influence within the non-regime areas through their cooperation with other rebel groups, even in areas where they may be militarily weak.

For example, in the southern and northwestern areas of the country, JAN has fought alongside many FSA-affiliated brigades and other alliances against regime forces. In other areas, JAN had proven to be capable of military advances on its own without support from other brigades. The ability and willingness to enter into larger networks of violence has expanded JAN's influence within the non-regime areas considerably.

Moreover, JAN demonstrated a larger geographic reach than other rebel groups and has been active in most major battle areas in the country. Upon entering the Syrian conflict, JAN fighters had adopted more guerrilla tactics targeting regime security forces, including car bombs and attacks on security installations. These occurred throughout the country and were not confined to one governorate or city, which allowed fighters a degree of mobility and also allowed them to evade besiegement from regime forces. The success of JAN's operations coupled with gradual regime retreat due to FSA military advances allowed JAN's leadership to recruit more Syrian fighters, especially from the rural areas that were increasingly outside of regime control. This allowed JAN's fighters to grow and coalesce into larger units and brigades, which encouraged more strategic military activity that was focused less on attacking regime security forces and more on acquiring and controlling territory.

Its renewed military strategy and initial successes in defeating regime forces fostered greater cooperation with FSA brigades and allowed JAN fighters to more solidly root themselves in non-regime areas and begin social service provisions. This gave the organization a base to begin establishing their administrative authority in Syria. While the provision of social services has been an important area of JAN's activities, the group has also devoted considerable effort to the creation of Shari'a courts in non-regime areas.

Unlike ISIS- or PYD-controlled areas, JAN does not control contiguous territory. Moreover, JAN has relied extensively on cooperative relations with other armed rebel groups, as discussed in Chapter Three. Indeed, relations between JAN and many FSA brigades have been cooperative and have led to the sharing of resources and the formalization of governance structures. For example, JAN has been very active in water and food provision and has extended its efforts into areas that are not directly under their territorial control. The group has put great effort into fostering relations with certain rebel groups, especially in the northwest, in order to gain a foothold within the rebel movement. Such relationships give JAN a wider reach and enhance their military strength considerably. Typically, cooperative relations around social services provision have provided opportunities to establish more formal institutional structures, especially in regard to law.

The main administrative strategy pursued by JAN translates military operations into shared governance. For this reason, JAN has cultivated strong relations with other Salafist-jihadist groups and other armed groups. Their governance strategy has been to pursue mixed-authority institutions in which JAN shares responsibility with other groups. The main focus here has been on Shari'a courts. In 2013, for example, the Aleppo Shari'a Committee (ASC) was formed with JAN as one of the five founding members (four other brigades participated). Although the committee eventually expanded to fifteen members, JAN has exercised major influence because of the relative weakness of the other members and has devoted considerable resources to strengthening the courts. The model was replicated throughout the country in areas in which JAN is active, especially in Deir ez-Zour where a similar Committee has been established (called the Mujahideen Shura Council) with subordinate offices and departments.

Even in areas that have not formalized shared governance in the form of Committees or Councils, there are similar arrangements. The Kafr Nabel Shari'a Court is another example of the patchwork of authorities that underpin administrative structures. In mid-2014, the court was controlled by JAN, the Foursan al-Haq brigade (an FSA affiliate), and the Souqour al-Sham brigade (affiliated with the Islamic Front), which upheld the court's rulings. Similar courts have appeared throughout the country, especially in the areas where JAN has been most active: Dar'a, Eastern Ghouta (Damascus), Deir ez-Zor, and Aleppo. JAN's governance strategy has been successful because they have relied on alliances to build stronger networks to provide social services, coordinate military activities, and implement Shari'a law. The fusion of social and military strategies has been important to JAN's ability to build these alliances. Moreover, unlike ISIS, which is mostly composed of foreign fighters and foreign leaders, JAN's base was predominantly Syrian. The group has demonstrated a remarkable flexibility in adapting to local conditions and not overly disrupting local traditions and power structures, for example, in their morphing into Hayat Tahrir al-Sham in response to various military setbacks. Instead, they have integrated themselves into existing rebel networks and into the social bases of these networks.

Conclusion

Until late 2015, the defining feature of the Syrian conflict was the military and political stalemate. This stalemate emerged out of the tensions and contradictory policies of Western, Arab, and regional states, all of which effectively adopted a military solution to the Syrian crisis. The strategies to achieve this manifest in two ways: first, most efforts at international, multilateral peace negotiations were rendered meaningless and consistently stymied, and, second, they supported different armed groups on the ground. For supporters of the opposition, this meant funneling resources to FSA, ISIS, and JAN/HTS affiliated Fronts, as well as smaller brigades. This meant that many of the armed groups were strong enough to fight on the battlefield without being strong enough to overtake each other. Such balances produced territorial fragmentation in Syria as regime authority contracted and competing armed groups stepped in to fill the vacuum.

As this chapter has shown, the different projects that emerged in non-regime territories were radically different. Many were ad hoc and unsustainable, others had the pretentions of establishing statehood, while the Kurdish-led project was intent on positioning the territory as a strong, decentralized power in a postconflict, federal Syria, or as an altogether independent state should Syria's geography be reconfigured once the conflict ends. The combination of international conflict over Syria and the fragmentation of Syrian territory were the main features and drivers of the stalemate that defined the conflict until late 2015.

At that point, the large-scale Russian intervention set in motion a process that would decidedly tip the conflict in the favor of the regime-aligned forces. Russian intervention would return territory to regime control (even though this was largely governed by militias outside of formal state authority), force the international community to accept Russian designs for Syria through the Astana political process, destroy the armed opposition and their main supply routes, and fundamentally alter the course of the Syrian conflict. The breaking of the stalemate is explored in the next chapter.

<table>
<tr><td>**5**</td><td>After Aleppo:
Breaking the Stalemate _____</td></tr>
</table>

By mid-2015, the Syrian conflict landscape had more or less hardened. Front lines between regime and non-regime areas had slowly been established; even if the authorities that exercised control were constantly shifting. The country was very loosely divided among five identifiable, if fluid, territorial arrangements: the regime and its aligned forces controlled territory from Damascus through to the north-western coastal areas; the PYD-led forces controlled pockets in northeastern Syria along the Syrian-Turkish border; ISIS controlled large swathes of the less densely populated eastern Syria; southern areas along the Jordanian and Golan borders were controlled by FSA and some Islamist factions; while the northern parts of the country between regime- and PYD-held areas were dominated by Islamist factions mainly led by groups such as JAN and Ahrar al-Sham.

This is what Syria's geography looked like on the eve of the Russian intervention. At that time, Western intervention had been ruled out. Local armed groups had begun to cement their control of key areas, mainly those that were of strategic economic benefit, such as border crossings and checkpoints. Each identifiable unit had its own internal economic logic as well, leading to the emergence of multiple Syrian war economies, all of which were tethered to different border-lands. For example, FSA units in the south were dependent on the free flow of supplies and fighters from Jordan, while

Islamist factions in the north, which controlled the Aleppo–Turkey supply route, relied on Turkish entry points.

The Syrian war economies were necessary for the sustenance of armed groups as well as to their material and social reproduction. As the formal economy collapsed and more Syrians turned to violence as a means of survival, the war economies provided opportunities and incentives for violence. Thus, warlordism began to take root and, increasingly, armed groups fought each other and the regime-aligned forces for access to the material benefits of war. It is not surprising, then, that the Russian intervention targeted these supply routes and sought to suffocate the armed groups and prevent their reproduction.

In this chapter, we explore how transformative the Russian intervention that began in September 2015 has been for the Syrian conflict. We begin by looking at how political processes failed to end the conflict and why the Russian intervention was necessary to break the stalemate. We then move along a timeline of events, showing precisely how and why Russian intervention cut off particular supply lines: first in the south, then the east, and then on to Aleppo, where the major armed factions had coalesced for one final stand. It is after Aleppo, after a bloody, disastrous, and catastrophic few years of violence and conflict, that the conflict's trajectory takes an almost irreversible turn toward a Russian-designed solution to the conflict. Thus, after exploring the intervention itself and its aftermath, the chapter explores how the Russian intervention is making multilateral politics possible where they have otherwise failed since the conflict began in 2011.

Failure of peace efforts

There has been no shortage of attempts by international bodies to solve the Syrian conflict. Beginning in mid-2011, the United Nations in particular was involved in mediation efforts that have evolved as the conflict expanded. Unfortunately, none of these efforts created the space for serious peace negotiations and most parties involved simply participated in them for cosmetic reasons. Often times, the same states participating in peace negotiations were the ones fueling the violence. The section below explores some of these efforts as well as the reasons behind their failure.

The United Nations Security Council

The United Nations Security Council (UNSC) has been in permanent paralysis regarding the Syrian conflict. The five permanent members—Great Britain, the United States, France, China, and Russia—have pursued their policies outside of the UNSC in large part because of the conflicting interests represented by China and Russia, who are generally supportive of the Syrian regime on the one hand, and the U.S., Great Britain, and France, who have declared policies of regime change on the other. The paralysis of the UNSC has meant that the United Nations has played a rather limited role in the conflict, being increasingly confined to humanitarian aid work with little progress made by UN-sponsored mediation talks. Since the outset of the conflict, the UNSC has passed a number of resolutions regarding Syria. Because of disagreements and conflict between the permanent members these resolutions have largely ignored the security situation and have focused predominantly on humanitarian issues.

The UNSC has passed three resolutions that form the pillars of the humanitarian response: resolutions 2139, 2165, and 2191. These resolutions were consistent in their demands for a cessation of violence, demilitarization, the protection of civilians. Resolution 2139 even went so far as to demand the comprehensive implementation of the Geneva Communique of June 2012 calling for a political transition. Without any significant political pressure exerted by the UN on any of the warring sides, the security and political elements of the resolutions rang hollow. The more substantive aspects of the resolutions—the ones where the international community could actually affect the conflict—had to do with humanitarian assistance. More specifically, the resolutions called for the lifting of sieges on populated areas and the safe passage of

UN humanitarian agencies to conflict zones, while calling on member states to increase funding for humanitarian efforts.

While such resolutions were never seriously going to bring about a political transition, they held out the greatest prospect for a collective, international response to the humanitarian catastrophe. Yet the number of Syrians living in areas that were outside the reach of aid agencies doubled from 2.5 million in 2013 to 4.8 million at the start of 2015 (Norwegian Refugee Council, 2015, p. 13). The World Bank estimated in 2016 that more than 13.5 million Syrians needed some form of aid (World Bank, 2016). In 2014, UN humanitarian convoys had reached just over 1 million Syrians, which was 1.8 million fewer than the year before. Further aggravating the situation is the dramatic reduction in contributions from member states to UN aid agencies, who received a 96 percent reduction in food aid in 2014 (Norwegian Refugee Council, 2015). In 2017, UNHCR requests to member states had reached a staggering $4.63 billion (UNHCR, 2017). Such reductions in food aid parallel reductions in money and other resources channeled to international nongovernmental organizations (INGOs). The trend in addressing the humanitarian situation is a negative one: as humanitarian needs increase, access to the most affected populations is decreasing while aid resources dwindle.

Deliberations at the UNSC about Syria did not take place until early 2012, almost one year after the uprising began, after the failure of a League of Arab States initiative to end the conflict. A resolution calling for an end to violence and a political transition process that involved Assad handing power to his vice-president was drafted but eventually vetoed by China and Russia. Supporters of the resolution easily had it passed in the General Assembly but the vote was of no consequence because it was nonbinding and could not actually commit the UN and its member states to any action on Syria. With stalemate at the UNSC level, the UN initiated mediation talks. Since 2012, there have been three different Special Representatives for Syria—Kofi Annan, Lakhdar Brahimi, and, since July 2014, Staffan de Mistura—who have been dedicated to bringing about a political settlement to the conflict.

Geneva I

Kofi Annan began his tenure as special envoy by proposing a six-point peace plan that built on the Arab League initiative and was intended to serve as a transitional plan. Annan was successful in ensuring the deployment of a UN observer mission to Syria, which began in April 2012 and was eventually suspended because of violence and a lack of cooperation by the regime in August. While this was occurring, Annan was also able to gather representatives of the UN and Arab League, and the foreign ministers of the major regional and international acting nations, including the U.S., U.K., France, Russia, Turkey, China, Kuwait, Iraq, and Qatar, in Geneva to negotiate and adopt a plan for mediation and political transition. In the absence of a UNSC resolution, the Geneva process became the focus of international efforts to end the Syrian conflict.

On 30 June 2012, Annan presided over an Action Group on Syria and thus initiated the first process to bring together the international community to solve the Syrian conflict. Curiously, there were no Syrian representatives from the regime or opposition present at the conference aimed at deciding Syria's future. The intent, rather, was to bring together supporters of the regime and the opposition to negotiate and agree upon principles that would guide a solution. Among the principles that the parties agreed to were an end to violence, humanitarian aid access, the release of all political prisoners, the resignation of President al-Assad, and a Syrian-led transition that would lead to a multiparty democratic system. The final communique called for the transition to include regime and opposition members in government; the participation of all major Syrian parties in a national dialogue; a reform of the constitutional and judicial systems; and free, democratic elections.

Not surprisingly, the Syrian regime and the main opposition group, the National Coalition, accepted these ideals and pledged support for the Geneva process. Such support did not, however, come without conditions and caveats. The regime, for example, rejected participation of "terrorists" in the political process, while opposition groups demanded that Assad resign as a precondition for the implementation of the plan (Asseburg and Wimmen, 2014, p. 3). While regime and opposition rejection of Geneva was an important factor in derailing the process, the actual commitment of the international community to the implementation of the plan was also seriously in doubt. Many regional states, including Saudi Arabia and Iran, have never been fully committed to an international process to solve the Syrian conflict and have instead viewed the conflict through their narrow geopolitical prisms. The process was thus never given the full political support of the major regional powers who had ability and opportunity to invest the political resources in the Geneva process and bring about a resolution to the conflict. The military solution—and not the international process started in Geneva—was the preferred method of conflict resolution for the regional parties.

International actors were also not fully committed to the process. Western states had placed a tremendous amount of faith in a process that they were reluctant to support with political pressure on regional actors or Syrian opposition groups. Although many Western states had shunned the arming of Syrian rebels, they similarly failed to support the development of the Syrian grassroots. They did not help to develop the administrative and governance capacity of groups attempting to establish alternative institutions in non-regime areas. Meanwhile, the Russian and Chinese delegations were highly skeptical of the process and eventually contributed to its collapse because of their opposition to the plan's agreement on a transition that involved the resignation of Assad—and other preconditions that had been insisted upon by Arab and Western states. The collapse of the Geneva process eventually led to Annan's resignation and his scathing criticism of the Syrian regime and the international community, noting in a press conference announcing his resignation that "without serious, purposeful and united international pressure, including from the powers of the region, it is impossible for me, or anyone, to compel the Syrian government in the first place, and also the opposition, to take the steps necessary to begin a political process" (Gladstone, 2012). When asked what the future of the peace process he started would be, Annan claimed that "the world is full of crazy people like me, so don't be surprised if someone else decides to take it on" (NYT, 2012). A few weeks later, Algerian diplomat Lakhdar Brahimi took Annan's place as the UN Special Representative on Syria.

Geneva II

Brahimi's appointment as Special Representative brought some initial optimism that an international peace process could be revived. Facts on the ground had changed and it was believed that the regional climate was perhaps more conducive to a collaborative peace process. The advent of ISIS and other radical jihadist groups had created a greater urgency for Western and Arab states to resolve the conflict and the military option preferred by regional players was leading to nothing but stalemate. In this context, Brahimi attempted to restart the Geneva process.

Unlike the first round, there would be Syrian representation at the talks, held in Montreux in January 2014, with both regime and opposition representatives committed to attending. By this stage of the conflict it was clear that the main opposition group, the National Coalition, no longer enjoyed any legitimacy on the ground in Syria and could not serve as the representative of the armed groups or the internal political opposition. The Coalition was wholly unable to generate consensus among Syrian opposition and armed groups around the need for a political solution. Nor could it ensure the support of various opposition factions for the negotiations. Immediately after accepting the invitation to the talks, the Syrian National Council withdrew from the National Coalition in protest. The leaders of the major armed Fronts, including Ahrar as-Sham and the Islamic Front, immediately rejected the talks, while others, including the now-defunct Syrian Revolutionaries Front (SRF), supported the talks and had even requested the right to send representatives. The Kurdish PYD had similarly asked to send a delegation, which was rejected by the organizers. Although Geneva II was heralded as being more inclusive of Syrian representatives, the mosaic of opposition groups was not sufficiently represented.

Such incoherence and conflict between the different opposition and armed groups reflect how precarious the situation is on the ground. The armed groups were outside the influence of the external opposition, and the overwhelming majority of armed groups rejected the talks as pointless political theater, effectively pledging commitment to a military solution. The Coalition and its various political factions were left with an inescapable dilemma: how to engage in a political process with an entrenched regime that was unwilling to meet the basic demand of the resignation of President Assad. For all the talk of transition and democracy that had permeated the first round of Geneva talks, the opposition was unable to realize this core demand of the opposition groups.

The failure of the Geneva Process to bring about any substantive changes in the conflict, let alone to move the various parties toward a resolution, is indicative of the inability of the international community to bring political pressures to bear on the regime, rebels, and opposition groups to resolve the conflict. There is no doubt that the regime and its state supporters had never taken the Geneva platform seriously as a forum for political transition that would remove Bashar al-Assad. In the second round of talks in January 2014, for example, the regime's negotiators framed the conference as a "counter-terrorism" effort in an attempt to reframe the conflict within the broader global war on terror. Such intransigence, however, was not the sole reason for the collapse of the Geneva Process. Although most parties to the conflict did attend, they did not do so in good faith. Most participants from the regime and opposition camps did not demonstrate a commitment to a political solution. The National Coalition suffered from the defection of key allies and a strong perception of illegitimacy that undermined their ability to seriously negotiate a political solution. For the regime, it was clear that their commitments led instead to maintaining a military solution to the conflict; they did not lead to an internationally driven process largely outside of their control. International actors, such as the United States, were mostly ambivalent and unwilling to offer much by way of political incentives to bring the parties closer to a political solution. At the same time, the two rounds highlighted the failures of the Syrian opposition to shape events on the ground. Many of the groups fighting inside of Syria, and many of the nonviolent groups, rejected the very premise of the Geneva Process and the prospects of negotiating with the regime. As the external opposition lacks legitimacy both inside of Syria and in the international community, its participation can be seen as an effort to assert itself as a legitimate actor in the Syrian conflict and to present itself as not only a partner in peace, but as an alternative to the regime. Their participation in the talks did not increase the opposition's legitimacy and did very little to unify opposition groups. It highlighted the fissures and detachments between them. The total rejection of Geneva II by the armed groups who at that point were exercising the most influence on the ground in non-regime areas was a further nail in the Geneva Process coffin.

It is thus a mischaracterization to suggest that the Syrian opposition landscape was split over the question of whether to participate in Geneva II. It is more accurate to suggest that the overwhelming majority of violent and nonviolent groups rejected dialogue with the regime, especially if that dialogue did not carry a precondition of al-Assad's immediate removal. Groups such as Jabhat an-Nusra and ISIS, who at this point were the strongest actors in the non-regime areas, categorically rejected Geneva II, as did many of the other armed groups, including the powerful and relatively organized Islamic Front. Of the armed groups inside Syria, only the FSA pledged support to the Geneva Process. This, however, should be understood within the framework of the FSA's general political and military fragmentation and decentralized leadership. Such a decision then cannot be said to apply to all brigades associated with the FSA but rather to the representatives of the central command. Whether fighters on the ground would have obeyed any ceasefires or demilitarization measures associated with the Geneva process is unlikely.

The political opposition was equally in favor of rejecting the talks. On the eve of the Geneva II talks, the National Coalition itself was not unanimous in its support of the talks. The decision to participate in the talks—which was taken days before they would start—was not approved until the Syrian National Council, a third of the Coalition delegates, had withdrawn from the body in protest against the prospect of negotiations and the failure to secure al-Assad's resignation as a prerequisite for talks. By the time of approval, only fifty-eight of the original 121 Coalition delegates had voted to support attending Geneva negotiations.

Leading up to the Geneva negotiations, the influence of regional and international actors on Syria's opposition groups was becoming more and more obvious. Decisions taken by these groups were no longer autonomous or independent, but heavily influenced by the main international players in the conflict. However, throughout the conflict, the interests and political goals of these external actors have not coalesced and are more conflictual than cooperative. Such discord among the international parties to the conflict was quite evident around the Geneva II negotiations. States have gradually grown to frame the conflict in counter-terrorism terms and to regard the rise of ISIS, Jabhat an-Nusra, and other Islamist groups as more threatening to security than the conflict itself. To this central geopolitical concern over expanding Islamist influence we can add the continued flow of refugees, the ongoing negotiations with Iran over its nuclear weapons program, and the potential violent spillover effects of the Syrian conflict, as the main interests of the Western powers. The Geneva process has thus morphed into a sideshow for larger geopolitical issues.

The regime itself has been under very little pressure from its main international backers to offer concessions through the Geneva Process. Iran and Russia have little appetite for ceding political ground to Qatari- and Saudi-backed groups, let alone supporting a political transition process that would remove al-Assad and, potentially, the main pillars of the security apparatus. Thus while all parties involved, from the UN to the major international players, through to the regime and the National Coalition, pledged support for the Geneva process, it ultimately failed because of a lack of political will, a poor negotiating framework, and the commitment to a military solution by most of the regional powers.

Local freezes?

Kofi Annan and Lakhdar Brahimi eventually resigned from their positions because of an unwillingness on the part of warring sides and their regional patrons to take a political settlement seriously. Brahimi's resignation in May 2014 led to the appointment of Staffan de Mistura as the new Special Representative. De Mistura's strategy was fundamentally different from that of his predecessors. Instead of focusing on larger peace plans for Syria, he has devoted energy to local "freezes" in Aleppo. These freezes are essentially short-term ceasefires negotiated in specific areas where fighting is most intense and are aimed at accomplishing two key goals: first, to allow for humanitarian aid to reach the most affected areas, and, second, to build momentum and confidence to spread the freezes and move toward a larger political settlement.

The plan was drawn from a report prepared by the Center for Humanitarian Dialogue in Geneva and was adopted after secretive consultations between regime and opposition figures. Rather than focusing on the formation of a transitional government, the plan envisions a series of steps to be undertaken over a two-year period, beginning with local freezes and the expansion of local administrative capacity, and then followed by parliamentary and local elections. A new parliamentary system would be established that devolves powers from the President to the Prime Minister. Unlike the Geneva process that imagined a transitional government and new elections as the beginning of the transition process, de Mistura's plan calls for a series of steps prior to a transitional government being established.

This bottom-up approach to a political settlement is radically different from the Geneva process model developed by de Mistura's predecessors. The Geneva process relied on a political model that aimed at a grand bargain between Syrian parties and regional players. Increasingly, however, the talks were disconnected from events on the ground and were not inclusive of the main parties to the conflict, raising serious doubts about whether an agreement would actually lead to a cessation of violence. The strategy pursued by de Mistura instead relies on engaging local actors involved in fighting and encouraging the reduction and freezing of violence to facilitate the delivery of humanitarian aid. Aleppo, Syria's most devastated city, would be de Mistura's test lab.

Although this strategy is a unique deviation from the strategy of his predecessors, it is not without problems. Its prospects for success are best assessed retroactively: the reality is that the emergent post-intervention order has sidelined the UN, the Geneva process, the concept of local freezes, and de Mistura himself. De Mistura was unable to secure the regime's acquiescence to the freezes, and unable to enforce a moratorium on air raids and barrel bombing in Aleppo, which are the primary cause of casualties in that city. The freezes required the regime's forces to honor agreements, and this simply never happened (*Guardian*, 2012). The possibility of "frozen" areas becoming cleansed of fighters and leaving civilian areas entirely unprotected and at the mercy of regime bombardment risks turning these areas into killing fields rather than safe havens. Moreover, the plan did not have any clearly defined incentives for fighters to lay down their weapons and it is unclear how local freezes would not simply encourage fighters to move from one district to another. While regime officials have met the suggested plans with caution and public optimism, some Fronts have already rejected the plans as unrealistic.

Ultimately, the United Nations has failed to bring about peace in Syria. Bâli and Rana (2017) chart out two common arguments for this failure: first, that the UN efforts have precluded a settlement to the conflict by pressing powerful states to negotiate when they were unprepared to do so, and, second, that the UN has legitimized Assad by insisting on negotiating with the regime, thus preventing the possibility of real peace emerging. Critiquing these two common narratives, the authors instead argue that the failure of the UN peace processes can be attributed to the systematic undermining of the UN processes by regional states who have privileged their own strategic interests over humanitarian or postconflict resolution needs. As discussed below, this means that regional states have pledged cosmetic support to the UN processes while putting forth their own strategies and plans for Syria.

The Moscow Process

The local freeze plans have had a lukewarm response in many Western capitals. For Russian officials, however, such plans have emerged as a parallel track to a recent Russian political initiative to end the conflict. Both de Mistura's plan and the Russian plan reflect alternatives to the Geneva process. Both were born out of the stagnation of the Geneva process and the recognition that it was not moving the parties any closer to a political solution.

In late 2014 the Russian Foreign Ministry proposed hosting a series of talks between regime officials and the Syrian opposition. Deputy Foreign Minister Mikhail Bogdanov was placed in charge of organizing the talks, which were to take place in early 2015. The attendees from the opposition consisted entirely of individuals and groups that were part of the regime's loyal opposition, not a serious threat to the regime. The five opposition parties represented at the talks were never serious actors in the uprising and have only survived as parties because of their loyalty to the regime, or, as one observer put it, they are "nothing more than the other face of the regime" (Pizzi, 2015).

Although the Russian Foreign Ministry declared that the basis of the Moscow process was the initial Geneva Communique, it is clear that they never took seriously the responsibility to address many of the deficiencies and problems of the Geneva process. Rather, the Moscow process merely reproduces the regime's narratives of the conflict and does not represent a serious attempt at reconciliation. For this reason, all major opposition parties and armed groups rejected the talks as illegitimate because they do not satisfy any of the key demands of the opposition, such as the necessity of a political transition, or fundamentally alter the regime's control of the political system.

The extent to which the Moscow process reflects the regime's strategic interests is reflected in the eleven Principles (Barmin, 2015) of a resolution adopted at the talks:

1. Preservation of the sovereignty of Syria
2. Countering international terrorism and fighting terrorism and extremism in Syria
3. Resolution of the Syrian crisis through peaceful political means on the basis of the Geneva Communique of 30 June 2012
4. Syria's future will be determined by the free and democratic expression of its people
5. Rejection of outside interference in Syria's affairs
6. Ensuring the preservation and continuity of state institutions, including the army
7. Ensuring civic peace through equality of all Syrians
8. Equality of all citizens before the law
9. Rejection of all foreign forces on Syrian territory without the consent of the Syrian government
10. An end to the occupation of the Golan Heights
11. Lifting of sanctions against Syria

Declarations that followed the adoption of the principles focused mainly on urging the international community to alleviate the humanitarian catastrophe and to support the regime's efforts to eradicate terrorism in Syria. As such, the negotiations avoided serious discussion of any of the substantive demands of the opposition and armed groups. In particular, the fate of President al-Assad was not a topic of discussion, and fundamental changes to the distribution of power through constitutional, legal, or political reforms were not taken seriously. This even led one of the delegates from the Syrian Kurdish community to declare that all of the negotiations and the adoption of principles actually reflected the regime's lack of desire for political change and refusal to recognize Kurdish autonomy and self-rule in the northeast.

Not surprisingly, Iran has supported the talks as an alternative to the Geneva process. And while the United States initially dismissed the talks, Russian Foreign Minister Lavrov and U.S. Secretary of State Kerry met in March 2015 to discuss the prospects of future talks and new diplomatic efforts to end the Syrian conflict. Ultimately, despite being competing alternatives and radically different visions of what a political solution in Syria could look like, the Geneva and Moscow processes suffer from major flaws that cast serious doubt on the prospects for diplomatic resolution to the conflict in the short term. First, the major international actors have not demonstrated a willingness to privilege a political solution over a military one, and neither have their proxies in Syria. The FSA has pledged lukewarm support to negotiations but it is unclear whether they would comply with any ceasefire or demilitarization measures. The remaining armed Fronts have all rejected international negotiations. Second, the negotiations have failed to demonstrate to the regime or opposition groups that negotiations are in their best interests. International mediation efforts have thus lacked incentives for parties to enter into serious political dialogue. This is in part an outcome of the regime's calculation that it has the military advantage, but it is also a product of the opposition's fragmentation, which has precluded the realization of a larger political solution to the problem that is inclusive of all major forces and which could guarantee a cessation of violence. Third, negotiations have not led to any tangible benefits for Syrians. It remains to be seen how de Mistura's plans for humanitarian aid will unfold but even on this issue of humanitarian access the regime has remained stubborn.

Russian intervention

Russia's intervention into the Syrian conflict began in September 2015 after a formal request from the Syrian regime. Up until that point, Russia had been the regime's staunchest ally, alongside Iran, and was responsible for political, military, and financial support that prevented the regime from collapse. At the international level, Russia had shielded the regime from censure and was one of the main reasons behind Western hesitation to intervene directly in the Syrian conflict. The regime's request for Russia to intervene must thus be seen as an act of weakness and not one of strength—despite the tremendous material and military support provided by Russia, the Syrian regime was unable to stem the tide of the conflict and was, at best, only able to maintain a stalemate. Syria's major regional supporter, Iran, explicitly approved the Russian intervention and provided political, if not material, support. While there is no clear consensus on why Iran would have done so, this has led to one observer referring to Iranian–Russian relations as a "marriage of convenience" (Kozhanov, 2016).

The intervention must thus be seen first and foremost as an attempt to break the military and political stalemate that defined the conflict up until that point. Why the Russian establishment favored intervention at that point, as opposed to earlier in the conflict, is a complicated question with multiple answers. They range from a genuine fear of the regime's collapse, a desire to test out new weaponry, a sense of impending victory, and a desire in balancing regional forces' power in Syria in Russia's favor. All of these explanations have some merit but are not sufficient to explain Russia's intervention. Regardless of the intention behind it, the intervention has had serious consequences for the conflict's trajectory.

The initial stages of the intervention did not reveal a clear, discernible military or correlate political strategy (Kaim and Tamminga, 2015). This fueled speculation among many inside and outside of Syria as to how Russia's long-term motivations—beyond regime preservation—were driving the intervention. This also raised questions about the extent to which Russia was committed to intervening and how much military power would be directed toward the Syrian conflict. The initial weeks of the intervention did not shed much insight into any of these issues and "strategic ambiguity" came to define the initial stages of the intervention (Sage and Davis, 2015).

Russian military planes commenced the intervention with attacks in the core and surrounding areas of Homs and Hama, two of the largest cities with a rebel presence. These attacks targeted various FSA and Islamist armed groups in the areas, the core of the armed opposition to the Syrian regime. Days later, Russian planes attacked ISIS and JAN targets in the Homs governorate and in the eastern parts of Syria, especially around Palmyra. Attacks were also recorded in Hama and Raqqa governorates against ISIS, Jan, and other Islamist armed groups.

As the intervention proceeded throughout the rest of the year, a two-pronged strategy slowly emerged. The first identifiable strategy was to suffocate supply lines of the various armed groups. The attacks against ISIS, for example, in Palmyra were mainly targeting the T-4 highway that was essential to linking ISIS areas in Raqqa governorate to Palmyra and further west in Syria. Highways, and not just command centers and training areas, became significant targets of Russian intervention. The second strategy that emerged reflected the deep, growing cooperation between Russian military forces and the regime-aligned forces on the ground. Aerial attacks were almost always followed by on-the-ground offensives by regime-aligned forces. Slowly, these forces were recapturing territories that armed groups withdrew from following Russian attacks.

By early 2016, the Russian intervention had expanded to include warships and submarines, with reports of large troop contingents operating on the battlefield. At this time, the first major rebel supply route was cut off by regime-aligned forces in Western Latakia governorate in areas that were used by armed groups to bring supplies and fighters from Turkey. The so-called Latakia strategy brought contiguous territory under regime control from Damascus to the Turkish border, the first time this had happened since early in the conflict. The focus on Latakia, and the quick success it yielded, portended the next months of the Russian intervention.

When the offensive started, many parts of Latakia governorate had been under rebel control. In fact, in late 2015, small villages and towns had changed control between regime and rebel forces as many as four times in a single month. The fighting there was intense and reflected the deep stalemates throughout the country. However, by December, joint Syrian-Russian aerial attacks, coupled with a Hizbollah-led ground offensive, captured the strategic mountainous areas and by early January 2016 armed groups controlled only a handful of small villages. Within a month, the entire governorate was under regime control. The recapture of Latakia governorate was the first in a series of relatively quick military victories.

The next major success also occurred in northwestern Syria where Russian and regime-aligned forces cut off a major rebel supply route from Turkey. From 2012 until early 2016, a supply route had been established that is often referred to as the Kilis highway as it begins in the Turkish city of that name and comes south across the Syrian border to Azaz and then into Aleppo. This was thus the most significant supply route for armed groups in Syria because it linked them to Turkey. By February 2016, however, the supply route was effectively cut off. Regime-aligned forces, led by Hizbollah, overtook rebel areas north of Aleppo near the besieged villages of Nubl and al-Zahra, while PYD-led forces, now a major player and beneficiary in the post-intervention conflict landscape, defeated rebels in and around Azaz, only a few kilometres from the Turkish border. The PYD forces cut off the major supply line—the Castello Road—leading directly into Aleppo City. Not only did the suffocation of the Kilis–Azaz supply route dramatically harm the rebels, it portended new forms of military cooperation in Syria in which the PYD-led SDF would play a major role (discussed below).

Such was the trajectory of the conflict in 2016. Russian-led aerial and maritime attacks, supported by ground troops drawn from a hodgepodge of regime-aligned forces, from local and regional militias to the SDF, slowly forced armed groups out of towns and villages and away from their supply routes. The suffocation of supply routes was the single most important factor in breaking the military stalemate in 2016.

Without supply routes, the ability of armed groups to sustain themselves, let alone govern areas under their control or fight on the battlefield, was severely undermined. Paradoxically, in the context of the retreat of armed groups and the increased cooperation of Russian, Syria, Lebanese, and Syrian Kurdish forces, a political solution to the conflict seemed plausible to contemplate.

Given their increased confidence and the speed at which rebel supply routes fell, the Russian government put forth a "cessation of hostilities" agreement, essentially a ceasefire, which would begin in late February 2016. While the collapse of the agreement was entirely predictable—the Russian government insisted on an exemption to attack "terrorist" targets—the ceasefire raised the possibility of a formula, albeit a dangerous one, for the cessation of major hostilities in Syria. Specifically, the Russian government's insistence on the possibility of a truce with some groups, while engaging in continued conflict with others, raised the spectre that the Syrian conflict could be both solved and continued at the same time. It would be "solved" insofar as major hostilities had subsided and all major armed groups had accepted the dictates of a Russian-led plan for Syria, while it "continued" in the form of sustained violence against any groups or areas seen as sympathetic to "terrorists," the convenient, catch-all label used to refer to all armed elements in Syria. This, of course, is not to absolve armed groups of their culpability in the destruction of Syria and the overall humanitarian crisis. Rather, it is to suggest that the Russian government wanted to hold the key for deciding what political actors can and cannot participate in any political agreement on Syria.

Indeed, such a vision for the future of Syria—one in which armed elements remain active in the country, thus justifying continued intervention—seems to have taken root among all of the major players by mid-2016. That virtually all of the ceasefire agreements signed by various armed groups and the Syrian regime collapsed is an indicator of how little faith either side had in them. Nevertheless, the political and military space for the armed groups, to say nothing of the political opposition, has shrunk significantly in the aftermath of the intervention, to the point where very few options remain. As I discuss later in the chapter, the space for conflict or negotiation between regime forces and rebel groups is so small that most observers have declared the conflict virtually over.

Yet there will indeed remain remnants of the conflict for years, if not decades, to come because the intervention has not entirely eliminated armed elements. Beginning in 2014, regime advances in and around key areas, especially in Homs and Hama cities, led to a series of negotiations between regime and rebel forces that led to the latter's guaranteed free passage out of the conflict zone, typically to Idlib. Since then, this strategy has been replicated in many other parts of the country, whereby besieged rebel groups were offered the opportunity to leave areas encircled by regime forces. These have been referred to by the regime as "reconciliation agreements" and typically exchanged regime control for the safe passageway of rebel fighters, along with their weapons and families, to other parts of the country. Because of the shifting nature of the conflict landscape, this often meant passage to Idlib—today, the last rebel stronghold in Syria. The "reconciliation agreements" have been a novel innovation in the regime's pacification strategy and have been employed throughout the country. While they have indeed reduced violence, serious analysis of their outcomes reveals that they have not alleviated the causes of conflict or initiated any substantive reconciliation processes (Adleh and Favier, 2017). Instead, they have been used as a strategy of pacification and displacement of civilian populations, exacerbating already difficult conditions.

These agreements have allowed armed elements to survive and persist in pockets of the country, with Idlib being the last major area of concentration for these groups. The FSA's Southern Front was decimated, ISIS's territorial control has shriveled away to virtually nothing, and Idlib, with its Islamist-dominated landscape, has emerged as the last bastion of any significant rebel control. Meanwhile, regime-aligned forces, such as Hizbollah, and those perniciously affiliated, such as the SDF, have increased their power and control of the conflict landscape, a landscape that looks significantly different than it did when the initial military stalemate began to take hold in 2013.

The Battle of Aleppo

Nowhere is the changing conflict landscape more evident than in the fate of Aleppo, Syria's second city and the site of massive, incomprehensible destruction and loss of human life. To understand the political and military significance of the Battle of Aleppo and its recapture by regime-aligned forces in late 2016, some background information on the city and its role in the uprising is important. Syria's commercial capital prior to the conflict, Aleppo had a population of around 2.5 million spread across more than fifty distinct neighborhoods. Of this population, approximately half were living in large informal settlements (Aleppo Urban Development Project, 2009). The city's population as well as the number of informal settlements had grown significantly since the 1970s and 1980s when rural migration induced by structural changes in the agricultural sector brought economic migrants to the city. The population growth did not disrupt the social landscape of the city, with Christians, Kurds, Alawites, Circassians, Turkmen, Yezidi, and Ismaili communities co-existing with the majority Sunni Arab population.

During the uprising in 2011, local Aleppines did not protest in large numbers against the regime, nor did armed groups emerge from within the city's civilian population. Indeed, until mid-2012, Aleppo was relatively stable compared to other parts of Syria. However, as armed groups, especially those affiliated with the FSA, made repeated advances in the urban peripheries, military attacks began in the main cities, including Aleppo. By 2012, FSA-affiliated brigades had entered Aleppo and established a presence. Regime contraction in the city and the onset of conflict fatigue and depleted military resources meant that significant parts of Aleppo fell to rebel hands rather rapidly. By 2013, Aleppo had been carved up between regime forces and the armed opposition, which were increasingly in conflict with one another over control of key supply routes in and out of Aleppo. The division and fragmentation of Aleppo today reflects the stalemate that emerged around mid-2013. While the front lines of the conflict have not significantly changed since then, the composition of the armed groups within the majority of the city has indeed changed, with varying battalions and fronts taking and exchanging power with one another. While the conflicts between armed groups are complex, control over supply routes is an important factor. The Killis corridor that links northern Aleppo areas to the Turkish border crossing at Bab al-Salamah, which supplies everything from humanitarian goods to food to weapons, has been a particularly important supply route.

All major armed coalitions were present in Aleppo on the eve of the Russian intervention because of its strategic access to Turkish supply routes, which are essential to the survival of the armed groups. This is why many of them engage in conflict to control highways, routes, checkpoints, and border crossings. Such geographic control allows these groups to reap the benefits of the war economy and maintain their military entrenchment in Aleppo. The FSA's Command was once strong in Aleppo but shared control of the non-regime areas with the SILF, the SRF, PYD, and Jabhat an-Nusra, all major coalitions with affiliated brigades scattered throughout the city and its countryside. In other words, virtually all major armed actors were present in Aleppo and tried to lay claim to part of its territory. Relations between these groups were rarely cooperative and they were mostly engaged in conflict with one another as they attempted to expand their geographic and military control. In addition to this, regime forces, including the Syrian Arab Army, National Defense Forces, and militia groups, were present in Aleppo as well.

Aleppo city and its countryside were also home to thousands of fighters with fluid affiliations with larger units and brigades. The many fighters divided into smaller groupings never coalesced into a larger unit capable of coordinating and overtaking regime forces. Rather, the opposite occurred. Most fighters turned against each other and allowed the regime forces to remain entrenched in the parts of the city under their control. All of these coalitions alternated between conflict and cooperation in vying for as much control of the city as possible. Over time, this fluidity made defense of areas under rebel control virtually impossible. Years of barrel bombs and relentless aerial attacks slowly began to shrink the non-regime areas until finally, in late 2016, Aleppo fell to regime forces.

Aleppo was thus seen as a "prize" in the larger conflict and, like Damascus, the group that controlled it was to have a military and political upper hand on adversaries. Its strategic significance paralleled its emotional significance and thus the loss of Aleppo to regime forces was a major blow to rebel prospects and a major boon to regime loyalists, who, perhaps rightly, saw in the Battle of Aleppo the beginning of the end of the Syrian conflict. Indeed, events since then have suggested that most armed and opposition groups have conceded defeat after the Battle as major supply routes and the prospects for rebel unification have disappeared in the aftermath of the Russian intervention. Meanwhile, the Battle of Aleppo reveals the basic strategy of the regime and its Russian allies toward rebel areas: they are besieged, pummeled into submission, and then offered meagre humanitarian relief (Böttcher, 2017). This strategy positions the regime as liberators among the besieged populations.

Impacts of the Russian intervention

The Russian intervention so fundamentally changed the trajectory of the Syrian conflict that the major drivers and dynamics that had characterized the political and military stalemate up until 2015 have radically shifted. Indeed, there is no more serious talk of a stalemate in Syria. Quite the opposite has occurred, in fact, as most observers now have set their sights on the coming reconstruction period as the next phase of Syria's conflict. But, like most conflicts, Syria's is not linear. There is no clear, definitive break between a period of conflict and peace, of violence and nonviolence. Many patterns established during the first few years of Syria's conflict will indeed persist for years and decades to come—war economies, criminality, violence against civilians, poverty, displacement, and international intervention—regardless of whether this new period of the conflict suggests otherwise. We can certainly expect the conflict to endure in many forms.

This means that while the political and military stalemate has been broken, a new conflict order has emerged. In the following section, I explore two key impacts of the Russian intervention that will shape Syria's immediate political future. The first concerns the rise of the SDF and what this may mean for the future political order after Russian intervention. The second impact is in the new political process aimed at imposing a postconflict order in Syria. Whereas a political solution to the conflict was beyond the commitment of the major players in the first few years (as discussed above), today the Russian intervention has created a new framework for a political process that has the support of former regional adversaries and the regime itself. No matter how brutal or undemocratic, or how the peace will perpetuate the war, the reality of the Astana process is that, for the first time since 2011, there is a political formula on offer for the future of Syria that most major players have acquiesced to and endorse.

The rise of the SDF

In the aftermath of the Russian intervention, the SDF have become one of the most powerful and politically important actors in the Syrian conflict. The rise of the SDF, however, predated the intervention, as they have functioned as an umbrella for armed groups since 2014. There are two principal factors behind the rise of the SDF and its central role in Syria's conflict today that this section explores. First, the SDF has since 2014 been the main actor fighting ISIS in the northeast of the country. For this reason, the SDF has been the direct beneficiary of U.S. airstrikes, and some of the brigades with the SDF have received material and logistical support as well. The SDF has thus been a direct beneficiary of the Western interventions against ISIS and has served essentially as a Western proxy force in the fight against ISIS. Second, the SDF, and its principal Kurdish factions, have had a stable, if uneasy, relationship with the Syrian regime. At many times since the conflict began, Kurdish parties have been accused of complicity with the regime and many oppositionists have long accused the PYD of supporting the regime. In response, many PYD officials and supporters argue that they remain committed to political change in Syria, if not to the tactics and methods adopted by armed groups. The reality, however, is murkier than either opposition or PYD supporters suggest, as the regime and PYD have co-existed in a conflict that has thus far been conducive to their limited (if not public) cooperation (Stein, 2017). As we will see below, there are limits to the cooperation.

While the SDF is dominated by the PYD, it does contain many Arab, Turkmen, and Syriac armed groups under its umbrella, which gives it the appearance of being a broad, multi-confessional coalition. In reality, the SDF is a PYD-dominated actor. While officially founded in 2015, the SDF brought together a number of brigades that had already been fighting together since 2014 against ISIS in the north and northeast of Syria. These groups included the Syriac Military Council, an Assyrian- and Syriac-armed brigade formed in 2013, the Kurdish Women's Protection Units (YPJ), the YPG, and five other brigades that had already been cooperating on the battlefield under Syrian Kurdish coordination. Since the formation of the SDF a number of other armed brigades have joined the network and fought under its central command.

There are a number of reasons behind the expansion of the SDF, but perhaps the most important is their battlefield successes. These successes were directly tied to both U.S. and Russian intervention, which provided the aerial cover for ground movements. Much like in the rest of Syria, aerial intervention provided the immediate cause of battlefield changes in favor of the regime and its aligned forces. As SDF forces advanced against ISIS, more and more brigades pledged allegiance to the SDF and began fighting under their banner. As the SDF advanced and absorbed these new groups, many of which were localized, smaller units that had been operating in specific geographic areas of the country, they began to create military councils under which these new groups could operate and function.

Indeed, this is precisely how the advance of SDF forces has unfolded in Syria: battlefield victories are followed by the absorption of smaller fighting units that are organized under the institutional structure of a military council that is given responsibility for securing newly acquired areas. By the end of 2015, the SDF had absorbed a mix of tribal militias and former FSA battalions into its structure, almost doubling the size of the group. In mid-2016, the SDF had tripled in the number of aligned battalions, many of which were not Syrian Kurds, but mostly Arabs and Turkmen. Some of the groups that had joined the SDF had existed prior to this period, but most were formed hastily out of the aftermath of SDF victories, suggesting opportunism. Other groups, such as the Free Raqqa Brigade (FRB), simply changed their names and joined the SDF. The FRB had previously fought under the decidedly Islamist name of the Jihad in the Path of God Brigade. The emergence of such new formations to take advantage of the SDF advances has persisted since.

As more battalions were absorbed into the SDF and more territory came under its control, the SDF had to create subsidiary structures. These came in the form of Military Councils. The first of these was created around March and April 2016 when the Manbij Military Council was created with the aim of taking over, securing, and governing Manbij. The Council absorbed battalions that had been active in the immediate area, including the Northern Sun Battalion, which had absorbed a number of unaffiliated fighters by 2016, and was heavily dependent on U.S.-led airstrikes against ISIS-held areas in and around Manbij. A year later, in March 2017, the Council had successfully controlled the city and had formally relinquished control—without conflict—to the Syrian regime. This was not simply an act of restoring sovereignty to the regime but an attempt to create battlefield distance between the SDF and Turkish army forces as well as Turkish-supported brigades operating west of Manbij. The complexities of the new battlefield realities often brought SDF-regime-Turkish forces together into both conflict and cooperation.

Other councils were created as the SDF made similar advances. A few months after the creation of the Manbij Military Council, the al-Bab Military Council was created in al-Bab. Not long afterwards, the Jarablus Military Council was created in Jarablus and its surrounding areas, followed by the Deir ez-Zor Military Council close to the end of 2016. In each case, the Military Councils were established to coordinate battalion and brigade armed activity in the specified areas. In this way, the SDF was able to both absorb new fighters and their units, while giving them a clear command structure under which to operate. As the SDF expanded, so did the central power of its main power broker, the PYD.

However, the expansion of the SDF coalition has not been without its own military and political problems. While the SDF has been successful in articulating themselves to the U.S. and Western observers in general as a multi-ethnic, multi-sectarian coalition, it is unclear how much legitimacy the SDF indeed has on the ground. Whether fighters have pledged allegiance to the SDF out of loyalty or expedience is unclear. Considering the vast numbers of defections to the SDF it is likely that loyalty is one of the more unlikely reasons. There have also been substantiated reports of SDF infighting, particularly among groups that were once loyal to Turkish intelligence. Other SDF brigades have confronted the PYD on issues of regime loyalty and support. Thus, the expansion of the SDF has not meant cohesion or continuity. Indeed, the flurry of battalions and brigades rushing to join the SDF is typical of battlefield alliance shifts in Syria. By 2017, many former FSA brigades were actually defecting back to the regime-aligned forces, creating a complicated, tenuous, and violent game of conflict and cooperation in northern Syria.

The SDF has been the beneficiary, thus far, of these games as U.S. air cover has provided some level of protection against Turkish incursions and regime frustration with political developments in the Kurdish areas, which are two substantive outcomes of the SDF advances (Knapp et al., 2016, p. 252). The Turkish regime has not viewed the SDF's advances favorably. On the one hand, the emergence of a contiguous, Kurdish-governed territory along Turkey's border is inimical to core Turkish regional interests. On the other hand, the SDF has proven to be much stronger on the battlefield against both ISIS and Turkish-led brigades. Repeatedly throughout the conflict's latter years, the Turkish army has threatened to intervene to prevent the joining of Kurdish-led territory. At times, these interventions have occurred but they have been limited and targeted. The intolerability of a Kurdish-dominated order on its border has been enough to warrant Turkish intervention. There are thus limits to the SDF's battlefield expansion. Similarly, the expansion of the SDF has changed the political landscape of the Syrian conflict in two main ways: first, with the rise of the DFNS as an administrative and institutional reality, and, second, with the rise of a new "Kurdish question" that demands political resolution, *vis-à-vis* the Syrian regime, in Syria's political future.

Geneva, Astana, and beyond

The Astana talks represent a radically different approach to peacemaking in Syria than that proffered by the Geneva process. Although the two are intended to be complementary efforts to resolve the Syrian crisis, the Geneva process lacks substance, a legitimate process, or buy-in from the major parties. In many ways, then, the Astana talks are a more accurate indicator of what Syria's postconflict future may look like. If that is the case, then the ideals of the revolution that brought people to the streets en masse from 2011 onwards will have been seriously betrayed.

It is important to consider not only what solutions Astana proposes, but what problems it presents as needing to be solved. One of the significant features of Astana is the role prescribed to international actors as caretakers of a post-conflict Syria. While not framed as such, the Astana process has produced a framework for "de-escalation zones" in which there would be an agreed-upon cessation of hostilities between regime and rebel forces (al-Jazeera, 2017). These zones would be patrolled by foreign troops and monitored by one of the three tripartite powers participating in the talks: Russia, Iran, and Turkey. Essentially, the de-escalation zones are believed to be future zones of influence in which each of the three countries exercises major influence over the political actors in that territory. While the central state would obviously continue to exist, its sovereign powers and reach would be severely compromised by what amounts to the creation of guarantor powers. In this way, the Astana process articulates the Syrian problem as one of international rivalry that can be solved through carving out particular spaces for each country to exercise influence in as "guarantors" (Russian Federation, 2017).

A second important feature is the total absence of a political process to accompany the ceasefire. This is the central criticism of opposition groups, who have been reluctant to support a process that will not lead to some form of political change, whether in the leadership of the country or the basic structure of the political system. Political reforms or changes of any sort are simply not on offer in the Astana process. For many, including the increasingly irrelevant United Nations, this is because a framework for a political process exists in the form of the Geneva process. For Staffan de Mistura, the Astana and Geneva processes are linked, as each attempts to accomplish what the other is incapable of securing: Astana seeks the ceasefire that has eluded Geneva; while Geneva seeks the political solution that evades Astana.

The main problem with this thinking is that it assumes that the parties are equally committed to both processes. This is a significantly flawed way of seeing the two processes; while they may be parallel, they are certainly not equal. This is in large part because the post-Russian intervention period is one in which the regime and its allies have a serious battle-field advantage such that they are not inclined to yield any meaningful political concessions or to engage in large-scale restructuring of the political system. After years of fighting and bloodshed, so the argument goes among regime loyalists, now, after gaining the military advantage, is not the time for political concessions. Whereas the Geneva process attempts to extract such concessions from the regime and to support a restructuring of the political system inclusive of general opposition demands and some opposition actors, the Astana process does no such thing, instead maintaining the political status quo under the umbrella of dividing Syria into territorial spheres of influence.

Thus, while the United Nations has blessed the Astana process, concretized with the passing of Resolution 2336 in December 2016, they are distinct processes that will have radically different outcomes if they ever were realized. It is worth delving into the content and substance of the Astana process to get a better sense of precisely why this is the case. The process began, not as a multilateral effort among concerned states, but as an agreement between the Russian and Turkish leaders, Vladimir Putin and Recep Tayyip Erdogan that was entered into in early December 2016. Not long after that, Iran was invited to form a third in a tripartite power to oversee the talks. On 20 December 2016 the United Nations passed Resolution 2254 calling for a ceasefire and political settlement in Syria, and 11 days later Resolution 2336 was passed in support of the Astana process.

When formal negotiations began in late December 2016 they were premised on a ceasefire between the regime and various rebel forces. Various groups, especially ISIS, JAN, and the YPG, were excluded from the ceasefire, and thus from the negotiations. This reflected an exclusion of the major armed groups that were driving the Syrian conflict. A number of armed groups did agree to the terms of the ceasefire and were thus invited to participate in the Astana process, including: Sham Legion, Jaysh al-Islam, The Levant Front, Jabhat ahl al-Sham, and, notably, Ahrar al-Sham. The latter group was by far the most powerful of the armed groups invited to Astana. Perhaps in an attempt to save face and maintain credibility among the armed groups, Ahrar al-Sham's leadership vigorously denied agreeing to the ceasefire. Although denying their participation in the talks, the groups' leadership has been deeply involved in them. Mohammed Alloush, the political head of Jaysh al-Islam, has assumed responsibility for the negotiations on behalf of the armed groups. In contrast, the Geneva talks are led by the Higher Negotiations Committee (HNC), which is made up of the political opposition. Thus, Astana gives agency and legitimacy to the military actors, while the Geneva process favors political actors who are not major players on the battlefield.

The participants at Astana differ and the basis of the negotiations is radically different than the Geneva process negotiations. The Astana discussions are more reflective of the regime and its allies' visions for a future Syria, one that excludes major opposition groups. On offer are a series of major reforms that were entirely crafted by Russia, including a new draft constitution for Syria, a model of decentralization and a new federal structure, a slight shift in power and responsibility from the Presidency to the Parliament, and the enshrinement of secularism in a new constitution.

The progression of the Astana process, despite its initial obstacles, contrasts sharply with the parallel Geneva process, which has continued despite changing battlefield dynamics. The third round of Geneva talks were shortlived because a regime offensive north of Aleppo ruined any possible opportunity at progress. Regardless, the HNC, which led the Geneva talks, was not excited about the prospects of negotiating with the regime in the first place. The talks, which were supposed to begin in early 2016, accomplished nothing because of the regime's offensive. Prior to the beginning of the talks, the HNC had refused to attend until a ceasefire had been agreed upon. Unable to guarantee a ceasefire, UN envoy de Mistura was left without any way to incentivize regime or opposition participation.

All was not lost, however, as a fourth round of Geneva talks began again a year later in February and March 2017. These talks did not include direct negotiations between regime and opposition officials and they only lasted eight days. Given how disastrous the previous rounds of talks were, this was a major achievement. Nevertheless, the Geneva process remained weak, ineffective, and for all intents and purposes a wholly cosmetic process that the major players do not take seriously. Besides the exclusion of major domestic actors, such as the PYD, and regional ones, such as Iran, there is the substantive issue of whether the opposition participants have any legitimacy to negotiate a political solution to the Syrian crisis. Perhaps the best indicator of this problem is the total rejection of the role the HNC has played in the negotiations, and indeed the negotiations themselves, by the major armed groups inside of Syria. Thus, although both Astana and Geneva are supposed to be based on realizing UNSCR 2254, which calls for a postconflict transition in Syria that includes a new constitution and political structure, among other things, the reality is that the latter process is more reflective of the battlefield and the major players subjugating Syria. This is perhaps why many consider the Astana process as the most realistic way forward for the Syrian conflict, regardless of how problematic it is.

Conclusion: Internationalizing Syria's future beyond the stalemate

In response to the question of whether the Syrian regime has prevailed in the conflict, former U.S. Ambassador to Syria Robert Ford stated this: "Yes. The war is winding down little by little. Assad has won and he will stay [in power]. He may never be held accountable, and Iran will be in Syria to stay. This is the new reality that we have to accept, and there isn't much we can do about it" (Karam, 2017). Such thinking was impossible prior to the Russian intervention, when the consensus was that Syria was locked in a stalemate. This chapter has outlined how attempts to solve the Syrian conflict through a political process have failed and how Russian military intervention into the conflict made a political process possible. That process, however, reflects an imagined Syrian order far from the hopes and dreams of the opposition, protesters, and anti-regime activists. It is a far cry from a perfect vision for regime loyalists either, as decision-making and sovereignty have been diminished as Syria falls under the tutelage of a tripartite agreement between Russia, Iran, and Turkey.

For decades Syrians and the regime that ruled over them prided themselves on their sovereignty and sovereign decision-making. In the decades to come, Syrian political authorities will be beholden to regional powers whose interests are inevitably at odds with those of average Syrians. Syria's conflict was internationalized virtually from the start, but the Astana talks have set in motion a process whereby Syria will be geographically and politically divided among various external patrons who will exercise substantive control over Syrian political and economic life. Syria's future is thus one of shared suzerainty between Turkey, Iran, and Russia, the tripartite powers that have emerged from the failed peace processes of 2011–2016 and who have laid claim to patronage over Syria by virtue of their military strength on the battlefield. The peripheralization of Qatar, Saudi Arabia, and Western countries should not be mistaken as a victory for Syrian sovereignty or for the Syrian regime. One set of overlords was simply exchanged for another.

As Syria's future becomes internationalized, the battlefield will continue to shift and change. Despite the growing battle-field supremacy of regime-aligned forces, there is no reason to believe that the armed groups will simply disappear. There are entrenched interests that have developed over the course of the conflict, and the continued misery and poverty induced by the war will continue to incentivize violence and criminality. Their capacity has been degraded but there has also been a dramatic change in the composition of the armed groups inside of Syria. The major players today are no longer ISIS and JAN, but Hizbollah, the SDF, and HTS. The latter has come to dominate the armed groups' landscape. Today, most armed groups are not fighting for regime change but are deeply embedded in economies of violence that are fueling the conflict. Syria's war economies exist alongside battles for territory and battlefield strength. The two often intersect and cohere.

This all raises the question of what kind of peace is Syria headed toward. That question is taken up in the concluding chapter.

Conclusion: The Coming _____
Authoritarian Peace

In the preceding pages, I have attempted to outline what I see as the main factors that gave rise to a political and military stalemate and the consequences of the rupture of that stalemate after the Russian military intervention that began in 2015. The goal of my analysis in this book has been to introduce readers to the main parties to the conflict and also to help the reader think analytically about why the Syrian conflict has taken on this particular trajectory. At this point, it is worth cautioning you, once again, about thinking that the conflict has a linear path. As I have tried to describe throughout the book, the conflict has many dynamics that are driving violence, the humanitarian crisis, and, ultimately, the prospects for a political resolution. With this in mind, it is difficult to chart what the future may hold for the millions of Syrians for whom the only certainty right now is uncertainty. Today, many analysts have declared the conflict virtually over. This is perhaps one thing that regime loyalists and oppositionists can agree on. A cursory view of the analysis of Syria today demonstrates a shift from thinking about battlefield alliances and territorial fragmentation to questions around the coming reconstruction period. Thus, rather than asking how or why battlefield changes are occurring, analysts have begun asking how best to direct reconstruction resources toward certain ends. Long gone are serious discussions of Syrian political life after the collapse of the regime.

In this chapter, I consider what peace options were available for the Syrian conflict, what peace options are emerging in relation to events on the ground, and what an alternative peace could look like. The contradiction and tension between the latter two—the reality and the vision—hold in them the key for Syria's future and will determine the key question facing Syrians and the world today: under what conditions will peace come to Syria, and how can violence and conflict, today and in the future, be addressed?

Between liberal and authoritarian peace

The approach preferred by the international community to solve violent conflicts is that of liberal peace. This takes as its starting point the need to integrate multiple actors into the postconflict state. The models articulated by the Geneva process are largely based on the liberal peace, which has been the basis of many ideas about the Syrian conflict, including ideas about transitional government. In the liberal peace approach, planners argue that the establishment of strong state institutions is the best means of resolving conflict. This is what Beswick (2009) calls the "single sovereign" problem. Planners attempt to reinscribe sovereignty into the postconflict state by strengthening state institutions and integrating former adversaries into the new state. In this model, conflict is disincentivized by offering the material and political benefits of institutional access to the former conflict participants through their cooptation and integration into the postconflict order. These rewards come in the form of official positions, bureaucratic appointments, and so on. One only needs to look to Syria's neighbor Lebanon for an excellent example of a liberal peace approach to conflict resolution. The logic of this approach is simple: economic and political power accrued from integration into the state outweigh the benefits of conflict. Strengthening state institutions makes the sovereign state (rather than the battlefield) the locus of deliberation and debate, the central provider and distributor of services and aid, and reestablishes the state's monopoly on violence.

These approaches are based on the faulty assumption that conflict occurs solely because different actors seek access to the state. This premise is extremely problematic in most conflict spaces but especially so in Syria, where the conflict has evolved from demands for political rights and regime change to a complicated violent conflict in which different groups pursue radically different and competing agendas, very few of which have anything to do with integrating into a post-conflict state order. Today, the conflict requires resolution on multiple levels, beyond a single bargain between the major regional powers or a political agreement that integrates warlords and oppositionists into a rejuvenated state.

To this end, a number of new and old formulas were proposed by commentators to solve the Syrian conflict. The diverse range of policies includes a commitment to arming the rebels, relegitimizing the regime and making it a counterterrorism partner, economically and administratively supporting non-regime areas, military intervention, reinvigorating the Geneva process to undermine Astana, or linking resolution of the Syrian conflict to a larger regional settlement. Yet, these policies aimed at resolving the Syrian conflict do not meaningfully address its underlying causes and the consequences of its violent evolution. The goal of most peace agreements is simply to stop violence and not to rectify the social and political catastrophes wrought by it. Indeed, the liberal peace approach is the standard approach to conflict resolution and has produced the norms, strategies, and expectations of most planners' and analysts' approaches to resolving the Syrian conflict.

An important intervention into the debate about the utility of the liberal peace approach that is directly relevant to the Syrian case has been provided by David Lewis, who argues that the liberal peace approach's hegemony among policy makers reflects a type of Western-centrism that takes Westphalian sovereignty as the aspirant form of political authority in the international system (Lewis, 2017). Consequently, by centralizing and normalizing the liberal peace we miss how other illiberal and authoritarian models for peacemaking have emerged in today's world. He calls these new forms of peacemaking "authoritarian peace" and cites Russia's bombardment of Aleppo as a key example of the structure and form of this approach to peace, which is neither liberal nor peaceful. The major point that Lewis is making, and which is relevant for our purposes here, is that there are other ways in which states can and do make peace beyond the liberal model. Those forms of peacemaking ultimately reproduce an authoritarian, illiberal order, not a liberal one. The elements of Syria's emergent authoritarian peace are explored in the subsequent section.

Syria's authoritarian peace

A liberal peace, let alone a progressive postconflict polity, has not emerged in Syria. The momentum today in the aftermath of the Russian intervention is toward an authoritarian peace in which regional and domestic actors cohere around illiberal, authoritarian practices. We can identify at least five features of Syria's coming authoritarian peace based on the Astana process (discussed in Chapter Five).

Regional suzerainty

The central feature of the Astana process is that it cedes major political decisions to a tripartite alliance of regional powers: Russia, Iran, and Turkey. These three countries have emerged as the most influential and important actors in the conflict today, largely at the expense of the Arab Gulf states who were informally aligned with Turkey for years during the conflict. Today, Turkey, which once actively called for the removal of the Assad regime and is directly responsible for some of the Syrian devastation, has shifted its policy 180 degrees to now support the continuation of the regime in more or less its current form. The three countries will shape the future direction of the country's foreign policy and will exercise de facto veto power over policies that are in their zones of influence. For Turkey, these zones of influence are in the northern borderlands, an important concession given the emergence of the DFNS and a militarized Syrian Kurdish element that could seriously threaten Turkish interests and ignite conflict in Turkey proper.

In exchange for a major role in Syria's future, Turkey has been forced to reduce support and cover for the major armed groups that it had been supporting. This has left those groups without a major patron and has isolated them, militarily, materially, and politically, from further support. Many of these groups showed up at Astana reluctantly, which reflected their battlefield weakness and their susceptibility to Turkish political pressure. Some of the major issues moving forward are whether the regional tripartite powers can keep their end of the bargain and ensure that the armed groups (whether regime or rebel forces) respect ceasefires, whether the regime itself will accept suzerainty, and whether the tripartite powers will maintain enough coordination to prevent violent episodes among competing battlefield loyalists.

In with the old, out with the new

Almost none of the political opposition demands are realized in the emergent authoritarian peace. The one possible exception is a clause in the draft constitution put forth by Russia that shifts some of the power from the Presidency to the Parliament. Yet, beyond this, none of the major political reforms advocated for by the opposition, let alone removal of the President himself, have been realized. This is simply a re-rigging of the Syrian political architecture to shore up the regime. While over the long term a strong Syrian Parliament may prove vibrant and a major center of power beyond the Presidency, it is certainly not the major concession oppositionists fought and lost their lives over. Similarly, Syria's draft constitution entrenches secularism even further by abolishing Islamic jurisprudence as a source of law.

Two other elements of power sharing have been proposed but are complicated by the presence of the DFNS administration. These are provisions for decentralized authorities to emerge in a newly designated federalist system. This could conceivably pave the way for integrating the DFNS into a federalist Syrian structure, despite this being against the wishes of the Syrian regime (Said, 2016). These proposals are consistent with the efforts to decenter the power of the Presidency, but it is unclear whether they will be accepted by the regime or how the federalist structure will actually materialize. The larger point here is that these minor concessions do not represent the kind of regime change envisioned by oppositionists.

Regional conflict complex

Syria is not only subject to the tripartite rule of regional powers; it is now embedded in a regional conflict complex (Pugh et al., 2014) that stretches across its borders. While Hizbollah and Lebanese army forces battled armed groups in Arsal on the Lebanese-Syrian border, evacuees were being shuttled to the Iraqi-Syrian border in a prisoner exchange deal. Shifting armed groups from place to place within Syria and the region has become a common and disturbing trend in the Syrian conflict. In the aftermath of ceasefires, armed fighters were given passage, in many cases to Idlib, in return for giving up fighting in specific areas.

Another element of the emergent regional conflict complex is that various states retain the right to intervene should they choose to do so. Turkey continuously threatens intervention against the SDF even though it is committed to the Astana process, the U.S. continues to attack ISIS forces, and Russian forces have not declared any intention to leave Syrian soil. Quite the opposite, in fact, as it is expected that the Russian military presence will increase in the years to come. There is also increased threat from Israel (Calamur, 2017), which continues to bomb Syrian territory at will and has declared an increased Iranian presence in Syria as grounds for further attacks. Prior to 2011, the Syrian regime had been successful in maintaining a cold peace with the Israelis for forty years, and in preventing any foreign role that undermined state sovereignty, as happened in Lebanon—ironically during the years of the Syrian presence. Such realities are no more.

De-escalation and continued conflict

The Astana process does not actually conceive of a total elimination of violence. Instead, it identifies four de-escalation zones in which armed groups can continue to be present but are safe for humanitarian relief and refugee return. These are in Idlib province, the Al-Rastan area north of Homs, Eastern Ghouta, and southern areas around Dar'a and al-Quneitra. The process does not contain any pretensions toward a full return of Syrian sovereignty or the extension of regime control over all the territory. Instead, what the de-escalation zones accomplish is a temporary truce to facilitate some relief while maintaining the right of armed groups to exist and operate in these areas. Any breaking of the ceasefire by the armed groups would stop humanitarian aid and relief.

The larger point here is that the Astana process accepts the continued presence of armed groups and the possibility of continued violence in the future. How these armed groups respond to the ceasefires and the political process in general will determine the future of violence in the country. If the authoritarian peace is as suffocating and violent as the conflict itself, these de-escalation zones are likely to remain anything but.

Socioeconomic deprivation

Despite repeated reference to humanitarian relief, there are no serious reconstruction plans for Syria to alleviate the horrific socioeconomic deprivation wrought by the conflict. Syria's reconstruction process will be ad hoc, disconnected from larger policy goals, and likely to concentrate in regime loyalist areas. Alongside the continued presence of armed groups and the constant threat of intervention from one of a number of regional states, the continued socioeconomic deprivation experienced by Syrians is unlikely to be alleviated anytime soon.

What, then, does the authoritarian peace solve? The emergent order undermines Syrian sovereignty, subjects the state and its citizens to a violent regional conflict complex, and fails to address the long-term generational needs of Syrians who have suffered tremendously through war. The authoritarian peace, in contrast to the liberal peace, does not carry with it the pretensions to sovereign re-inscription into the state, liberal and democratic politics, or robust relief and reconstruction. In many ways, the brief discussion of the five features here reflects the actual designs of the authoritarian peace: more or less cessation of violence, underpinned by regional agreements to commit more violence if necessary, legitimized by cosmetic political reforms that may not have a serious impact on the distribution of political power, and the continued support of a hollowed-out regime that oversees a weak and inefficient bureaucracy incapable of carrying out reconstruction plans, let alone financing them. This "better-than-conflict" peace is exactly what it promises to deliver: reduced violence and regime continuity.

Conflict legacies .

This concluding section asks a question that should dominate discussion concerning Syria for decades to come: how does the emergent order confront the long-term consequences of the Syrian conflict? Here, I identify three issues—fragmentation, a social and humanitarian crisis, and reconstruction—that are unaddressed in the emergent authoritarian peace.

Fragmentation

During the course of the conflict, Syria was de facto divided into competing centers of authority and control. The country's northwestern, southern, and northeastern areas were divided from one another and from the central heartland as competing authorities, from ISIS to the PYD, took control over territory and established alternative centers of administrative and political power. While many of these governance arrangements were ad hoc and reflected battlefield alliances, and were thus temporary, they have left a lasting legacy for the Syrian population. For many Syrians, in the absence of the state, armed groups and their attendant administrative apparatuses became the sole source of services and justice. The country was thus both territorially and administratively fragmented. Syrian children's education—when they received it—was severely disjointed and based on radically different curricula from others. Justice and law became subject to a series of legal courts, ranging from revolutionary courts that began in Manbij to the Shari'a courts that came to dominate the legal landscape in the northwest of the country. Various laws—mostly not codified and thus open to interpretation—were created in different parts of the country, reflecting the aspirations and disciplinary impulses of the various armed groups that happened to be governing over an area. Public executions in ISIS areas, for example, became common. While these temporary, ad hoc architectures of governance exist in virtually all conflicts, they are rarely integrated in any meaningful way into the postconflict order. In many ways, this reflects the liberal peace approach to re-inscribing sovereignty into the central state, but it can also be seen as an effect of the decentralized and informal ways in which administrative power emerges during the conflict. Carpenter et al. (2013) have referred to these forms of governance as "alternative" in that they represent a temporary constellation of actors who emerge to fulfill specific administrative needs in local areas. This has meant that, in some areas of the country, Syrians have gone years without any administrative relationship to the central state, as the armed groups controlled all issues of basic governance and justice. While the long-term impacts of such arrangements are difficult to gauge, we can identify a number of ways in which fragmentation has affected Syrians and their relationship to the state. First, many Syrians have figured out how to live without the state. This has increased their dependency on armed groups, of course, but also on informality and criminality. The return of the state, so to speak, in areas that were previously under rebel control does not mean that the state will function smoothly and that residents will continue to refer to the state for anything other than birth, death, and marriage certificates. Even in areas under regime control, regime-aligned militias have taken on roles for justice, dispute mediation, and welfare provision similar to those that armed groups provided in non-regime areas. The rise of these new authorities undermines the authority and legitimacy of the state while giving Syrians alternative means of procuring goods and services. This legacy will not easily go away. Second, the Syrian criminal code, its education curriculum, and indeed the entire architecture of justice and laws, has been turned inside out by the conflict as competing practices and institutions took root. Sewing back together anything resembling a national policy on these major issues and laws will be difficult. Again, while the state may be able to ostensibly extend its violent authority to many parts of the country, it will find it difficult to assert its bureaucratic authority to shape, control, and implement national policies, whether in health care or education. This portends a continued disconnected future for Syrians, especially those in remote areas or areas that are still experiencing violence. Finally, Syrians have grown accustomed to making demands on authorities other than the state. In some cases, these demands have been institutionalized, such as in the case of the DFNS, where new curriculum has emerged, along with a radically different legal system from that of the central state. In such cases, how the DFNS gets integrated, or not, into the future political system will have serious consequences on relations between the state and its citizens, how the latter make political demands, and what the expectations are of political authorities moving forward.

Social and humanitarian crisis

The demands of ending violence in many conflict zones usually outweigh agreement over other key areas of postconflict life. In many postconflict countries, social policy is severely neglected at the expense of purely political questions. To put it simply, postconflict planners focus almost exclusively on the political and institutional arrangements of the state at the expense of thinking about key questions of social provision and social policy more broadly. Here, social policy refers to policies that directly affect the lives of those in postconflict zones, whether related to housing, food distribution, employment, services, or, in the case of displaced people, repatriation. Many of these areas are severely neglected in postconflict spaces; in perpetrating such neglect, planners unintentionally reproduce grievances and problems associated with the conflict.

In Iraq, for example, the Coalition Provisional Authority (CPA) had no defined social policy when it took over control of Iraq. The set of ideologically driven policies pursued by the CPA disempowered the state and dramatically reduced the capacity of the public sector to engage in the reconstruction process. Despite years of displacement under the Saddam Hussein regime, the CPA did not even develop a policy for the repatriation of refugees. Unfortunately, such experiences for the displaced have been replicated in many other conflict zones.

Unfortunately, the emergent authoritarian peace does not seriously or substantively address the social and humanitarian crisis. This would require a concerted and long-term commitment from the international community, including states and INGOs, to the provision of resources and support services to local government bodies and civil society to provide postconflict reconstruction services. Yet, the emergent order is largely outside of international sanction and support, which means that there will be limited external involvement in Syria's reconstruction. Nevertheless, future Syrian planners must consider that social policy must address multiple crises at once: the brain drain, the collapse of the health care system, unemployment, refugee and IDP repatriation, and the physical reconstruction of homes, among other crises. Doing so requires more than just the coordination of federal, governorate, and local bodies within Syria; a sustained effort will be required on the part of the international community to channel needed resources to these bodies in order to assess, develop, and implement reconstruction plans that address the humanitarian crisis. Whether this materializes or not remains to be seen.

Although such programs are not contained in the provisions of any Astana peace discussions, they are nevertheless prerequisites for addressing the conflict and preventing it from being intractable. Reinvigorating Syria's social service provision system and establishing a strong social safety net would not only encourage repatriation but would foster social stability and help Syrians return to some degree of normalcy in the years and decades after the conflict ends. A commitment from international donors and actors to the long-term social stability of Syria will be as important to the stability of the country as any political agreement hatched in Geneva or elsewhere. Social stability in Syria will not follow from a political agreement to end the conflict. Such stability requires a material basis. As Cocozelli (2006) has argued, social policy is largely absent in postconflict reconstruction plans, where planners typically focus on normative macroeconomic indicators to assess the economic well-being of the country.

Moreover, when social policy is incorporated into postconflict plans it is often done on a project basis and is not pursued holistically in relation to other social issues. Any solution to the Syrian conflict must thus take social policy seriously and incorporate a robust, holistic plan to address the short- and long-term social and humanitarian crisis wrought by the conflict. This will necessarily include engagement with local, national, and international actors. How this can happen in the context of Astana remains to be seen. While such engagement will certainly raise coordination and financing issues, progress on social issues will be a vital component of stability in Syria after the conflict ends. Rather than building from scratch, any solution should engage the ongoing efforts of Syrian civil society (discussed in the previous chapter) and of informal social networks to provide social services and relief to Syrians. Working through these existing networks will not only strengthen them but will incorporate diaspora and local activists into the postconflict order. The subsequent discussion around reconstruction highlights how absent social policy is from the authoritarian peace.

Reconstruction

In 2017, the World Bank estimated that the total loss of GDP in Syria amounted to $226 billion, while around a third of all houses were destroyed or damaged and more than half of all education and medical facilities were destroyed (World Bank, 2017). These staggering figures do not even begin to express the enormity of Syria's reconstruction needs in the coming generations. They do, however, point to the totality of the destruction and the necessity of immediate relief and reconstruction. There are two central, related questions when it comes to reconstruction in Syria today. The first is: how can reconstruction occur in the context of an authoritarian peace, and who will guide and finance reconstruction? The liberal peace approach to peacemaking, although having been criticized for focusing on peacemaking at the expense of reconstruction, nevertheless places importance on linking peace to material benefits. This often entails attempts to centralize and coordinate efforts from local actors, the postconflict state, INGOs, and the international donor community. What links the important cog in that architecture—the donor community—the postconflict space is the international legitimacy afforded the peace process. In many postconflict states, the involvement of the UN in brokering or monitoring peace has given the appearance of international consensus and legitimacy for the postconflict process.

No such legitimacy exists in Syria, where the emergent authoritarian peace has been imposed by battlefield gains that produced very little, if any, political concessions to the opposing political and armed forces. Thus, Syrian reconstruction will not occur within the context of a major international effort to rebuild the country. Indeed, many countries, especially the U.S., seem uninterested in navigating Syria's reconstruction terrain. There is a dilemma faced by states who do not support Syria's authoritarian peace, let alone the continuation of the regime: how to provide humanitarian and reconstruction support while not legitimizing or empowering the regime? This is an unsolvable dilemma given how deeply connected regime cronies are to the existing reconstruction process (*The Economist*, 2017). What we can reasonably expect, then, is limited international involvement in the Syrian reconstruction process. This involvement may even be limited to humanitarian relief efforts and IDP resettlement. While major IFIs such as the World Bank and IMF have jumped on the reconstruction bandwagon and have begun to produce reports about how best to move forward with reconstruction, their involvement may be limited by pressures imposed by Western states who have very little interest in providing the Syrian regime with the material resources to shore up their postconflict legitimacy.

The second major question is how reconstruction can even begin with such profound levels of violence still occurring throughout the country. The example of Homs may give us insight into what Syria's reconstruction future may actually look like. In that city, the UNDP recently declared that 99 percent of war debris was cleared and that the central markets were open for business, while barely a few miles away Russian and regime airplanes maintained a siege against villages in the Homs countryside. Such radical parallels—an "open for business" approach while a suffocating economic and military siege occurs a few miles away—is perhaps the best example of what Syria's reconstruction future may look like: profound violence occurring alongside modest, and important, improvements in material life.

Conclusion

In the conclusion to the first edition of this book, I suggested that the political and military stalemate would shape Syria's conflict in the years to come. Today, it is the breaking of that stalemate and the emergence of an authoritarian peace that will shape Syria's future. A structure for the gradual de-escalation of violence seems to be in place and a crucial regional tripartite agreement is emerging. Both bode well for the fate of the Syrian regime, and represent a death knell for those who still believe in the ideals of the revolution. Perhaps for the optimistic the revolution can continue through different means. However, today, pessimism and pragmatism reign. The morphing of the conflict into a violent contest among unsavoury, violent, criminal, and illiberal forces delivered the fatal blow to the revolution long before the Astana process. This process is where Syria stands today, between "victory" over rebel forces and the daunting reality that years of conflict have induced physical and emotional destruction that may never be repaired.

It is important to restate the obvious here: that nobody has won this war. Celebration and jubilation among regime loyalists mask the trauma that the country has endured and will continue to endure as it emerges from the aftermath of the destruction. There is no time for celebrating the outcome of the conflict today. Everyone has lost.

Afterword

In a recent exchange with a reader in the Letters page of the *New York Review of Books*, columnist Charles Glass argued that the original *casus belli* of the war—regime change—was no longer relevant to understanding the conflict or the goals of its various actors. The Syrian war had moved beyond the original question of whether, how, and when the regime would fall and what authority would replace it to a much more complicated state in which the current war was defined by many overlapping conflicts. While I have rarely agreed with Glass's analysis of Syria, I agree that regime change as envisioned by the original protest movement and organized opposition is no longer a plausible outcome in the Syrian conflict. Where does this leave our analysis and understanding of the Syrian conflict? Since the completion of this book, a number of developments have reinforced the main analytical point presented in the preceding pages – primarily, that the Syrian conflict is complicated, messy, multi-dimensional, and currently entering a new phase in what I called the "authoritarian peace." In the following pages, I hope to explore some of these events and contextualize them within the authoritarian peace.

The continued bombardment of Ghouta, east of Damascus, has captured headlines in recent months. This area of the country has been decimated by years of bombardment, sieges, and economic suffocation, and was one of the last remaining rebel strongholds left in the wake of the Russian intervention. Many armed groups had a significant presence in Ghouta, including some of the more prominent Islamist groups such as Ahrar al-Sham and Tahrir al-Sham. As the regime intensified its onslaught of Ghouta in recent weeks, many of these groups were totally destroyed, forced to surrender to regime forces, or subject to forced transfers as in other "local truces" negotiated throughout Syria. As these groups dwindled, more territory came under government control, leaving Douma as the sole area of Ghouta under the control of Jaysh al-Islam.

At the time of writing, a brutal chemical attack in Douma was followed by an agreement between the Syrian regime and Jaysh al-Islam, in which the latter's fighters and supporters would be guaranteed safe passage to Idlib while the regime would assume control over the area. The Idlib strategy has been deployed since as far as back as 2014 when the regime would guarantee secure passage of fighters from various parts of Syria to the northwestern governorate. The "liberation" of these areas from armed groups has continued since then and has been a prominent conflict management strategy. The premise of the strategy is simple: to depopulate recalcitrant areas and to establish regime presence and new political realities. The successful deployment of this strategy in Douma has returned more than 125,000 civilians to government control and eliminated a major rebel stronghold so close to the Syrian capital, Damascus.

Aside from this, the Idlib strategy also portends what future violence may look like in Syria. When this book was completed, there remained three significant areas of non-regime control. In addition to Ghouta, these areas included Idlib and the northern areas under Syrian Kurdish control. Having survived the decimation of destruction that was the fate of so many other armed groups, the SDF was poised to be a major player in post conflict Syria. Indeed, many people inside and outside of Syria seriously contemplated rapprochement between the regime and SDF and possibly even a federalist post conflict arrangement. Yet, in merely a few weeks, a Turkish military offensive into Afrin effectively decimated the SDF as a major military force. In the aftermath of the Turkish incursion and in an attempt to maintain Kurdish political relevance in Syria's emerging authoritarian peace, the PYD established a new party called the Syria Future Party, in a sort of political rebranding. The common assumption about the change has been that the SDF's American allies forced it upon them. If so, this would point to a disturbing reality for Syria's Kurdish political parties: their American allies are more than willing to force adjustments on them but unwilling to prevent a Turkish decimation of their military capacities.

While making sense of the Trump administration's policies toward Syria has been difficult, in the aftermath of the chemical weapons attack in Ghouta there has emerged some clarity. Despite a multi-pronged, targeted attack against regime installations, the threat of sustained US intervention has been effectively removed by President Trump's repeated declarations that he wants to remove US forces from Syria. While the USA attacked regime targets, it was simultaneously trying to whip up regional support for an Arab-led stabilization force to replace its troops in the northeast of Syria. While Egypt immediately rejected the plan, Saudi Arabia has publicly stated its willingness to explore the possibility. Supporters of sustained US intervention were delivered another blow when the US bombing campaign halted mere hours after it started. Thus, out of the fog of war and President Trump's often-contradictory tweets about Syria has emerged a US policy of disengagement. Chemical weapons use may be a red line, but it is not enough of a red line to deepen US engagement in the country.

In the absence of a major shift in US policy, the regional situation that will shape Syria in the coming months and years will be determined by the tripartite powers and their appetite (or not) for further destruction of the country to advance their specific geopolitical goals. The two looming confrontations that regime-aligned forces will face in the coming months are, first, with the Kurdish political and military elements, and, second, with the remnants of the armed groups currently based in Idlib. It would appear that any sort of political accommodation with any of these groups is outside of the tripartite consensus for Syria, given Turkey's unopposed intervention into Afrin. As we enter the authoritarian peace phase of the conflict, such military realities will likely produce a sustained insurgency campaign, further justifying continued fighting and the creation of recalcitrant territories in Syria that can be acted upon with prejudice and violence. In this stage, however, territory is unlikely to be controlled as it was during the period of stalemate and may come to resemble more of an insurgency. The presence of violence, not its absence, will continue to define the authoritarian peace.

This peace is also consolidating around property confiscation, a key economic strategy that has followed the regime recapture of key areas of the country. In this strategy, a number of laws have been passed to concretize depopulation and to initiate a process of social erasure whereby Syrian citizens' relationship to their towns, cities, governorates, and even their homes is severed. Through these laws, the government has legalized the process of depopulation and dispossession and has used property transfer as a means of enriching state coffers, private economic interests, and the militias that have contributed to and enforced depopulation. These laws include Law No. 23 (2015) that expedites property expropriation; Law No. 11 (2016) that suspended property transfers in non-regime areas; Law No. 33 (2017) that completely transforms the issuance and management of property documentation; and Law No. 4 (2017) that alters the civil status code.

The reconstruction project in Syria is emerging with two central features: first, there is less emphasis on addressing the humanitarian crisis, including the repatriation of refugees and the internally displaced through comprehensive social programming, housing developments, and the revival of social services, especially outside of the cities. In other words, the reconstruction phase has thus far focused solely on clearing debris, rebuilding some infrastructure, and providing procurement opportunities for regime-aligned business-people. All of this is occurring absent a national plan for reconstruction. Second, most existing projects focus on urban areas at the expense of rural regions, which were heavily devastated during the war. By all accounts, all policies passed under the framework of reconstruction have been devoted to shoring up urban areas.

As all of this unfolds, the narrative wars in Syria continue to be fought. Nothing displays these wars better than the aftermath of the chemical attack when so many people, from established journalists to Russian twitter bots, peddled narratives that the attack was orchestrated by everyone but the Syrian regime itself. Campaigns of misinformation and uncertainty have defined these narrative wars today and will continue to do so for as long as the conflict drags on. These narrative battles are more than simply disputes of truth or untruth but reflect the multiplicity of ideas and narratives around the conflict as well. Conflicts are messy. They are multidimensional. And they also tell many, many stories.

In the preceding pages, I have tried to tell some of these stories and to provide a narrative that traces the evolution of three distinct phases in the Syrian conflict. The first phase was one in which the possibility of the revolution winning or the regime falling was seriously contemplated. The regime or revolution phase occurred early in the conflict and was defined by questions about regime endurance, opposition stability and cohesion, and the role that international powers would play in the conflict. The second phase began as militarization led to a proliferation of violence and the geographic fragmentation of the country in ways that produced a political and military stalemate. The third phase of the conflict began when that stalemate was broken by the Russian intervention in 2015 that produced the conditions of possibility for the emergence of Syria's authoritarian peace.

The events that have occurred since the completion of the book suggest that the argument about an authoritarian peace will be borne out and that the tripartite powers, along with their Syrian regime allies, will shape the future of Syria in violent, exclusionary, and destructive ways.

References

Abbas, H. (2011). The dynamics of the uprising in Syria. *Jadaliyya*, 19 October.

Abboud, S. (2009). Syrian trade policy. In S. Abboud & S. Said, *Syrian Foreign Trade and Economic Reform*. St. Andrews, Scotland: Lynne Rienner Publishers.

———. (2012). Economic transformation and diffusion of authoritarian power in Syria. In L. Sadiki and Heiko Wimmonen (eds.), *Unmaking Power: Negotiating the Democratic Void in the Arab Middle East*. London: Routledge, 159–177.

———. (2013a). Capital flight and the consequences of the war economy. *Jadaliyya*, 18 March.

———. (2013b). Syria's business elite: Between political alignment and hedging their bets. *SWP Comments*. August 2013.

———. (2015). Locating the "social" in the social market economy. In R. Hinnebusch & Tina Zintl (eds.), *Syria: From Reform to Revolt*. Syracuse, NY: Syracuse University Press, 45–65.

———. (2017). The Economics of War and Peace. *The Century Foundation*. 31 January.

Abboud, S. & B. Muller. (2012). *Rethinking Hizballah: Legitimacy, Authority, Violence*. Farnham: Ashgate.

Abu Hamed, A. (2014). Syria's local coordination committees: The dynamo of a hijacked revolution. In *Knowledge Programme Civil Society in West Asia Special Bulletin*, 5, May.

Abushakra, R. (2013). Main Syrian opposition group in exile chooses government. *The Wall Street Journal*. 12 November.

Adleh, F. & Favier, A. (2017). "Local Reconciliation Agreements" in Syria: A non-starter for peacebuilding. *Middle East Directions*, European University Institute.

Al-Jazeera (2017). Syrian de-escalation zones explained. *Al-Jazeera*. 4 July.

Al-Wasl, Z. (2015). Interim govt. faces severity of financial crisis as funds deplete. *The Syrian Observer*, 24 March.

Alagha, J. (2006). *The Shifts in Hizbullah's Ideology*. Amsterdam: Amsterdam University Press.

Ali, Abdallah Suleiman (2015). Jabhat al-Nusra slammed for not severing ties with al-Qaeda. *Al-Monitor*, March 11. Trans. Rani Geha.

Ali, Nour (2011). Syrian regime steps up propaganda war amid bloody crackdown on protests. *The Guardian*. 20 July.

Aleppo Urban Development Project (2009). *Informal settlements in Aleppo: Rapid profiles of all informal settlements in Aleppo*. Aleppo: Aleppo Urban Development Project.

Allison, R. (2013). Russia and Syria: Explaining alignment with a regime in crisis. *International Affairs*, 89(4): 795–823.

Allsopp, Harriet (2015). *The Kurds of Syria: Political Parties and Identity in the Middle East*, London: I.B. Tauris.

Anden-Papadopolous, K. & Pantti, M. (2013). The media work of Syrian diaspora activists. *International Journal of Communication*, 7: 2185–206.

Anna, C. (2015). Report says 640,200 Syrians live under siege. *The Columbian*. 20 March.

Aranki, D. & Kalis, O. (2014) Limited legal status for refugees from Syria in Lebanon. *Forced Migration Review*, 47 (September): 17–19.

Aras, B. & Falk, R. (2015). Authoritarian "geopolitics" of survival in the Arab Spring. *Third World Quarterly*, 36(2): 322–36.

Asseburg, M. & Wimmen, H. (2014). Geneva II—A Chance to Contain the Syrian Civil War. *SWP Comments*, 10 (January): 1–7.

Bâli, Aslı & Aziz Rana (2017). The Wrong Kind of Intervention in Syria. In Karim Makdisi & Vijay Prashad (eds.), *Land of Blue Helmets: The United Nations and the Arab World*. Oakland: University of California Press.

Bank, André & Roy Karadag (2013). The "Ankara Moment": The politics of Turkey's regional power in the Middle East. *Third World Quarterly*, 34(2): 287–304.

Barmin, Y. (2015). Moscow's 11 principles for peace in Syria. *Russia Direct*. 29 January.

Batatu, H. (1999). *Syria's Peasantry, the Descendants of Its Lesser Rural Notables, and Their Politics*. Princeton, NJ: Princeton University Press.

Benraad, M. (2011). Iraq's tribal "Sahwa": Its rise and fall. *Middle East Policy Council*, Spring 18(1).

Boex, J., Kimble, D. & Pigey, J. (2010). Decentralized local government as a modality for post-conflict recovery and development: An emerging natural experiment in Northern Uganda. *Urban Institute Center on International Development and Governance*. IDG Working Paper No. 2010-01.

Böttcher, Annabelle (2017). Humanitarian Aid and the Battle for Aleppo. *Center for MellemØstsudier News Analysis*. January.

Byman, D. (2014). Sectarianism afflicts the New Middle East. *Survival: Global Politics and Strategy*, 56(1): 79–100.

Cairo Center for Human Rights (eds.) (2014). *Al-khlas am al-kharab? Suriya 'ala muftarak al-taraq*. Cairo, Egypt: Cairo Center for Human Rights.

Calamur, Krishnadev (2017). Why Israel is worried about Syria. *The Atlantic*. 7 September.

Carpenter, Ami, Anu Lawrence & Milburn Line (2013). Contested authorities alternatives to State law and order in post-conflict Guatemala. *Journal of Law and Conflict Resolution*, 5 (3): 48-61.

The Carter Center (2013). *Syria Countrywide Conflict Report #1*. Atlanta: The Carter Center.

Charap, S. (2013). Russia, Syria and the doctrine of intervention. *Survival: Global Politics and Strategy*, 55(1): 35–41.

Coles, I. (2015). Iraqi Kurds say Islamic State used chlorine gas against them. *Reuters*. 14 March.

Dahi, Omar S. & Munif, Y. (2012). Revolts in Syria: Tracking the convergence between authoritarianism and neoliberalism. *Journal of Asian and African Studies*, 47(4): 323–32.

Dannreuther, R. (2015). Russia and the Arab Spring: Supporting the counter-revolution. *Journal of European Integration*, 37(1): 77–94.

Daoud, D. (2014). Hezbollah: The party of Iran, not Lebanon. *The Washington Institute*. 3 December.

Dark, E. (2014). Syrian regime ignores supporters' rising anger. *al-Monitor*. 7 October.

De Châtel, F. (2014). The role of drought and climate change in the Syrian uprising: Untangling the triggers of the revolution. *Middle Eastern Studies*, 50(4): 521–35.

Dib, Kamal (2013). *Azmah fi Suriyah: infijar al-dakhil wa 'awdat al-sira' al-dawli 2011-2013*. Beirut, Lebanon: Dar al-Nahar.

Dreyfuss, B. (2014). US should back Syria's Assad against ISIS. *The Nation*. 3 July.

Droz-Vincent, Philippe (2014). State of Barbary (Take Two): From the Arab Spring to the return of violence in Syria. *Middle East Journal*, 68(1): 33–58.

Durac, V. (2015). Social movements, protest movements and crossideological coalitions: The Arab uprisings re-appraised. *Democratization*, 22(2): 239–58.

el-Hokayem, E. (2007). Hizballah and Syria: Outgrowing the proxy relationship. *Washington Quarterly*, 30(2): 35–52.

_____. (2013). *Syria's Uprising and the Fracturing of the Levant*. London: Routledge.

el-Husseini, R. (2012). *Pax Syriana: Elite Politics in Postwar Lebanon*. Syracuse, NY: Syracuse University Press.

The Economist (2017). Syria's new war millionaires: For the new elite, peace would be bad for business. *The Economist*. 1 June.

Evans, D. & Karouny, M. (2013). Iranian Guards commander killed in Syria. *Reuters*. 14 February.

Farouk-Alli, A. (2014). Sectarianism in Alawi Syria: Exploring the paradoxes of politics and religion. *Journal of Muslim Minority Affairs*, 34(3): 207–26.

Fisher, N. (2014). Foreword: The inheritance of loss. *Forced Migration Review*, 47(September): 4–5.

Fouad, Fouad et al. (2017). Health workers and the weaponisation of health care in Syria: a preliminary inquiry for *The Lancet*— American University of Beirut Commission on Syria. *The Lancet*.

Fox, W. (2007). Fiscal decentralization in post-conflict countries. *Fiscal Reform and Economic Governance Project: Best Practice*. (http://www.fiscalreform.net/)

Gelvin, J. (1999). *Divided Loyalties: Nationalism and Mass Politics in Syria at the Close of Empire*. Berkeley: University of California Press.

Gladstone, R. (2012). Resigning as envoy to Syria, Annan casts wide blame. *New York Times*. 2 August.

Goodarzi, J. (2009). *Syria and Iran: Diplomatic Alliance and Power Politics in the Middle East*. London: I.B. Tauris.

_____. (2013). Iran and Syria at the crossroads: The fall of the Tehran-Damascus axis? *Viewpoints*, 35: Wilson Center.

Gorenburg, D. (2012). Why Russia Supports Repressive Regimes in Syria and the Middle East. *PONARS Eurasia Policy Memo 198*. June 2012.

Gorman, S., Malas, N. & Bradly, M. (2014). Brutal efficiency: The secret to Islamic State's success. *The Wall Street Journal*. 3 September.

Guardian (2012). Syrian forces shell central Homs, breaking ceasefire, activists claim. *The Guardian*. 14 April.

Haddad, B. (2004). The formation and development of economic networks in Syria: Implications for economic and fiscal reforms, 1986–2000. In Heydemann, Steven (ed.), *Networks of Privilege: Rethinking the Politics of Economic Reform in the Middle East*. New York: Palgrave, 39–78.

———. (2011). *Business Networks in Syria: The Political Economy of Authoritarian Resilience*. Stanford, CA: Stanford University Press.

———. (2012a). Syria, the Arab uprisings, and the political economy of authoritarian resilience. *Interface*, 4(1) (May): 113–30.

———. (2012b). Syria's state bourgeoisie: An organic backbone for the regime. *Middle East Critique*, 21(3) (Fall).

———. (2015). Four years on: No easy answers in Syria (Part II). *Jadaliyya*. 30 March.

———. (2016). The debate over Syria has reached a dead end. *The Nation*. 18 October.

Hashem, A. (2015). Iran's new strategy in Syria. *al-Monitor*. 15 May.

Hassan, H. (2013). The Gulf states: United against Iran, divided over Islamists. In Barnes-Dacey, Julien, and Daniel Levy (eds.), *The Regional Struggle for Syria*. European Council on Foreign Relations, 17–24.

Henderson, E. & Singer, D. (2002). New wars and rumors of new wars. *International Interactions*, 28(2): 165–90.

Heydemann, S. (1999). *Authoritarianism in Syria: Institutions and Social Conflict 1946–1970*. Ithaca, NY: Cornell University Press.

———. (2007). Upgrading authoritarianism in the Arab world. *The Saban Center for Middle East Policy at the Brookings Institution*, 13 (October).

———. (2013a). The big picture: Envisioning a best possible peace for Syria—and what it will take to reach it. *Foreign Policy*. 6 December.

———. (2013b). Syria and the future of authoritarianism. *Journal of Democracy*, 24(4): 59–73.

Hinnebusch, R. (1989). *Peasant and Bureaucracy in Ba'athist Syria: The Political Economy of Rural Development* (Westview Special Studies on the Middle East). Boulder, CO: Westview Press.

———. (1990). *Authoritarian Power and State Formation in Ba'athist Syria: Army, Party, and Peasant* (Westview Special Studies on the Middle East). Boulder, CO: Westview Press.

———. (2001). *Syria: Revolution from Above*. London: Routledge.

———. (2009). "The Political Economy of Populist Authoritarianism." In *The State and the Political Economy of Reform in Syria*, edited by Raymond Hinnebusch and Søren Schmidt. St. Andrews, Scotland: St. Andrews Papers on Contemporary Syria, Boulder: Lynne Rienner Publishers.

———, ed. (2010). Agriculture and Reform in Syria. Boulder, CO: Lynne Rienner.

———. (2012). Syria from "authoritarian upgrading" to revolution? *International Affairs*, 88(1): 95–113.

Hsu, Carolyn L. (2007). *Creating Market Socialism: How Ordinary People are Shaping Class and Status in China*. Durham, NC: Duke University Press.

Hubbard, B., Krauss, C. & Schmitt, E. (2014). Rebels in Syria claim control of resources. *New York Times*. 28 January.

Hughes, G. A. (2014). Syria and the perils of proxy warfare. *Small Wars & Insurgencies*, 25(3): 522–38.

International Crisis Group (2013). Syria's Kurds: A struggle within a struggle. *Middle East Report 136*. 22 January.

———. (2014). Flight of Icarus? The PYD's precarious rise in Syria. *Middle East Report 151*. 8 May.

International Rescue Committee (2017). First-of-its kind survey of Syrian school children shows math and reading skills devastated by war, *IRC Press Release*.

Ismail, S. (2013). Urban subalterns in the Arab revolutions: Cairo and Damascus in comparative perspective. *Comparative Studies in Society and History*, 55(4): 865–94.

Kahf, M. (2014). The Syrian revolution, then and now. *Peace Review: A Journal of Social Justice*, 26(4): 556–63.

Kaim, Markus & Oliver Tamminga (2015). Russia's Military Intervention in Syria: Its Operation Plan, Objectives, and Consequences, *SWF Comments #48*.

Kaldor, M. (1999). *New and Old Wars: Organized Violence in a Global Era*. Stanford, CA: Stanford University Press.

———. (2012). *New and Old Wars: Organized Violence in a Global Era*, 3rd ed. Cambridge: Polity.

Karam, Joyce (2017). Assad has won says former US ambassador to Syria, *The National*, 28 August.

Kaylah, Salamah (2013). *Al-Thawrah al-Suriyah: waqi'uha sayruratuha wa-afaquha*. Beirut: Atlas lil Nashr wal Intaj al-Thaqafi.

Khaddour, K. (2014). Securing the Syrian regime. *Sada*. Carnegie Endowment for International Peace. 3 June.

Khashanah, Khaldoun (2014). The Syrian Crisis: A systemic framework. *Contemporary Arab Affairs*, 7(1): 1–21.

Khoury, Doreen (2013). Losing the Syrian grassroots: local governance structures urgently need support. SWP Comments #9. Berlin: German Institute for International and Security Affairs.

Khoury, Philip S. (1983). *Urban notables and Arab nationalism: The politics of Damascus 1860–1920*. Cambridge: Cambridge University Press.

Kirisci, K. & Salooja, R. (2014). Northern exodus: How Turkey can integrate Syrian refugees. *Foreign Affairs*. 15 April.

Kleinfeld, R. (2013). The case for arming Syrian rebels. *The Wall Street Journal*. 24 February.

Knapp, Michael, Ayboga, E. & Flach, A. (2016). *Revolution in Rojava: Democratic Autonomy and Women's Liberation in Syrian Kurdistan*. London: Pluto Press.

Kozhanov, Nikolay (2016). *Russia and the Syrian Conflict: Moscow's Domestic, Regional and Strategic Interests*. London: Gerlach Press.

Kurdistan National Congress (2014). Canton based democratic autonomy of Rojava: A transformation process from dictatorship to democracy. May.

Landis, J. & Pace, J. (2006). The Syrian opposition. *Washington Quarterly*, 30(1): 45–68.

Lawson, F. (1997). Private capital and the state in contemporary Syria. *Middle East Report 203: Lebanon and Syria, The Geopolitics of Change*, 8–13, 30.

Leenders, R. (2012). Collective action and mobilization in Dar'a: An anatomy of the onset of Syria's popular uprising. *Mobilization*, 17(4): 419–34.

Leenders, R. & Heydemann, S. (2012). Popular mobilization in Syria: opportunity and threat, and the social networks of the early risers. *Mediterranean Politics*, 17(2): 139–59.

Legrand, Felix (2016). Foreign backers and the marginalization of the Free Syrian Army. *Policy Brief*, Arab Reform Initiative.

Lekas Miller, A. (2014). Syria's White Helmets—The most dangerous job in the world. *Waging Nonviolence*. 25 September.

Lesch, D. (2013a). *Syria: The Fall of the House of Assad*. New Haven, CT: Yale University Press.

———. (2013b). The unknown future of Syria. *Mediterranean Politics*, 18(1): 97–103.

Lund, A. (2012). Syrian jihadism. *UI brief #13*, Swedish Institute of International Affairs.

————. (2015). Who are the pro-Assad militias? *Carnegie Endowment for International Peace*. 2 March.

————. (2016). Origins of the Syrian Democratic Forces: A primer. *Syria Deeply*, 22 January.

Lewis, David (2017). The myopic Foucauldian gaze: discourse, knowledge and the authoritarian peace. *Journal of Intervention and Statebuilding*, 11(1): 21–41.

Lynch, M., Freelon, D. & Aday, S. (2013). Syria in the Arab Spring: The integration of Syria's conflict with the Arab uprisings, 2011–2013. *Research & Politics* 1(3).

Macias, A. & Bender, J. (2014). Here's how the world's richest terrorist group makes millions every day. *Business Insider*. 27 August.

Mackreath, H. (2014). The role of host communities in north Lebanon. *Forced Migration Review*, 47 (September): 19–21.

Malantowicz, A. (2013). Civil war in Syria and the "new wars" debate. *Amsterdam Law Forum*, 5(3): 52–60.

Matar, Linda (2016). *The Political Economy of Investment in Syria*. New York: Palgrave.

Miles, T. (2014). WFP suspends food aid for 1.7 million Syrian refugees. *Reuters*. 1 December.

Moret, E. (2015). Humanitarian impacts of economic sanctions on Iran and Syria. *European Security* 24(1): 120–40.

Mufti, Malik (1996). *Sovereign Creations: Pan-Arabism and Political Order in Syria and Iraq*. Ithaca: Cornell University Press.

Mustafa, Faruq (2013). *al-Kurd al-Siriyun wal harak al-dimuqrati*. Beirut: al-Dar al-Arabiyah lil Ulum Nashirun.

Nielsen, R. (2015). Does the Islamic State believe in sovereignty? Islamism in the IS Age. *Washington Post*, February 6. 28–31.

Norwegian Refugee Council. (2015). Failing Syria: Assessing the impact of UN Security Council Resolutions in protecting and assisting civilians in Syria.

Oesch, L. (2014). Mobility as a solution. *Forced Migration Review* 47 (September): 48.

O'Toole, J. (2012). Billions at stake as Russia backs Syria. *CNN Money*, 10 Feb.

Owen, R. (2012). *The Rise and Fall of Arab Presidents for Life*. Cambridge, MA: Harvard University Press.

Perthes, V. (2011) The political economy of the Syrian succession. *Survival: Global Politics and Strategy*, 43(1): 143–54.

Phillips, C. (2015). Sectarianism and conflict in Syria. *Third World Quarterly*, 36(2): 357–76.

Pierret, T. (2013). External support and the Syrian insurgency. *Foreign Policy.* 9 August.

Pierret, T. & Selvik, K. (2009). Limits of "authoritarian upgrading" in Syria: Private welfare, Islamic charities, and the rise of the Zayd Movement. *International Journal of Middle East Studies,* 41(4): 595–614.

Pizzi, M. (2015). Syrian opposition to snub Moscow peace talks invite. *Al Jazeera.* 17 January.

Rawan, B. & Imran, S. (2013). Framing the Syrian uprising: Comparative analysis of *Khaleej Times* and *The New York Times. Journal of Social Sciences and Humanities,* 21(1).

Rubenstein, L. (2011). Post-conflict health reconstruction: Search for a policy. *Disasters* 35(4): 680–700.

Ruiz de Elvira, L. (2013). The Syrian civil society in the face of revolt. *TEPSIS Papers,* October 2013, 1–5.

Russian Federation (2017). Memorandum on the creation of de-escalation zones in the Syrian Arab Republic. *The Ministry of Foreign Affairs of the Russian Federation.* 6 May.

Saadullah, V. (2014). Syrian Kurdish refugees struggle to find affordable housing. Trans. S. Utku Bila. *Al Monitor.* 6 October.

Sadiki, L. (2011). The Bouazizi "big bang." *Al Jazeera.* 29 December.

Sadjadpour, K. (2013). Iran's unwavering support to Assad's Syria. *Carnegie Endowment for International Peace.* 27 August.

Sage, Christopher & Michael Davis (2015). Understanding Russian Strategic Ambiguity in Syria. In Mohseni, Payam (ed.), *Disrupting the Chessboard: Perspectives on the Russian Intervention in Syria,* Belfer Center for Science and International Affairs, 24–6.

Sahner, C. (2014). *Among the Ruins: Syria's Past and Present.* Oxford: Oxford University Press.

Said, Rodi (2016). Syria's Kurds rebuked for seeking autonomous region. *Reuters.* 17 March.

Salloukh, B. F. (2013). The Arab uprisings and the geopolitics of the Middle East. *The International Spectator: Italian Journal of International Affairs,* 48(2): 32–46.

Sayigh, Yezid. (2012). The coming tests of the Syrian opposition. Carnegie Middle East Center, April 19 (http://carnegie-mec. org/2012/04/19/coming-tests-of-syrian-opposition-pub-47877).

Seale, P. (1990). *Assad: The Struggle for the Middle East.* Berkeley: University of California Press.

Seeberg, P. (2014). The EU and the Syrian crisis: The use of sanctions and the regime's strategy for survival. *Mediterranean Politics,* 20(1): 1–18.

Seifan, Samir (2010). *Al-ather al-ijtameeah al-seeaset al-iqtisad fi suryeeah*, Syrian Economic Society, Damascus, Syria, 9 February.

Shaery-Eisenlohr, R. (2008). *Shi'ite Lebanon: Transnational Religion and the Making of National Identities.* New York: Columbia University Press.

Slavin, B. (2015). Shiite militias mixed blessing in Iraq, Syria. *Al Monitor.* 2 February.

Sood, A. & L. Seferis. (2014). Syrians contributing to Kurdish economic growth. *Forced Migration Review*, 47 (September): 14–17.

Sottimano, A. (2008). Ideology and discourse in the era of Ba'athist reforms: Toward an analysis of authoritarian governmentality. In Hinnebusch, Raymond (ed.), *Changing Regime Discourse and Reform in Syria.* Boulder, CO: Lynne Rienner.

Stacher, J. (2012). *Adaptable Autocrats: Regime Power in Egypt and Syria.* Stanford, CA: Stanford University Press.

Staniland, Paul (2012). States, Insurgents, and Wartime Political Orders. *Perspectives on Politics*, 10(2): 243–64.

Steenkamp, Christina (2014). *Violent Societies: Networks of Violence in Civil War and Peace.* London: Palgrave.

Stein, A. (2015). Turkey's evolving Syria strategy: Why Ankara backs Al-Nusra but shuns ISIS. *Foreign Affairs.* 9 February.

———. (2017). Reconciling U.S.-Turkish Interests in Northern Syria. *Council on Foreign Relations Discussion Paper.* February.

Strategic Comments. (2012). Russia's Syrian stance: Principled self interest. *Strategic Comments*, 18(7): 1–3.

Sulayman, Bahjat (2015). *Ma'jara wa yajri fi Suriyah: mu'amarah am thawrah?* Sfax, Tunisia: Dar Biram lil Nashar wal Tawzi.

Suleiman Ali, A. (2015). Noose tightens around Jabhat al-Nusra. Trans. S. Abboud. *Al Monitor.* 18 March.

Taylor, P. (2015). "It's God's gift." Islamic State fills coffers with Iraqi government cash. *The Guardian.* 21 April.

Tejel, Jordi (2008). *Syria's Kurds: History, Politics and Society.* London: Routledge.

Tilly, Charles, Doug McAdam & Sidney Tarrow (2001). *Dynamics of Contention.* Cambridge: Cambridge University Press.

Trombetta, L. (2014). The EU and the Syrian crisis as viewed from the Middle East. *The International Spectator: Italian Journal of International Affairs*, 49(3): 27–39.

Umar, Idris (2016). *Suriyah: min al-idtihad al-siyasi ila al-karithah al-insaniyah.* Cairo: al-Maktab al-Arabi lil-Ma'arif.

United Nations Children's Fund (2013). *Syria's Children: A Lost Generation?*

United Nations High Commission for Refugees (2014). *Syria Response Plan.* New York: United Nations.

———. (2017). *UN seeks $4.63 billion to aid Syrian refugees and host nations.* UNHCR.

USAID (2015). *Crisis in Syria.*

Utas, M. (ed.) (2012). Introduction: Bigmanity and network governance in Africa. In *African Conflict and Informal Power: Big Men and Networks.* London: Zed Books, 1–34.

Valeriano, B., & V. Marin (2010). Pathways to interstate war: A qualitative comparative analysis of the steps to war theory. *Josef Korbel Journal of Advanced International Studies,* 2: 1–27.

Von Maltzahn, N. (2013). *The Syria-Iran Axis: Cultural Diplomacy and International Relations in the Middle East.* London: I.B. Tauris.

Wakim, Jamal (2012). *Sira' al-quwa al-kubra 'ala Suriyah: al-ab'ad al-jiyu siyasah li azmat 2011.* Beirut, Lebanon: Sharikat al-Matbu'at lil-Tawzi wal Nashr.

Wall Street Journal (2011). *Interview with Syrian President Bashar al-Assad.* 31 January.

Wezeman, P. (2013). Arms transfers to Syria. In *SIPRI Yearbook 2013: Armaments, Disarmament and International Security.* Oxford: Oxford University Press, 269–73.

White, B. (2012). *The Emergence of Minorities in the Middle East: The Politics of Community in French Mandate Syria.* Edinburgh: Edinburgh University Press.

Wieland, C. (2012). *Syria—A Decade of Lost Chances: Repression and Revolution from Damascus Spring to Arab Spring.* Seattle, WA: Cune Press.

Windrem, R. (2014). Who's funding ISIS? Wealthy Gulf "angel investors," officials say. *NBC News.* 21 September.

Wintour, Patrick (2016). Syrian peace talks in peril after opposition's chief negotiator quits. *The Guardian,* 30 May.

World Bank (2016). *MENA Quarterly Economic Brief.* Washington: World Bank. January.

———. (2017). *The Toll of War: The Economic and Social Consequences of the Conflict in Syria.* Washington: World Bank, 10 July.

Index